GROWTH AND GUILT

The increasing exploitation of the planet is the subject of ever more frequent debate on the limits of growth and development. Technology's boundless growth seems irreconcilable with the finiteness of the earth. Potential solutions are almost always technical, but is it truly possible to deal with the excesses of our civilization without considering the psychological dimension?

The idea of continuous growth is relatively recent. Previously, agrarian modes of culture held sway and notions of measurement, reflecting the seasons, were circular rather than linear. The history of the west is the rejection of this paradigm, relegating it to more primitve peoples and supplanting it with aspirations to unlimited expansion. When did this race towards the limitless begin?

The Greeks, who shaped the basis of western thinking, lived in mortal fear of humanity's hidden hunger for the infinite and referred to it as *hýbris*, the one true sin in their moral code. Whoever desired or possessed too much was implacably punished by *némesis*. Yet the Greeks themselves were to pioneer an unprecedented level of ambition that began to reverse that taboo.

If it is true that no culture can truly repudiate its origins, and that gods who are no longer potent can vanish but still leave behind a body of myth which continues to live and assert itself in modernized garb, then our concern with the limits of growth reflects something more than an awareness of new technological problems – it also brings to light a psychic wound and a feeling of guilt which are infinitely more ancient.

Luigi Zoja is a Jungian analyst based in Milan. From 1984–1993 he was the President of CIPA (Centro Italiano di Psicologica Analitica) and from 1989 he has held the position of Second Vice-President of the International Association of Analytical Psychology. This is the second of his books to appear in English. *Drugs, Addiction and Initiation: The Secret Search for Ritual* was published in Boston (SIGO) in 1989.

'Very clear and well written,
a scholarly text with a wealth of historical and mythological material,
but above all the first book telling us that unlimited development is a
perversion, not a psychological necessity.'

Francesco Rutelli, *Mayor of Rome, former Italian Minister of the
Environment and Head of the Green Members of Parliament.*

GROWTH AND GUILT

Psychology and the limits of development

Luigi Zoja

Translated from the Italian by Henry Martin

London and New York

First published as *Crescita e Colpa*
by Edizioni Anabasi Spa Milano in 1993

First published in English in 1995
by Routledge
11 New Fetter Lane, London EC4P 4EE

Simultaneously published in the USA and Canada
by Routledge
29 West 35th Street, New York, NY 10001

Typeset in Palatino by
Ponting–Green Publishing Services, Chesham, Bucks
Printed and bound in Great Britain by
TJ Press (Padstow) Ltd, Padstow, Cornwall

British Library Cataloguing in Publication Data
A catalogue record for this book is available from
the British Library

Library of Congress Cataloging in Publication Data
A catalogue record for this book has been requested

ISBN 0–415–11660–0 (hbk)
ISBN 0–415–11661–9 (pbk)

For Eva

CONTENTS

Part III From the Greeks to the Present

Part IV Nemesis Returns

Part I

THE PROBLEM

PART 1

THE PROBLEM

I

THE MYTH OF GROWTH,
THE MYTH OF LIMITS

Europe has conquered the world, and on a scale more vast than any of its wars. The Euro-American way of life has spread across the whole of the globe, assuming the status of the first planetary culture in human history. Yet this enormous achievement seems to strike no chord in our emotions. Like the technology on which it rests, it seems to have no soul. The victory of the west – or of its technological civilization, flanked by market economy, representative democracy, and the morals of consumerism – has created no epic in its own celebration.

Such a grandiose scale of hegemony has never before been witnessed. The non-European civilizations that have not already succumbed are currently doing their best to enter the world of technology; they are likewise in the throes of converting themselves to the ideologies and ways of life that accompany technology. All attempts to curb such tendencies have proved entirely fruitless, and by now this process of development is also fully underway in the countries that once pursued the experiment of Marxism. Yet the fact that the western way of life has defeated or converted all others produces no sense of excitement; it does not inspire us to assume victorious attitudes. Western triumph over the peoples of Asia Minor once found celebration in the *Iliad*; the routing of Islam was immortalized in the *Chanson de Roland*; the *Nibelungensage* is the epic of Europe's repulsion of enemy hordes that arrived from the east. But today, at the time of the achievement of its total and global supremacy, the west remains silent. One can only wonder why.

To reply that epic poetry has ceased to exist as a viable genre would be simply to beg the point. The limits of epic poetry were already clear to Herodotus, and to narrate the story of the Persian Wars – which he saw as a sequel to the Trojan Wars – he invented new forms of expression that consisted of a mixture of myth and chronicle. Cinema, today, might take on the task of re-inventing an epic tradition. Or does it make more sense to imagine that the west relinquishes self-celebration because its victory has not been the fruit of the adventures of individual heroes or exemplary protagonists, such as the Captains of ancient Greece or the Paladins of

3

medieval France? Such a reply seems even more suspicious. Our world knows no heroes since all of us have played an active part in the expansion of the technological west; we all share equal status in the story of its victory. "Today, there are no longer any protagonists; there is only a chorus."[1] But we do not recognize ourselves in this victory; instead, we are ever more fascinated by the rural and primitive worlds that are now on the verge of disappearing.

A modern-day epic could again take the form of a mixture of history and myth, which is not, however, to imply that fact would give way to fantasy. Fact itself can have the presence of myth, since epic simply recasts facts into forms that allow for a style of majestic narration, and they come to be charged with transcendental overtones. The original meaning of "myth" had nothing to do with declaring a story to be fictional rather than true. "Myth" was synonymous with "language," or with narrative in its broadest, most general, and most authoritative form, charged with emotion and the power to persuade. Myth speaks with a voice that seems to arise from the very events it narrates, and it typically possesses the power to mold human beings into a semblance of the forms that it uses to capture their attention. Myth is the repository of a destiny, even perhaps while omitting to describe it.

Myth is the part of history that refers to no previous explanations. No ulterior origins lie farther to its rear. It is the part of history that deflects the movements of its personages into confirmations of ancestral expectations and it routs all personal intentions on the part of its narrator. Myth constrains the narrator to follow a rhythm inherent in the myth itself. Myth is that "past" which even in the past was never a present, but which claims none the less to be a part of every present. Myth is autonomous, or independent of everything other than itself; but it constitutes and imposes a bond that events are forced to respect. While distant, it is also ever-present.[2]

But to offer a simple description of myth is still to offer too little. Myth possesses a peculiar relationship with the person who recounts it and also with the listener, since in addition to being a narrative form, it is also an interior space. Myth is the site of our most peremptory mental images. This fact is very clear to the politicians who govern us, and they are often prone to abandon rational arguments – which very few are likely to want to hear – and to replace them by myths; myths function even without being heard, since they seem to speak truths that we have always known. Myth is society's first medication, arresting time and restoring us by sending us back to the roots of things. One can know a myth by heart and yet tirelessly return to hearing it told, year after year, always the same.

Human beings need narratives in order to identify with figures or models of human behavior. Things are not sufficient, since they offer no respite from solitude. But technological civilization ignores the need for

the production of mythic event and instead is committed to the manufacture of objects of use, which are alien to the functions and purposes of
narrative. These objects are the victors. Technological civilization thus
stands at a special distance from the passions of myth: Weber describes
our civilization as disenchanted, or *entzaubert*. In the realm of the victory
of things, the sources of action no longer reside in the states of mind of
individuals: action is objective, and the course of action can programmed.
It is in much the same way that the victory of things banishes emotion and
makes itself an impossible theme for narrative or for epic celebration. The
achievements of technology are immediately distributed, but difficult to
mythologize. Progress today is so swift that we constantly exploit its
most recent innovations without having been able to establish any profound connection with the culture from which it derives. Technology has
beneficiaries, but no fathers. Its victory has its chroniclers and archivists,
but no narrators.

Here we can add a second consideration. The problem of the lack of an
epic form of expression for the praise of the victory of technological
civilization also coalesces with a moral problem. Technological civilization
forswears the celebration of its triumph not only because of its loss of
access to the elevated planes of mythic language, but also because it
harbors doubts and feelings of guilt about the meaning of its achievements.
The achievements of western mankind are ever less experienced as a
victory over the men of other civilizations; they seem instead to represent
the general defeat of men by things. Some of us sometimes wonder why
the west directs its pacifism against itself and not against its adversaries,
and one has to respond that the source of western pacifism is embedded
in the west's sense of guilt. It represents a need to make peace with all of
those parts of ourselves that the modern world has bruised and mangled.
Our universal victory bears the burden of a guilt that derives from
technology's original sin.

If we seek out the mark of that sin, we will soon discover that the absence
of a canon of mythic description in the ways in which we depict our world
is really no more than apparent.

Unlike all preceding civilizations, whether European or otherwise, the
world of technology exposes its belly primarily by taking recourse to the
modes of critical thinking, ever further exploring the heritage and increasing the scope of what we refer to as *Kulturpessimismus*. The intellectuals of
the western world have the impression of now for the very first time living
out the story of a form of life that does not love itself. Suicide among such
people is now more frequent than ever before. The future is an eddying
maelstrom that first engulfs our gaze and then sucks us down to its depths.
Technological civilization has compiled something more than a body of
critical descriptions of itself: such self-descriptions amount in fact to a cycle
of negative epics, or of epics in reverse. They graft history onto a myth that

narrates destruction rather than creation. As though returning to an ancient Greek idea, such visions describe the succession of the generations as a linked series of degenerations. The Greek version of the tale sees mankind as already having fallen from a former and indeterminate golden age to the age of iron; the modern myth, on the other hand, sites the lowest point of human life not in the present, but in an ominous future.

At a time when medical progress had begun quite effectively to beat back illness as a cause of death, Malthus predicted demographic disaster. Marx belonged to the era in which the industrial revolution was beginning to reveal its scope, but saw it as the harbinger of social catastrophe. The critical spirit of the twentieth century has grown even more intense – especially since the period of the two world wars – pushing ever further forward in an ever greater number of fields, from sociology to history, anthropology and ecology. By now it directs its attention to the state of the whole of the globe. The world ever increasingly presents itself as a single thing, or as an integrated whole in the sway of technological and territorial interdependencies, and one foresees an interlocking series of collapses and disasters that will show their effects, with no respect for geography, on all the various sectors of civilized life. Frightened and regressive modes of thought dwell on the possible death of western civilization and of everything that the west produces, and all precisely at the very same time in which the tenets of western civilization seem once and for all to have widened their sphere of dominion to include the whole of the globe. In rational terms, western civilization conceives of itself as a positive force; but the narrative terms of its self-styled myth present it as something negative. This makes for a highly dangerous state of self-conflict. The west remains unconscious of the myth with which it describes itself, and unconscious psychic functions are always prone to turn against us.

Studies of the limits of the globe thus function on two different levels, shifting constantly back and forth between them. At the upper level we find immediate, articulate and historically responsible observation, no less technological than the world it attempts to describe. What we find at the lower level is much more pessimistic – prophetic, secretly inspired and a-historical. It is here that we find the seat of the narrative's "moral" element, which is of course the force that determines its shape and that structures the meaning of the negative epic. It formulates something more than any superficial lament on the loss of earlier and simpler times – a theme to be found in every age – and in fact it lends a voice to a much more vast and radical impulse that functions in much more thorough and sophisticated ways. One notes quite clearly that the various authors who deal with the subject of the limits of the globe start out from a number of highly contrasting points of view, and yet all of them reach conclusions that are charged with the same kind of pessimism; what they hold in common seems to derive less from the conscious elaboration of scientific data than rather from the activation of a single unconscious mythic idea.

The culture that lies at the basis of western civilization (if we accept a distinction between these often synonymous terms)[3] makes a remarkable departure from the cultures of nearly all other civilizations: the basic tenets that it consciously holds include an idea of productive technology as an agent of positive expansion. This culture, in short, is consciously committed to that "myth of growth" that in many ways accounts for the nature of the modern world. But this culture is also characterized by an accompanying unconscious fantasy in which it continues to nourish taboos and fears of punishment that in the past were associated with arrogance and excessive fortune. It therefore continues to live in fear of catastrophe, the forgotten denoument of its myth.

Unlimited growth is tantamount to the theft and unwarranted exercise of activities that belong to the gods. Anything that knows no limits is a part of their own and peculiarly divine prerogative.

One notes as well that the Latin words for "grow" (*cresco*) and "create" (*creo*) are intransitive and transitive valences of one and the same root, which is to say that growth and creation are the self-same act. We forget this fact because it manifests our sin of pride. Both are a question – growth internally, and creation externally – of causing the existence of a quantity that had no previous substance.

We are to see, moreover, that faith in the growth of human society, in the continuity of human development, and, more unconsciously, in a limitless course of history and an endless collective immortality (the vessels that respectively host them in the course of time) constitute expectations that do not date back to the origins of western culture. They are one of the products of western culture and they have slipped, like others, beyond its control. At the beginnings of western culture, things stood in fact quite differently. The myth of growth found its genesis in the disruption of the principles of moderation that originally flourished in ancient Greece.

The central part of our essay will therefore address the ancient culture of this country that cultivated the notion of limits and that likewise counts as the starting point of the history of our civilization. Our culture, after all, and rightly so, has been referred to as Hellenocentric.[4] Yet the decision to tread this path – like the exercise of any other option – none the less exhibits a certain one-sidedness. The later role of Christianity, which most certainly contributed to our notions of limits, will receive no more than indirect consideration. And the treatment of Greece itself will not be truly equable since the variety of its culture, its various epochs and its various states will remain unstressed so as better to savor its most essential traits. We know as well that the gods of Olympus do not date back to the origins of Hellenic culture and that the ways in which they were characterized were never truly stable or univocal. The religion that centered on Olympus had to conquer spaces that were occupied by the chthonian cults, by the mystery religions,[5] and also by the strange and overwhelming gods that came from the Orient.[6] Still, however, the gods of Olympus will serve as our general point of reference since they represent the forms of religion that were most widely practiced and their figures had the presence of already well-codified metaphors. And while recognizing the significance of Sparta, Ionia, Thebes, Corinth and Hellenized Macedonia, we will concentrate on Athens, seeing it as the most important of the city-states and as a crucible of unrivaled creativity. Our references, moreover, to the various historical phases of Greek civilization will primarily aim to relate them to the fifth century; this was the age in which the decisive developments that hold our interest can be seen to have crystalized as Athens affirmed and asserted its superiority. Our need, finally, to retrieve a sense of the essence of a Greek spirit – no matter if historical or intuitively reconstructed – will lead us to select our sources according to criteria that were dominant in ancient Greece itself. No matter how perfect they may have been, the figurative arts in ancient Greece were only accessory ornament, whereas the site of true creation was the word. Poetry derives from *poiéo*, the verb "do."[7] Our study will be based primarily on written documents.

The need for a paradigmatic vision of antiquity is mainly a modern need. When Greece and Hellenic culture were rediscovered, they came to be seen as an absolute ideal. Burckhardt and Nietzsche turned the Greeks into a metaphor of the very goals of education, and as such they initially enlivened the cultural life of nineteenth-century Germany and later contributed – here is the paradox – to the formation of modern thought.[8] This strong and highly concentrated image of Hellenic man is one of the tools that our recent culture has habitually employed for the stimulation of cultural growth – or of what the Greeks themselves referred to as *paideía*, which was a great deal more profound than any process of simple learning. Rather than in the documents that reach us from the past, the meaning of such an image is actually more to be found in the ways we currently use it. It is of less importance as a model that allows us to delve into the nature of antiquity than as a model for present-day life. Depth psychology goes about its tasks through the use of similar constructs. The unconscious is its principal working hypothesis, and that hypothesis is not verifiable. But the very notion of the unconscious has exercised significant influence, whether good or bad, on the shaping of modern culture.

This essay will attempt to explore the genealogy[9] of the Greek myth that set limits for desire. The task of following the myth's subsequent developments in the history of the west lies outside its scope, but it will none the less suggest hypotheses on the ways in which it relates to the modern state of mind that experiences the uninterrupted growth of our civilization as a source of guilt.

An essay on this theme was missing. It will contribute to revealing the extent to which scientific analysis, in today's criticism of unlimited growth, is indebted to a mythic tradition. This mythic tradition merits being taken as the object of a psychological study of its own, and such a study has the merit of concerning itself with spiritual needs that remain untainted by social and intellectual fashion.

The identification of a residual myth in such scientific studies may help to further the acceptance of their practical implications by furnishing them with a basis in collective psychology. Since the myth persists as a relatively stable model, or as a model that largely asserts its independence of specific historical circumstances, it merits attention not only as a precedent to current considerations but also as a possible guide. It contains proposals for moral behavior that are psychologically rooted in society, and thus for a practicable alternative to the forward propulsion of heroic models and their clash with the barrier of divine taboos. Consider for a moment the myth of Prometheus, which will later be one of our subjects of discussion.

Greek and Christian attitudes to myth were highly different from one another. Christianity was to redimension myth, curbing its indeterminate range of action and hemming it into the confines of Holy Scripture; and all of its multiformity had to be reduced to a sense of monotheistic uniformity. The position of myth in Greek civilization was absolute – in terms of its range of validity, in terms of its level of articulation, and also by virtue of its having being destined not so much to didactic purposes as simply to being listened to. The prejudices of the modern mind see knowledge as equivalent to the development of concepts, but that was surely not the case for the ancient Greeks. Myth and concepts were inextricably intertwined with one another and they developed in one another's company. There was no such thing as knowledge without myth.

Myth was always true, even if certainly not in ways that our own morality and rationality find it easy to accept. It pronounced no well-honed ethical principles such as one finds in monotheism or in philosophical reflection; and it paid no allegiance to the forms of rational cognition that have since become typical of science. But even if the basic forms of later modes and stages of knowledge were not revealed in myth, they were not necessarily extraneous to it. One does better to see them as unconscious structures that were held within it. The radical opposition of myth on the one hand and of science and philosophy on the other is a modern prejudice; and the appearance of science and philosophy in ancient Greece is seen by the modern mind as a sudden rupture or as the advent of a revelation. But there is also a continuity[10] between the traditional mythic thought of the Greeks and the surprising novelties that they authored. The aesthetic and psychological functions of myth were not unknown to the great innovators, whom we would be mistaken to imagine as having been always intent on challenging that tradition. After describing the "geographic" myth of the destiny of souls, Socrates comments:

A man of sense ought not to say, nor will I be very confident, that the description which I have given of the soul and her mansions is exactly true. But I do say, inasmuch as the soul is shown to be immortal, he may venture to think, not improperly or unworthily, that something of the kind is true.[11]

In the Greek community, myth occupied a central position; it nourished a stream of collective feelings and a reservoir of shared cultural images such as now are unknown in the drought of the modern world. It was rather like the single thread that runs through the whole of a knitted fabric. Aside from its religious importance for the individual, the function of myth for the collective mind was similar to the function of dream in the life of the personal psyche. Myths have been referred to as "the secular dreams of youthful humanity."[12] And just as the artificial elimination of dream produces pathology, thus clearly revealing the status of dream as a physiological and psychological need, the elimination of myth is accompanied by states of collective insecurity, proving its importance for the maintenance of historical continuity and sociological cohesion.[13]

Myth was essential to the thinking of the ancient Greeks, and their modes of cognition were thus quite different from the thinking of the monotheistic religions, where myth is preserved only in the background; and there is of course an even more radical difference between the thinking of the Greeks and the secular rationality of modern thought, where the loss of myth is total. Whereas the truths of scientific thinking are rooted into where they come from (turning their attention to causes), the truths of mythical thinking find their center in their destination (the revelation of meaning). Myth was committed not to objective truth but to salvation. In this sense, myth is properly considered to be true whenever it effectively performs a task that contributes to the health of the soul. The myth that we are about to relate was a life-giving force for ancient Greek civilization at the moment when it stood at the summit of its splendor and encountered its greatest danger. The myth made itself concrete by determining the form of a series of historical, artistic and military achievements. And having performed this task, it disappeared.

This book presents its readers with a question. Are the limits of the development of modern civilization an exclusively technical problem, or a psychological problem as well? Are there people who still believe in the myth that tells us that too much desire creates catastrophe? If the answer reads that the modern world can accept nothing other than exclusively external limits to otherwise infinite needs, the nature of the problem would be entirely political; and in all of their attempts to deal with it, the politicians have already given proof of their impotence. But we think that things stand differently. As a moral question that finds its basis in religious no less than in political terms, the widespread attempt to discern the limits of growth gives voice to expectations or presuppositions that are already seated in the minds of those who have turned their attention to the study of the global crisis. The notion of limits belongs to an unconscious myth, and unconscious myths make themselves manifest through a process of projection: limits thus come to be projected into the scientific data to which the scholar has access.

Among the ancient Greeks, the myth of limits did a great deal more than to offer any simple description of limits: it constituted limits and acted as its own agent. Early Greek civilization belongs to a context in which the human being had only recently left behind a condition of life that we presume to have been governed by instinct; self-limitation was one of the most intensely felt and generally applied of the factors that had to be called into play for the organization of the personality. Respect for what we have now become should not allow us to imagine that such a form of restraint – simple, ancient and charged with meaning – is definitively unproposable for the man of today.

To draw this premise to a close, the terms we have chosen to employ – developing a discourse on "limits" – require a few words of explanation, since the way in which we use them could appear to be too broad. We started out by asking ourselves whether needs and desires, if left entirely free, would be subject to infinite expansion, or whether instead they would reach a natural end. *Līmes*, in Latin, was a very simple word. It indicated the path that marked the borders of agricultural fields, and later it came to be applied to all frontiers. *Horus* was the corresponding term in Greek, and by extension it could also mean "rule" or "law."[14] Solon employed this word to describe the role he assumed as the vessel that contained all politics and morals; and we remember that his role was quite decisive for the future development of Hellenic culture.[15]

When I first began this book I was thinking in different terms – in terms of the notion of "just measure." But I then discarded this expression since it continues to contain an element of ancient ethics; it corresponds too precisely to the Latin notion of *aurea mediocritas* (the golden middle way).[16] So it seemed to run the risk of not referring with sufficient clarity to the current aspects of the problem. And that "just" seemed to harbor the shade of a foregone moral judgment.

Another possibility would have been to think in terms of the notion of "inhibition." "Inhibition," as defined by Freud, refers in fact to the limitation of a function of the individual.[17] And yet, even though Freud also makes use of this concept with reference to non-pathological situations, it now smacks too strongly of the clinic. It therefore contrasted with my aim to see the process of self-limitation as belonging to a much more general context – a context that surely no longer incarnates a myth or an ancient ethic, but where a myth none the less might hopefully continue to exist as the materializiation of a widely experienced modality of reason, and also as a civilized form of instinct.

Self-inhibition was certainly not invented by civilization and then subsequently imposed upon instinct. Quite the opposite is true. Nature itself is self-regulatory. Trees do not continue to grow to the point of touching the sky. And for a great deal of time, human beings quite naturally offered a series of similar examples of this need for limits. Limits were given a place in the commandments of pre-modern religion, and surely they are present in music. Men codified such limits while remaining unaware of simply giving an externally visible form to the needs of the human soul and the human ear.[18] Even in the twenty-first century, the newborn child and the animals whose instincts have been allowed to remain intact – animals which rank as anything more than pets – will not run the risk of over-eating. Civilization alone has toppled the hierarchy of the instincts and sent awry their principles of self-regulation. We have invented excess food and excess nausea as a way of attempting to appropriate the endless beatitude that rightfully belongs to the gods. Growth, which by now we believe to be life itself, is but one of its possible metaphors; and endless growth is nothing more than an ingenuous metaphor of immortality.

2

TOWARDS A PSYCHOLOGICAL TERRITORY

Psyché is the Greek word for "the soul," and psychology is literally the study of the soul, which means that it deals with entities that cannot be directly observed. We cannot study love, dependency and hate in the ways we study things and they can only be perceived as forces that make themselves visible in human behavior.

The psychology of real life, as opposed to experimental psychology, therefore makes use of metaphors as an indirect way of dealing with things that cannot be approached in any other way.

When we talk about geography, we no longer have any need for antiquity's mythographic models that describe the earth as a flat surface, held up by giants. An artificial satellite quite rapidly gives us a picture of the world that lies beyond the Columns of Hercules. But when it comes to discussing interior spaces and the various conditions and stages of development of the soul, there are no new technologies that can come to our aid. Once again, as always before, we have to turn to metaphors.

There is no way of being certain that technological developments may not one day make the qualities of the soul directly observable. And the metaphors that serve as our charts of the psyche might at that point prove to be as fully deficient as the ancient maps that show the world as flat. But for the present such metaphors still remain the instruments to which we have to turn for orientation; and just as the geography of the ancients gave pioneers a basis for the exploration of the physical earth, these metaphors have allowed our first advances in the exploration of the spaces of the soul.

Instead of inventing cold concepts, which would be free of all narrative quality, depth psychology[1] has frequently turned to the use of metaphors that derive from classical mythology, of which the first was the Oedipus complex. To return to recounting such myths can help us again to evoke the emotions they originally excited. In Greek and Roman mythology, the gods and all other higher powers were persons in every way similar to

13

human beings. We now no longer perceive them as external supernatural forces, but we continue to be open to their meaning and aesthetic power. Their apparent naiveté as theological constructs accords with a psychological truth: the activities that take place in the depths of the psyche (such as aggressiveness or love) have always been experienced as impositions, or as the invasion of the human individual by other active forces. In earlier times such forces were experienced theologically, as divine external entities; today they are experienced psychologically, or as interior drives more powerful than conscious intention. The relativization of the unity of the individual – the understanding that a plethora of forces is at play within the individual and that the individual's will is subject to powerful limitations – counts as one of the most important premises of depth psychology, and most particularly for the analytical psychology of C. G. Jung. An historical precedent for such a point of view can be found in the polycentric psychology that lies at the basis of Greek polytheism. Ancient mythology and the modern psychology that expresses itself through metaphors proceed along roads that are very close to one another, rather as though the millennia that separate these modes of thought were of very little importance. The interval between these two visions of the world ought to be a locus of progress. But progress does not seem to have conferred more importance on the role of human will, nor has it done very much to keep myth from continuing to lay its siege against the very roots of that faculty.[2]

Compared to the metaphors of myth, the metaphors employed by psychology have less emotional power; they are therefore less persuasive, or their powers of persuasion are not so direct and peremptory. But the metaphors employed by psychology take on the task of producing new levels of consciousness. To immerse oneself in myth can no longer mean to return to a liturgy that insists on resignation to destiny. It is instead a question of attempting to effect a reconstruction or re-appropriation of knowledge. Since this is their purpose, the metaphors employed by psychology, unlike those of myth, are in no way fatalistic. They always insist on the need for cognitive responsibility. It is true that there may perhaps be no such thing as cognitive responsibility,[3] just as the gods were fictitious. But it is equally possible that men now stand before responsibility in much the same way that men of the past stood before Olympus. The notion of responsibility could prove to be an efficacious and necessary tool, even in spite of referring to a myth rather than to any concrete reality. Every age considers its own particular convictions to be truths, and leaves every successive age with the task of proving that their only reality was as modes of communication. Myths, since they are forms of communication, are always relative. The value we attribute to the widening of consciousness, and thus to the assumption of greater responsibility, is itself another of the facets of the myth of growth that these pages hope to

14

explore. Rather than standing accepted as a sure and final value, it counts as a chapter of the story that we are now about to relate.

The conscious assumption of responsibility is nothing new. Fifth-century Greece was the scene of a suddenly more active awareness of human possibilities, and from at least that period onwards the Greeks were already much concerned with a particular form of responsibility that was crucial for the further unfolding of their cultural potential. The intensity of their interest in education (*paideía*) makes the Greeks quite different from the other peoples of antiquity and brings them closer to ourselves. But what the modern world calls "education" still says far too little about the nature of the commitments involved in the notion of *paideía*, which was a question of a great deal more than schooling for the young. *Paideía* was pertinent to every aspect of human development, independently of age and in every possible circumstance, and its concerns were never restricted to the simple transmission of knowledge. Its goal instead was to discover and develop the in-born gifts of which the seeds had been planted in man by nature, and it presupposed that no such seeds could germinate, grow, develop into plants, and finally bear fruit without proper cultivation. "Culture" and "cultivation" in fact were originally the very same word. The Greeks' most heroic achievement may perhaps have been *paideía* itself, and its birth remains virtually synonymous with the birth of everything we mean by "culture" itself, here thinking to allow that word the whole of the range of its highest connotations within a European context.[4]

The tasks assumed by *paideía* had nothing to do with questions of good and evil; they were wholly concerned with the individual's natural duty to develop the gifts conferred by birth and nature. In addition to revealing that the origins of *paideía* were aristocratic – even if Athens saw it as applying to all free men – the notion of in-born qualities also implies the existence of certain intrinsic limits that must always be respected: by persons who are not in possession of certain qualities, and by persons who have the duty of employing them. The words of the aristocratic Pindar probably give us the essence of Hellenic morality: "Become what you are by nature!"[5] The very notion of nature (*phýsis*) was itself a central and lasting invention of this particular period of Greek culture; without it, no such thing as the natural sciences could ever have developed.

The Greeks intuitively understood that the growth (*phýesthai*) of a plant was determined by a series of rigorous conditions, and they thus embarked on a general search for potentials and the norms that control the ways in which they unfold. Potential and its realization were facts to be looked for in everything around them, and no less in historical events than in the lives of individuals.[6] Speculation began to develop at unprecedented speeds and led to ever less interest in the gods, since the tales that were told of the gods had nothing to say about the hidden laws responsible for the growth in the world. *Paideía* came to be a question of completing the work of nature. And yet the development of the individual was never understood as the end in itself to which people today find it natural to aspire. The development of the individual was seen in terms of the individual's function as an organ of the city-state, and the ideal city-state of the aristocratic Plato was based on a "communist" ideal. Plato lived in an era in which the free man saw his first duty in useful work and service to the state.

Such rights and duties were felt with particular intensity in Athens, and the relation between them was clearer in Athens than elsewhere. Thucydides attributes this statement to Pericles: "In a word, then, I say that our city as a whole is the school of Hellas."[7] The growth of the individual took place inside society, just as the growth of plants took place inside nature; and both society and the individual had to give harmonious realization to the law that imposes growth on the one hand, and that limits it on the other. But Athenian society elaborated the guidelines of a project that was so completely modern as to seem not only grandiose, but tainted as well by presumptions of omnipotence; and it thus betrayed its own premises. Its novelties could not be reconciled with traditional religion. Traditional religion cast its lot with immobility, whereas the ever more impelling Athenian thirst for growth and knowledge was the beginning of that impulse towards the limitless with which we are here concerned. It is clear, however, that this world of new aspirations could not simply and suddenly eliminate the world of myth and religion. The new world came in many ways to be superimposed upon the older, and it permitted the continued existence of the world of tradition partly in unconscious forms, and partly in the conscious thoughts of the less cultured strata of society. This whole array of new attitudes infused unprecedented levels of energy into the life of the Greek city-states, and of Athens first of all, but this energy could continue to express itself for only so long as the Greeks could maintain a difficult balance between the individual and the state. The individual was committed to self-perfection, but the collective sense of the state had the power and proportions of a true and proper religion.[8] Individualism was the force that was later to come to the fore, as can be seen in art and literature. Though remaining entirely memorable, the art and literature that date from after the age of Pericles are far less concerned with aspirations to the absolute since they began to be made in the name of individual enjoyment and no longer for the purpose of collective worship of the state.[9]

It is interesting to note that reliance on mythological metaphors is not the only connection between this ancient civilization and modern depth psychology. When his studies led him beyond the pale of the traditional categories of normalcy and pathology, C. G. Jung proposed that the ideal route through the problems of the life of the psyche might be found in the "individuation process." This concept is generally held to derive from the ways in which Jung was influenced by Nietzsche and German romanticism. Nietzsche entitled one of his works *Ecce homo: How One Becomes What One Is*. But the roots of the notion of individuation are already to be found in Pindar's exhortation and in the similar maxim of the Delphic oracle: "Know thyself." And it is surely no accident that classical Greek literature lay at the roots of Nietzsche's thinking. Individuation is a question of being oneself and of living up to the duties and dictates imposed by one's own nature, and such things have nothing to do with any contrast between normalcy and pathology. The ideal Greek, when he committed himself to *paideía*, was likewise free of any dualism of good and evil that imposed a priori decisions about the ways in which he ought to conduct himself. His only necessary obedience was to what he discovered himself to be. *Paideía*, for Jungian psychology, is the historical archetype of the individuation process.

A psychology that works with metaphors and that regulates itself by appealing to myths stands necessarily at a distance from the customary models of scientific thought. Its mode of thought can seem to represent a kind of intellectual extremism, but still there is virtually no other possible route for a discipline that can take no recourse to laboratory measurements. The psychologist's task is to describe the immaterial forms of the soul,[10] and the nature of the discipline is essentially reflexive, which is to say that the psychologist works in a space where subject and object coincide.[11]

Its recourse to metaphor gives psychology a very particular place among the various forms of knowledge. Even the testing of hypotheses comes to depend on the metaphoric language in which one has chosen to couch them. Any number of critics[12] maintain that demonstrations of the theories of psychodynamics through the use of practical case studies boil down to nothing more than tautological variations of the metaphors that constitute their point of departure (the myths, for example, of Oedipus or Agamemnon, and so forth). And if we shift the system of metaphors that serves as our frame of reference, any single case can be seen to give rise to highly different conclusions, diagnoses and prognoses.

One has no other choice than to agree with such clearly grounded objections. But they none the less recede when we think of depth psychology not as a natural science, but rather as a form of knowledge in a much more ample sense where the psyche is dealt with not so much in terms of procedures (such as diagnosis, therapy and prognosis) that derive from a medical model as in terms of a process of education based on self-awareness.

The psyche's route of self-elevation – the progress of the soul – can then be expected to find its realization in forms that vary from case to case; they remain unpredictable, even while never being improvised. The process is analogous to the processes of interior growth that were once an integral part of religion and philosophy, or of culture[13] in general. Without necessarily having to refer to the Jungian notion of the "individuation process," this form of growth for adults is a modern version of *Paideía*.

An education can quite profitably proceed along any number of roads that by no means exclude one another. Knowledge and awareness can come to be enlarged in ways that are no less variable than the soul itself. The procedures of science are something quite different. In pursuing the purposes of education, every age has turned above all to paradigmatic narratives, or to its own particular myths. To remark, moreover, that depth psychology is an instrument of personal transformation rather than a scientific discipline is simply to note that its purposes have nothing to do with the explanation of fixed and stable entities; its goal is to *comprehend* the various and variable individuals whom it encounters along its way and to assist them in their processes of development. *To comprehend*, from the Latin *cum prehendere* (to take together) is not too different from the English *understand*, the German *ver-stehen*, and the Greek *epi-stámai* – which indicate occupying or standing in a single place. To comprehend an individual is thus to inhabit the same zone of the psyche; and this notion is of crucial importance in the practice of psychotherapy. Anyone acquainted with our field will know that the analyst with the most brilliant intellect is not necessarily the most effective, and may indeed be totally ineffective. What an analyst has to possess is empathy and the ability "to talk" the mythical language in which the patient will sooner or later address him/her. To achieve an understanding of psychic suffering, a part of the analyst's mind has to be distanced from rationality and proceed with lively feeling into the areas of the psyche inhabited by dream, instinct and madness, which are the areas where myth survives. When depth psychology examines the various conditions in which the psyche can find itself (melancholy, anger and so forth) its purpose has nothing to do with explaining a sickness or a more or less stable syndrome that lies hidden behind them; its purpose is simply to comprehend or understand the person who experiences them. Comprehension for depth psychology means establishing an identity of experience with the lives it observes, and thus to become a part of them, sharing their emotions and living their myths.

We will follow a similar procedure in the pages to come, attempting to reach a comprehension of now distant epochs. But distance does not make them inaccessible to intuition.[14] These, in fact, were precisely the epochs that produced the myths that today's psychology yokes to the wagon of the unconscious.

Aiming to comprehend rather than to explain is a question of suggesting images rather than of offering demonstrations, and as such it can seem to be limited. But the attempt to identify with the worlds we observe is more substantial than at first it appears to be. The analyst is accustomed to do so for clinical reasons: as part of a search for knowledge, but primarily to offer assistance in a process of transformation. By pointing out a pathology of today's civilization and tracing out its past I hope to do something of the same. In the company of the reader, I hope to be able once again to move into a territory where cures for this sickness still existed and to help them to benefit from their rediscovery: by participating, at least within the limits that a book can offer, in a therapy of civilization.

3

THE LIMITS OF ENDEAVOR IN NON-WESTERN CULTURES*

THE ORIENT

Holding and keeping a thing to the very full – it is better to leave it alone;
Handling and sharpening a blade – it cannot be long sustained;
When gold and jade fill the hall, no one can protect them;
Wealth and honor with pride bring with them destruction;
To have accomplished merit and acquired fame, then to retire –
This is the Tao of Heaven.

(Tao Te Ching, 9)

There is no greater crime than seeking what men desire;
There is no greater misery than knowing no content;
There is no greater calamity than indulging in greed.
Therefore the contentment of knowing content will ever be contented.

(Tao Te Ching, 46)

The Master said, Those who err on the side of strictness are few indeed!

(The Analects of Confucius, IV, 23)

The Blessed Lord Said:
"One has to understand what action is, and likewise one has to understand what is wrong action and one has to understand about inaction. Hard to understand is the way of work.

"He who in action sees inaction and action in inaction, he is wise among men, he is a yogin and he has accomplished all his work.

"He whose undertakings are all free from the will of desire, whose works are burned up in the fire of wisdom, him the wise call a man of learning.

"Having abandoned attachment to the fruit of works, ever content, without any kind of dependence, he does nothing though he is ever engaged in work.

20

"Having no desires, with his heart and self under control, giving up all possessions, performing action by the body alone, he commits no wrong.

"He who is satisfied with whatever comes by chance, who has passed beyond the dualities (of pleasure and pain) who is free from jealousy, who remains the same in success and failure, even when he acts, he is not bound.

"The work of a man whose attachments are sundered, who is liberated, whose mind is firmly founded in wisdom, who does work as a sacrifice, is dissolved entirely."

(*The Bhagavadgita*, IV, 17–23)

Whose senses have reached an even temper,
Like horses well trained by a charioteer,
Who has discarded self-estimation, who is free of influxes,
Even the gods cherish such a one.

(Buddha, *Dhammapada*, 94)

A western observer who turns their attention to India, China and Japan will surely grow aware of the manifold differences between Taoism, Buddhism, Hinduism and Confucianism, but is none the less likely to feel that they show a common ethical structure. The enormous distance that separates the west from the Orient causes its various worlds to be perceived as shadings of a single *Weltanschauung*. Our understanding of this *Weltanschauung* may perhaps remain partial and faulty, but still it can be of assistance in our attempt to understand ourselves.

We find ourselves faced not so much with a series of commandments or prohibitions that are at variance with our own, but indeed with a vision of human life to which the western mind is wholly alien. Eastern notions of rectitude, for example, place no immediate emphasis on distinctions between proper and improper action.

The Orient seems often to conceive of action itself as an evil. Or at least, to be more precise, it finds an example of evil in the illusion that setting our sights on goals can alter the conditions of human existence. Good, on the other hand, is identified with everything that serves to destroy the illusions of such an activistic attitude – though without impeding the performance of particular acts, which may even be seen as obligatory – and thus to lead us back to an absence of needs that accords with an idea of the whole. "The whole," moreover, is always close to what we would call "the void,"and at times they are even identical.

Oriental ethics – and especially Buddhist and Indian ethics – demands that the world be respected and treated as a given that the human being is not to attempt to modify. The ethical ideal is liberation from desire. Desire, which prods and disturbs us, is the seat of disorder, and it counts as the source of movement and becoming. This eastern attitude of

21

renunciation with respect to the transformation of the world is found not only in systems that are ruled by providential deities, but also, and even perhaps more fittingly, in others where the deities are indifferent, or even entirely absent.

There were no gods, for example, in the original form of Buddhism, and many western thinkers have therefore called it a philosophy rather than a religion. The ideal of conduct imparted by the Buddha resembles many of the prescriptions found in Yoga: withdrawal and detachment from the circumstances of the world, since they embody no more than illusion. It is true that later variations of Buddhism are less concerned with teaching withdrawal from action than with promoting a certain style or mode of action, but here again the primary purpose lies not in creating good, but in annulling the evil that resides in the pain of the world. Even while rejecting the rigors of asceticism, Gautama expressed no faith in action; his principle concern was to express mistrust for every form of excess. Such an attitude is common to all of the various modes of Oriental thought, and it holds considerable significance for the development of our theme. The very structure of Buddha's faith has nothing to do with inviting human beings to action as a way of pleasing God or meriting heaven. Among all the founders of religions, Siddharta Gautama, known later as the Buddha, is the only one who never spoke in the name of a god; he never even affirmed that gods or a god exist.[1] Confucius too presented himself primarily as an educator,[2] and never as the voice of a revelation.[3]

Oriental thought cannot conceive of a human being who is animated by an absolute thirst for conquest. Action is never based on pure, abstract idea, and is always in relation to specific goals. The action of the individual, or the space controlled by the individual's will, is of a very low order of magnitude, and generally far too slight to allow it to alter a destiny or to serve as a vehicle of meaning. Such attitudes of detachment, which are also embodied by the Indian notion of *karma*, are common to all of the doctrines of the Far East, and they help to explain why eastern cultures have been generally indifferent to history. History results from the work of incomprehensible superior forces and is once again a demonstration of the paucity and unimportance of human action.

Such low regard for history forms a singular link between Asia and the ancient Greeks,[4] relating as well to the Greek sense of fate.[5] Our own most typical assessments of the value of human action are quite different, in addition to ranking as much more recent. The Judeo-Christian tradition, and Protestantism in particular, sees human action as highly significant. Man is very small in comparison with God, but he has been created none the less in God's image. Man is the lord of the earth, the master of the fish of the sea, the fowl of the sky, and the beasts of the earth, and as well of all vegetable life.[6] Man, since he resembles God the Father and Creator, must in turn attempt to create, and to assume the responsibilities that accompany the act of creation. God has fashioned man from clay and made him similar to Himself. Man, in the Judeo-Christian tradition, is God's chosen creature, and the lives of those who adhere to this faith are dedicated to the constant effort of confirming the legitimacy of God's predilection. Man takes on the task of turning himself into another creative subject, shaping and constantly re-creating the world. He continues to shape the clay of which he himself was made. Since man was made in the likeness of God, he is also endowed with free will. If the Oriental conceives of themselves as a drop of water that flows within the cosmic current, the westerner might be thought of as a boat. No matter how frail this vessel may be, its place is on top of the water: it is not at one with the water, and it pursues a route of its own. But it can also founder.

At this point we can take a brief look at a few concrete examples of Oriental attitudes to technological innovation and economic growth.

Thanks to its contacts with Europe, Japan was acquainted with firearms in the sixteenth and early seventeenth centuries, and began to produce them on its own. The Japanese talent for improving the products they imitate is no recent acquisition. Some of the early firearms that Japan produced were of such high quality as to able to be reconverted and successfully used in the nineteenth and early twentieth centuries after having been abandoned for hundreds of years.

The end of this period of Japan's first opening to the west was quite rapid. Between 1616 and 1641 the European missions and commercial centers that were active in Japan were subjected to ever increasing restrictions that forced them finally to abandon the country. The new model of military action, ever more dependent on the use of firearms, disappeared along with them: Japan – in a case without precedent and never repeated – worked its way upstream, bucking the current of technological development, and gradually returned to the sword.[7] How can this be explained?

The conservative ideology of the aristocrats who scorned the new armaments, which were better suited to the infantry than to the cavalry, is an only partial explanation. All throughout history and in manifold societies, the aristocracy has typically objected to arms for combat at distance. In the war between Chalcis and Eretria, the contenders even took a solemn oath in which they renounced the use of bows and arrows and javelins.[8] But the usual conclusion, sooner or later, had been a surrender to the new technologies. In Europe too, the nobility initially held a very low opinion of firearms, but that did not allow them to halt their diffusion. Surely one has to remember that Japan is an island and found itself at considerable distance from other military powers of comparable strength; and one likewise has to consider that the enormous size of its class of

23

nobles and warriors (almost 2 million men, as opposed to a few tens of thousands in the European countries of the same period) made the country invincible even in the absence of the use of firearms. But these arguments relate to external enemies and overlook internal wars, which were surely not infrequent in Japan.

The desires of a particular caste are an insufficient explanation. And the same holds true for the will of the central government, which, just as in France and in England, restricted the possession of firearms and reserved their production to monopolies. But such edicts never achieved their goal in Europe, whereas they were wholly effective in Japan. No society listens exclusively to the voice of its legislators; laws have to agree with already accepted values. Japanese society was apparently much more amenable to the limitation of innovation, as represented by firearms. In the west, quite to the contrary, the rationale of firearms was inevitably seconded by a mode of thought that found its bearings in quantitative results. The west had already cast its lot with the forms of extroverted thinking, projected towards great inventions and discoveries, that would finally lead to the age of Enlightenment.[9] Firearms could not be banned, just as a system of economic expansion found it impossible to prohibit the lending of money for interest.

Japan's traditional preoccupation with military strength was not at all based on the kind of rational attention to concrete results that was found in the west. The heroic ethic of the Far East had a looser connection with the notion of victory. It often set restraints to its own aspirations, and at times it was openly fascinated by the image of defeat.[10] It found the proof of its own vitality not in the scale of its victories, but in its degree of successful adherence to its own essentially aesthetic principles. The Japanese soldiers who after the end of the Second World War remained for decades at their posts on remote Pacific islands know no western counterpart. They strike us as so remarkable for reasons that in fact have nothing to do with any material exploit: what makes them stand out is their commitment to an ideal that remains unconcerned with the achievement of military goals. The honor of the warrior resides in his serenity and detachment of spirit, and not in the measurable outcome of any battle that he wages.

The ethic of the artist and the soldier in Japan – no matter how strange it may seem to a western mind – were in this regard quite similar. An ancient tradition insists that the work of a Japanese artist intentionally includes a faulty detail: the artist is to use his very own hand to call himself back to a sense of modesty and to thwart the achievement of perfection.

It was only in Europe that the business firm developed as an institution in its own right, with a rational system of accounting entirely its own, and thus fully independent of the personal accounting of the family to whom it belonged.[11] This also marked the birth of a process of economic development that was based on entrepreneurial growth and no longer on the growth of personal needs.

Europe first entered into contact with China in the late Middle Ages, and the encounter took place on far from equal terms. With respect to scientific knowledge, technical know-how and the general level of civilization, China was quite superior to Europe.[12] And China maintained its advantage, albeit a dwindling advantage, throughout the following centuries; it was only with the start of the industrial revolution that Europe achieved a final and definite supremacy. One of the likely reasons why the Chinese economy did not accelerate in a similar way is that the Chinese found it difficult to conceive of a business enterprise as something independent of the person or family who controlled it. They were alien to the thought that an enterprise could be an entity with a life and dignity of its own, and devoted to an endless conquest of markets rather than to the satisfaction of more immediate and visible needs.

To shape such notions, Chinese thought would have had to construct a whole new series of abstract concepts[13] and to cultivate a lust for change and growth; desires and habits of mind that our own society quite naturally inherited from the late Greeks lay wholly outside of Oriental tradition. There is perhaps a shorter distance than at first there seems to be between the notion of knowledge as an external, rational and abstract entity – an entity not to be identified with the master through whom it speaks[14] – and the collective mental structures that lie at the base of technology and of Europe's industrial capitalism. The objectification of *lógos* permitted western thought to embark on a course of endless development that makes no reference to the person of the thinker; and the notion of the enterprise as an independent institution, distinct from the person of the entrepreneur, allowed businesses to expand, to increase the number of their financiers, to be bought and sold, and in short to embark on a similar course of limitless growth and mobility as self-sufficient organizations to which the personal lives of founders and subsequent proprietors are essentially irrelevant.

Competition for economic supremacy, as the phenomenon developed in Europe, also presupposes the high esteem with which westerners look at the very notion of activity. And the providential western God whose interventions serve good purposes flanks and completes the need for action with an incitation to the planning of foreseeable relationships of cause and effect. Things stood quite differently in China. The highest levels of knowledge in China were likely to be found among persons who were educated to the proper performance of their own particular tasks, but there was no such thing as an ideology that promoted the general improvement of the whole of human life. Chinese culture furnished no model of a god devoted to action, nor did it teach human beings to imitate god.

Economic growth, clearly enough, can never depend on psychological and cultural factors alone. The presence or absence of a number of quantitative parameters has to be thought of as crucial. But once these parameters are present and of an adequate order of magnitude, the decisive factor for development lies in a culture's attitudes, and not in the size of the market it offers. The inhabitants of China were far more numerous than the population of the whole of Europe. But this vast population was never transformed into a vast market. It is true that Chinese society was more rigidly articulated, in the sense that the dominant upper class and the general populace were separated by no such thing as a middle class with significant purchasing power, but this fact remains an insufficient explanation of the ways in which China differed from the markets of the west. Europe's conspicuous bourgeoisie was partly a cause and partly a result of economic development.

And here we can take a look at a specific and meaningful example of the ways in which Chinese attitudes differed from those of the west.

The period between the Renaissance and the industrial revolution saw a great deal of naval traffic between Europe and Asia. Ever greater quantities of spices, silk, cotton and so forth came to the west from the east. But for a great deal of time the west was seriously troubled by the fact that the east – and especially China, which was the Orient's major potential market – wanted almost nothing in exchange. And what excited China's interest least of all was the wealth of new manufactured products that were rapidly becoming a European speciality. The Europeans themselves were ever appreciative of their manufactures and simply could not understand that others might see things differently. China's limited purchasing power is here again no adequate explanation of languishing commercial exchange. The Europeans would have been quite happy with simple barter, or with Chinese purchases of European products in exchange for the European currency that China received for its own goods. But the Chinese market simply showed no interest in purchasing the novelties that Europe had to offer; the products that most acutely fueled the Europeans' desire for possession struck no chord in the Chinese imagination. Much of China's economic potential lay in the hands of mandarins and state officials with a refined humanistic and literary education and an aristocratic frame of mind, and they were wholly indifferent to novelties. At best, they simply ignored technology, and at times they viewed it with hostility. One remembers that gun powder was invented in China and that the country's acquaintance with artillery dated back to at least the thirteenth century (well predating Europe's); and yet the Chinese never created any true and proper system for a large-scale production of cannon and they showed no interest in buying such arms from the Europeans. This was also one of the ways in which China itself created the premises for the loss of its military superiority.[15]

There was only a single exception to the rule of China's indifference to western technology, and it here deserves consideration, since surely it serves to prove and not to confute that rule.[16]

Clocks were one of the very first articles to be industrially produced in Europe (starting as early as the fourteenth century) and for quite some time they were also one of the most profitable. These objects caused great excitement in China, and many were anxious to own them.

But the clock was not perceived as a revolutionary invention on the part of technology, and its use and appreciation did nothing to impose new ways of thinking or of looking at the world; perhaps quite entirely to the contrary. The clock, at least at first, was simply not perceived as a profane, manufactured object. Clocks, in fact, are different from other machines, since there is nothing that they really *do*. They bring about no state of motion in anything other than themselves; their only activity is to register a motion – the movement of the hours – that is already underway and that exists in its very own right. It is also important to remember that for quite some time – even indeed for centuries – these new devices were so imprecise as to require continual correction, and special attendants were often employed for precisely that purpose. Clocks were surely no example of the ways in which modern technology now imposes its tempos and modes of activity on the lives of human beings. It was quite the other way around. Clocks were wholly controlled and constantly re-adjusted by devoted human custodians who continually reset them to the proper time, as ascertained by former and more traditional techniques, which in fact were much more reliable. So the love of clocks had nothing to do with their physical or practical virtues; the value of clocks was metaphysical. They did not at all constrain the mind to grapple with their status as machines and directed it instead to the fact of time itself – to the fact of time as the universal vessel that contains and controls human life, and that we ourselves can in no way alter or direct. In a world that was not yet peopled by manufactured objects and where clocks themselves were the only technological invention with which people were generally acquainted, they constituted no real invitation to ponder the power of technology; they asked instead that the human mind reflect on the flow of life itself and on the scansions of eternal laws.

The clock found rapid popularity, in Europe no less than in China, as a symbol rather than a machine, and it inserted itself quite seamlessly into the religious spirit of the Middle Ages. For a great deal of time, clock-makers gave far more attention to flanking it with symbolic accessories than to the technological problem of making it function more precisely. Clocks provided various themes for philosophical and theological reflections, and for as long as they were primarily public objects, they belonged to the Church. They were associated with bells, and their valence as religious symbol was in some ways analogous to that of bells. It was only with the passage of time and with the gradual mass diffusion of the clock that these

27

new machines, like all machines, revealed themselves to be other than wholly natural. Having been born from mechanistic concepts, the clock was destined to accentuate the mechanistic characteristics of the culture that had created it.

> At the same time, the machine which had been devised to satisfy particular human needs created new ones. Men began timing activities that, in the absence of clocks, they had never thought of timing. People became very conscious of time, and, in the long run, punctuality became at the very same time a need, a virtue, and an obsession. Thus a vicious circle was set into motion. As more and more people obtained clocks and watches, it became necessary for other people to possess similar contrivances, and the machine created the conditions for its own proliferation.[17]

Our subject is the fatal craze for growth that typifies the western world. All of us experience the pace of time – immutable by definition – as having in fact been accelerated. So, for the east to have given the newly invented time machine a permanent place in a wholly static universe seems all the more significant.

In China, the clock continued for a great deal of time to exert its initial fascination, but no strong local market came into existence, and there was surely no Chinese industry for the production of clocks. Time moved the gears of the clocks, and clocks were not given the task of setting the times into motion. Clocks were valuable objects, but they remained without a place in the circulation of wealth. They played no part in trade and economics. The upper classes could in fact have afforded them, but to buy these machines was beneath their dignity. China's mandarins spurned all economic transactions that were less than absolutely necessary. And since they could not simply prohibit themselves from desiring such possessions, the problem found its solution in the feudal frame of mind that allowed the expectation of receiving clocks as gifts: an emblematic gift of time, and of a symbol rather than a mechanical object. So clocks flowed quite intensely from Europe to China, but only as a part of western attempts to curry the favor of the country's lords and court officials, who saw these gifts as their due and who accepted them easily and naturally. Simply to speak of corruption hardly does justice to such transactions. What we ought to see most clearly is a significant exception to China's indifference to the manufactured objects that Europe could offer, but in terms of a continued rejection of Europe's mercantile spirit. China's aristocrats clarified their relationship to Europe through the ritual of accepting a symbolic gift that reconfirmed their status as the masters of an eternally changeless world that knew no flow of history.

This anomalous form of importation was one of the expressions of a body of Chinese attitudes that totally discouraged the birth of a local industry for the manufacture of clocks – even in spite of a suitable work force and a more than adequate level of technical expertise.

PRIMITIVE PEOPLES

> How can you buy or sell the sky, the heat of the earth? The idea seems strange. . . . It is not man who has woven the fabric of life: he only holds the thread. Everything he does to that fabric is something he does to himself. . . . After all, are we not brothers? We will see. There is something we know and that the white man may perhaps soon learn: our god is his god. Perhaps you now think that you possess him, just as you would like to possess our lands; but you cannot. He is the god of men, and he shows the same amount of pity to all; so much for the white man, so much for the red man. This land is precious to him, and to damage the land is to despise its creator. The white men too shall disappear, earlier perhaps than the other tribes. If you dirty your bed, one night you will find yourselves smothered by your filth. . . . This is the end of life and the beginning of survival.
> (Seattle, Chief of the Dwamish, *A letter to President Franklin Pierce*)

Since the so-called primitive peoples were generally unacquainted with the art of writing, there are no written sources through which to examine their ethical norms in the past. We have to rely on their oral traditions. But little remains of these as well, owing to the ways in which Europeans have long since polluted, distorted and submerged their cultures.

Primitive peoples show a constant resistance to disruptions of the order of life as circumscribed by ritual, and they are likewise wary of accepting alterations in the rhythms of existence connected with the environment and the seasons. These attitudes generally come to expression in a mistrust of all activities that are not strictly necessary, and in a respect for "natural" limits, or for limits experienced as such. Though they normally make no use of any general concept of nature that resembles our own, primitive peoples hold their material lives and ethical systems in a state of equilibrium by means of the superstitions with which they constantly direct their attention to the surrounding physical world.[18]

The culture of such peoples develops in the spaces left open by nature, or in the folds that nature can be seen to offer; their cultures wound or modify nature as slightly as possible. There is thus a particular wisdom in the German term for the primitive peoples: *Naturvölker* literally translates as "peoples of nature."

The religious systems of primitive peoples show features that make them profoundly different from our own. The areas surrounding their villages are populated by spirits and deities who are infinitely more powerful than man; such forces, moreover, are not necessarily good and are often explicitly unjust.[19]

Changes in personal or environmental circumstances are almost always

29

seen to hold a meaning, and the terms of interpretation are likely to be magical. The workings of magic – and usually of evil magic – will be found most particularly in whatever departs from norm and predictability.

In religious, historical and economic terms, primitive cultures generally present themselves as closed systems, or as systems that foresee no possibility for true alterations or for evolution. Lévy-Bruhl speaks of "misoneism" (the rejection of the new) as a trait of primitive societies,[20] and Eliade remarks that primitive cultures articulate their rhythms in terms of an "eternal return" that expresses a "terror of history."[21]

The rejection of the new can be seen in the difficulties that primitives often experience in departing from previous ways of life and adopting new technologies. While showing remarkable ability in the use and control of the instruments with which their tradition has made them familiar, primitives may yet prove incapable of using the tools of the Europeans; their ability to deal with European tools can come to be impeded by magical interpretations of their functions, or by a tendency to endow them with autonomous and mainly threatening intentions. Even before taking the tools into their hands, they can be overwhelmed by fears that radically alter their ability to learn, and even their level of manual dexterity. Rather than simple technical apprenticeship, training in the use of European technologies presupposes the rupture of primitives' traditional cultural system and the gradual assimilation of a new one.[22] That, in fact, is what has almost always taken place. Very few peoples have succeeded in preserving their own customs and beliefs while taking possession of radically new technologies.[23] The use of the rifle is more than a new experience that belongs to primitives' physical world; it also alters the laws of their metaphysical world. To make use of the rifle means to manipulate the thunder of the heavens and the white people's magic. The arrival of the Europeans inevitably introduced a great deal of drama into the self-limited worlds of primitive peoples. To defend themselves they had to compete with the virtually unlimited forces and technologies of the new arrivals. But to compete on a terrain that presupposed no limits was already an act of self-betrayal that altered their former identity.

The problem of the "eternal return" underscores the radical difference between civilizations that are rooted in history and others that are rooted in myth. Historical civilizations have the firm belief that people have been entrusted with the responsibility of contributing to the change and improvement of their own destinies. Mythical civilizations, on the other hand, are alien not only to the concept of progress, but also to the very idea of historical change. Myth is their only reality and furnishes an explanation of the origins of everything: of human existence, of the gods and of nature. Man's only responsibility is symbolically to reproduce the genesis of the cosmos, reliving the myth that records it. Myth and the rites in which it reawakens contain all of the laws of life, including the laws of hunting and agriculture. And the purest examples of such forms of civilization are to be found in the primitive cultures.

From primitives' point of view, human life takes place within the immobility of surrounding nature and of the body of religious metaphors in which it finds expression. Variations of more than minimal importance to primitives' scheme of life could not be called impossible, but surely they cannot be thought about – which is even more basic – and are totally undesirable. It cannot be said that the primitive mind condemns the infraction of the limits of action and regards it as a sin, since any such mode of behavior lies normally outside of the range of their very powers of imagination. To conceive of any such sin, the primitive would already have had to take a step beyond their mental world. Whatever departs from that basic state of immobility will tend to be seen as unnatural and menacing.[24]

Wherever primitive peoples have been subjected to a vast and violent invasion on the part of Europeans and their customs, any number of the members of the native tribes felt immediate concern for something more than the actual events from which they suffered: the very arrival of white people was perceived as a fateful and fearsome occurrence.[25] The best-known example is furnished by the clash between the Europeans and the native peoples of North America. The economic immobility of the Native Americans was of an exquisitely religious nature and it was thoroughly disrupted by the nonchalance of the new traders. A profane and abstract concept that dwelled in the minds of the invaders – the notion of property as separate from its use – came suddenly to regulate relationships between nations and individuals.

> My reason teaches me that land cannot be sold. The Great Spirit gave it to his children to live upon, and cultivate, as far as is necessary for their subsistence; and so long as they occupy and cultivate it, they have the right to the soil – but if they voluntarily leave it, then any other people have a right to settle upon it. Nothing can be sold but such things as can be carried away.[26]

The religious concepts of many of the Native American peoples implied so drastic a limit for human intervention on the circumambient world as to make them suspicious of agriculture and to leave no more than a minimum of space even for the activity of hunting.

> You ask me to plow the ground! Shall I take a knife and tear my mother's bosom? Then when I die she will not take me to her bosom to rest. You ask me to dig for stone! Shall I dig under her skin for her bones? Then when I die, I cannot enter her body to be born again. You ask me to cut grass and make hay and sell it, and be rich like white men! But how dare I cut off my mother's hair?[27]

Part II

THE HELLENIC PAST

4

THE EGOISM OF THE ARCHAIC GODS

THE GODS AND THE FORCES OF THE PSYCHE

For a great deal of time the Greeks made use of their gods precisely for the purpose of keeping "bad conscience" at a distance, or for the purpose of being able to rest content with their spiritual freedom. Their use of their gods was precisely antithetical to the use of God in Christianity.

(F. Nietzsche, *Zur Genealogie der Moral*)

The function that Nietzsche attributes to the Greek gods – apparently referring to the gods of Olympus – excludes the notion of their serving as models of rectitude, but it hardly makes them insignificant as determinants of concepts of morality. In the earlier epochs of Greek civilization, the conduct of the gods remained unconnected to clear and invariable ethical principles and spoke instead of the extreme variability of the drives that reside in the unconscious. The gods were the locus of everything that found no proper habitat in the soul of a human being.

Whoever was engulfed by uncontrolled emotions felt tragically excluded from the community,[1] since self-control and moderation ranked high among the primary needs of a people whose titanic effort to create a civilized society was a still recent memory.

Rationality was still a fledgling and might easily have been endangered by overwhelming emotions. So, all such emotions were considered to be intolerable. They were things for which men could assume no responsibility; and therefore they had to be thought of as manifestations of external forces. These forces could then be considered to lie at the roots of all unforeseen or antisocial actions. The Greeks as described by Homer[2] had not yet developed a notion of the unity or homogeneity of what we now refer to, using a term not much different from their own, as the psyche.[3] Their souls were subject to invasion on the part of various forces, some of which were thought of as objective, and others as subjective. To speak of subjective forces as invading the soul is to imply that they lie outside of the ego while still belonging to some other part of the self, as in the cases

35

in which they correspond to corporeal functions. But the Greeks of Archaic times felt they had the right to treat such occurrences as external invasions that overwhelmed their will. They thus had quite a clear understanding of the conditionings to which the will is always subject. Unlike the men of later cultures, they did not yet conceive of the interior world as a single territory. *Daímon* and *theós* (which were very general terms) as well as *áte* (see note 1) *thymós* (the heart as the seat of the passions, and also, at times, as courage) and various other entities could shatter the will of the individual. Though their meanings could shift and were never precise, they personified parts of the soul.

As we approach the duel at the culmination of the *Iliad*, we find Hector outside the walls of Troy, alone in the face of Achilles and the Greeks. His father and mother implore him not to confront the enemy, but Homer implies that Hector does not even reply to them. His will is in the midst of a lacerating struggle with his *thymós*, almost as an interior prolog to his mortal battle with Achilles. The voice of his *thymós* suggests that there may possibly be peaceful solutions, and Hector has to fight against it, fending it off and bitterly reproaching it, in order to be able to reaffirm that his duty as defender of the city permits no compromise.[4]

Odysseus too, on arriving home and while still disguised as a beggar, passes a part of his sleepless night by arguing with his heart, which is impatient for revenge. His thoughts finally win the upper hand in their battle against his emotions and impart the order, "Endure, my heart [*kardía*]; a worse thing even than this didst thou once endure on that day when Cyclops, unrestrained in daring, devoured my mighty comrades."[5]

The personality of the Archaic Greek hero is highly fragmented and seems to lie in a state of transition from a discontinuous mode of the organization of the psyche – such as one finds in childhood or in certain psychopathological conditions – and the kind of mental structure that modern times would call sane and adult. It represents the state of gestation[6] that would later give issue to the individual psyche of the European man. "Individual," moreover, is to be taken both in its common meaning, as "personal," and in its etymological meaning, as "consolidated" or "indivisible."

This effort to give an interior organization to the components of the psyche that were still perceived as invasions on the part of outside entities was accompanied at the external level by an attempt – the beginnings of which date back to an unspecifiable time – to give system to the sphere of religious experience.[7] Even the gods of Olympus,[8] who were thought of as objective and definitely characterized entities, were held to be capable of invading the human soul: rather than liturgy, the fundamental relationship between man and the gods was invasion.

The true and proper gods sometimes found agents in other deities who had no personal names.[9] What differentiates the true and proper gods from these other entities (from whom, in part, they may have derived in more remote epochs) is that the gods had a face and a character of their own and that as time went by their influence on human life grew always greater. Even in spite of the various declinations of their names, the mutability of their attributes and the multiplicity of their cults, the deities were unique and individual figures, independent of the persons who perceived them, and with clear and unchanging characteristics of appearance and temperament. This accentuated anthropomorphism is the most fascinating and as well the most vulnerable part of Greek religion. Its pretensions to objectivity demanded a high and continuous level of social consensus.[10]

Whenever a god intervened in the life of a human being, it was generally the case that the human being would regress to states of mind that we can refer to as "primary," both in the sense that they are found in infants, and in the sense that they present themselves in such total and overwhelming ways as to make it impossible to break them down into constituent parts.

Though accepted, named and expressed in highly various ways, love, fear, rage and sadness are ageless and universal feelings that have little respect for the ways in which cultures differ from one another. The Archaic Greeks regarded such emotions with wonder, uncertainty and superstition and could confront them neither with will power – which came to be developed at a later date by Christian and philosophical asceticism – nor with psychological explanations. They had to be distanced from such emotions, knowing themselves to be menaced by the way they so frequently proved superior to intentions; they were therefore inclined to consider them to be true and proper deities that at times would take violent control of mortals. To protect themselves from states of possession, visions, dreams[11] and primary emotions, the Archaic Greeks expelled such psychological experiences and transformed them into disruptive deities who could be identified and cataloged. To turn them into deities meant, naturally enough, to renounce controlling them, but their anthropomorphic form made it possible to know and describe them and clearly referred to their human origins.

Ares thus corresponded to impetuous aggressiveness, Athena to controlled and intelligent combativeness, Apollo to the forces of serenity, Aphrodite to love, Chronos to sadness and so on. Such deities can be referred to as "emotional gods" (forces that preside over a specific and basic emotion) as distinguished from the monotheistic gods that are usually to be understood as manifestations of the absolute (which also explains the prohibition of making their graven images). Not even Zeus, the king of the gods, was fully independent; in book XVII of the *Iliad*, he seems to intervene on the side of both the Greeks and the Trojans, managing mostly to create confusion.

The Greek gods, naturally enough, could also affect human life in what might be called the more usual ways, as external agents. Apollo descended to the battlefield, protected the Trojans, assumed a disguise and successfully subjected Achilles to a ruse.[12] But the truly supernatural divine powers were those that came to manifestation as interior influences. Epic poetry was greatly in need of images, and the gods were therefore required to descend from Olympus and appear at the side of its human characters; but they performed their truest interventions by acting on the *thymós* of a human being: they took the form of irresistible emotions. Homer describes Hera as she encouraged the Greeks before the walls of Troy; but to tell us that they actually received her power, he explains that the goddess inflamed their *thymós*.[13] At the beginning of the *Odyssey*, Athena, disguised as a man, abundantly counsels the young Telemachus. Yet there is nothing divine about this lengthy dialog. It is only when the goddess, towards the end of the encounter, fills his *thymós* with power and decision that the son of Odysseus comes to understand that he has made the acquaintance of something supernatural.[14]

The monotheistic god gives man a center and a sense of the absolute; man knows that the Scriptures are the axis of the world and that he is made in the image of the Lord. The emotional gods of polytheism do something quite different; they endow the human being with states of mind that count as both peripheral and provisory. At any given moment, the individual can allow himself to be carried along by his state of mind, since he sees it to contain the will of a god; but he is always afraid of any stable identification with such a momentary state of mind; to allow such an identification would mean succumbing to a deviated destiny to which it corresponds and thus to a condition of non-freedom (if freedom exists at all in such a world).

The Greeks personified their emotions and turned them into gods for reasons that we easily intuit. In addition to allowing them to distance themselves from the primary emotions, such a tactic also helped to establish an attitude of reverential respect for the system of ethics that was coming into existence. If the Greeks created gods as a way of achieving liberation from intolerable emotions, the ensuing theology and religious ethics had to serve the purpose of holding the gods at an even greater distance. Their polytheism was trapped in a vicious circle and gave itself goals that were precisely the opposite of those assumed by Christianity. The religion of the Greeks was never to develop anything similar to the Christian effort to follow divine example (*imitatio Christi*); as Nietzsche remarked, it promoted the inverse course. The just man was expected *not* to reproduce the qualities of the gods. The very gravest of sins was *hýbris*, and one made oneself guilty of *hýbris* by transgressing the limits imposed by one's personal and individual condition. To excel in the possession of any particular quality was an act of arrogance and an outrage – the "out" of outrage relates to the possibility that *hýbris* derives from *hyper*, which is the corresponding word in Greek, and arrogance derives from *ad-rogare*, which is to ask, demand or appropriate something for oneself. To do so meant to subtract it from the god who represented it, and thus to whom it belonged.

At the time in which this polytheism was taking shape – which is to speak of far earlier periods that predate the formation of the notion of individual identity – the human being was allowed to follow no personal path that led beyond the realm of the predictable, as already determined by rite and custom. And the passions always ranged beyond predictability. So anyone who fell victim to the passions was quick to disengage from all personal responsibility, denying all relationship between his actions and his will. Just as a child denies knocking over a vase by saying "the vase fell," the Greeks – who can be thought of as pioneers who traveled the roads of the infancy of the modern psyche – dealt with intolerable actions of their own by attributing them to the gods.

Agamemnon makes just such a defense of his having stolen Briseis from Achilles:

> It is not I that am at fault, but Zeus and Fate and Erinys, that walketh in darkness, seeing that in the midst of the place of gathering they cast upon my soul fierce blindness (*áte*) on that day, when of mine own arrogance I took from Achilles his prize. But what could I do? it is God that bringeth all things to their issue.[15]

His closing words were no simple subterfuge that he employed as an excuse; they voice what in fact was a general conviction. Achilles was the injured party, and he too was shortly later to declare that the guilt for the wrong he had suffered lay not with his rival Agamemnon, but with father Zeus.[16] Even the rational Odysseus speaks of divine interference as he thinks back to Ajax, recalling that defeat had pushed him to madness and death: "no other is to blame but Zeus, who bore terrible hatred against the host of Danaan spearsmen."[17] Even Paris, who abducted Helen, knew that unbearable responsibilities are attenuated by the gods. His brother Hector reproved him and called him a spineless philanderer who had provoked so vast a war and yet avoided battle with Menelaus, the legitimately furious husband. Paris responded by drawing a distinction. In addition to insisting that he had not refused the duel and would indeed meet Menelaus, he further begged his elder brother not to hold him guilty for "the gifts of golden Aphrodite," which accounted for the wealth of erotic power that had found its culmination in his seduction of Helen. Even Hector by no means undervalued the gifts of the gods, knowing that a man in any case cannot choose them.[18] This safety net, moreover, would seem to have been quite ample: gifts of the gods (*dôra*) could explain a great deal more than a momentary loss of control; they could also furnish justification for the whole of a sustained and complex pattern of behavior. In the company of the woman he had stolen, Paris had faced all the trials of the long return voyage to Troy; and so as not to do things halfway, he had also seen to relieving Menelaus of his treasures.

Divine powers that make themselves visible in the emotions of human beings are even more typical of the lyric poetry of the centuries that followed the era of the epics.[19] Lyric poetry took no interest in external events and was wholly dedicated to the interior life of the feelings, thus helping it to nourish the seeds of a more mature form of individual identity.[20] In one of the most famous lyrics of all times,[21] Sappho begs Aphrodite not to torment her *thymós* with the pains of love and instead to intervene on the feelings of the person she desires. We are dealing here with something new. Emotion remains a property of which only a god can dispose, but the god is no longer felt to work in ineluctable ways; almost as though in a Christian prayer, the god is in fact invited to take part in an interior dialog.

Though the barbarians were normally treated as a group and not as morally answerable individuals, they too could be allowed the benefit of the law that saw final responsibility for human acts as lying with the gods. Herodotus was later to invoke it even while writing of the family of the king of Persia. His *History* recounts that Xerxes,[22] while about to begin to organize his mammoth expedition against the Greeks, was several times convinced to desist by his uncle Artabanus, who warned him against temerity. But every time he bowed to this prudent counsel, a tall and handsome man appeared in his dreams and forced him to persevere with his project, and with all of the *hýbris* that inspired it. Even while desiring to obey the dictates of reason, Xerxes "cannot do it."[23] Artabanus then dressed in his nephew's clothes and slept in his bed; his intentions almost might have been those of the modern man who lives outside of faith, since he had decided to prove that the figure in the dream had no objective existence. But the very same personage appeared to him as well. So this figure was something other, as we might say, than an image projected by Xerxes' unconscious; its reality lay outside of the persons of both of these men, and it enjoyed sufficient authority to be able to intrude into their interior worlds. On appearing in the dreams of Artabanus, the figure inquired "Art thou then he that would dissuade Xerxes from marching against Hellas?,"[24] and threatened to burn out his eyes. At this point the two Persians have no further doubt about the course to follow, and feel no responsibility for it. The expedition is necessary to fulfill the will of a god.

THE SENSE OF LIFE UP UNTIL THE FIFTH CENTURY

The Archaic Greek gods were superior forces, but they were not wise.[25] They paid no attention to human actions, except in those occasional instances when men excited their Olympian vanity. The Greek gods presided over an anthropomorphic theology, but it differed from the theology of every other major religion by being in no way anthropological.[26]

Man owed them nothing. He knew himself to be heroically alone.[27] That was the only true wisdom. The gods had nothing to do with it, if not by having provoked it with their endless foolishness.

Homer tells us that Zeus even pitied the animal who had to share the fate of man.[28] He tells us that happiness belongs to the moments in which the king of the gods deals good as well as evil, instead of evils alone.[29]

Even the lyrics seem to place more faith in death than in the gods.[30] This lack of trust in the gods was partly to survive until the fifth century, where similar tones appear both in theater and in the writing of history.[31]

It was precisely the awareness of having to count on themselves alone that gave the Greeks the power to confront their mortal battle with the Persians; and the same holds true for their desire to establish their continuity with the past, by means of historical research, and for their ability to examine future possibilities, by means of philosophy. Too gentle visions of life lull men and cultures to sleep, whereas struggle and pain stimulate invention and further understanding.[32] The Greeks had to come to terms with a stingy natural environment, and they likewise had to repulse a horde of barbarian invaders; but more than anything else – and none of the many studies of Greece has given this fact the importance it deserves – they had to do battle against their principal gods.

The Greek religion never took the form of an official institution, and it never created a true and proper class of functionaries and priests, even if such developments were common in the religions of other peoples. They thus appear – perhaps uniquely in all of history – to have waged a war of liberation against a foe that was neither a material enemy of the concept of nationhood nor an adverse social group. This conflict, no less mortal than the war with the Persians, took place within the solitude of the psyche. The Greeks did battle with the images which they themselves had shaped, since they had to redress the symmetry that balanced the greatness of the gods against the impotence of men. Their success in performing so great a task awakened a *hýbris* that was never to be abated. After defeating the gods of Olympus, many Greeks turned, with varying degrees of success, to the practice of less official religions which at that point seemed more closely related to their psychological needs. But the need for a new creed that fully acknowledged and respected the gods while affording men a sure perception of providence was never fully satisfied. When they encountered the advent of Christianity, their souls contained a void that needed to be filled.

MORALS

The struggle against the gods for a more just world was to last several centuries.

The Homeric ethic had offered a reference point that surely had been cruel, but it had also been charged with *páthos* and had as well been sufficiently simple to be found reassuring. The attributes of the individual were in no way uncertain or ambiguous; body and soul were inseparable; beauty and strength were moral qualities. Sin was expressed by facts, and not by any consciousness of guilt.[33] If Aphrodite assumed the guise of a mortal and deceived Anchises in order to seduce him, Anchises in any case had broken the law: not by virtue of promiscuity, which was no sin at all, but he had beheld the graces of a goddess.[34] Categories such as *areté* (virtue) and *agathós* (the good man) referred to the effective and useful individual who enjoyed success, and had nothing to do with any rejection of fraud. Odysseus' ability to lie with great astuteness received unconditional praise as an integral part of his wisdom. Though interior motives and feelings began to be subject to examination, men were not to be judged on the basis of their good or evil conscience, but only on the basis of facts. And the facts were decided by the gods, or, in the longer view, by the destinies which the gods also had to obey.

Homer sometimes presents us with a soul that begins to make choices; but then he is always quick to deny this incipient psychology and to reassert the primacy of religious absurdity as the force that establishes human destinies. Of all of Homer's personages, Hector is the most human and complex, and indeed seems almost modern. He shows courage and loyalty, fear of the enemy and respect for the opinions of his fellow citizens; he constantly reflects on the internal events that occur in his own soul. Yet Homer, almost seeming to be frightened by the affection he feels for this hero, immediately deprives him of the independence that he had already accorded him. Homer reveals Apollo to have ordered Hector not to advance against Achilles,[35] yet shortly before he had shown us Hector's attitude of well-reasoned prudence and allowed us to listen to his open admission of knowing himself to be the weaker.[36] He later describes Athena[37] as employing a deception to convince Hector to face Achilles; but there is no justification for divine intervention if not in the profundity of Homer's convictions. No such intervention is required by logic. In spite of his continuing fears and his unabated longing to make peace with the enemy, Hector's dialog with his own heart (*thymós*) had already convinced him that battle was the only possibility.[38]

If the Archaic Greeks established no link between objectively unjust actions and any subjectively experienced feeling of guilt, other lacunae were even more conspicuous. Their sense of morals could formulate prohibitions but would have found it extremely difficult to offer positive prescriptions or to define particular actions as good.[39] Rather than guided by an ethic, they seem to have been tormented by prohibitions and magical contingencies that have not a little in common with primitive "taboos."[40]

Relief from this awkward and painful condition was discovered in a slow rationalization of ethics, at least in so far as we are able to discern in a culture that had no sacred scriptures. A reorganization of religious thought attempted to free the human being from the grips of the absurd, and one sees this process already to have made itself responsible for the differences that separate the world of the *Iliad* from that of the *Odyssey.* Though nearly contemporary, these two epic poems may perhaps, in this respect, have been the work of different hands.

In the *Iliad*, each of the gods acts in his or her own right. Their rules of conduct are exclusively determined by the camp to which they belong: they are allied either with the Greeks or with the Trojans. Her desire to aid the Greeks allows Hera to consider it legitimate to neutralize her husband Zeus by means of fraud. She draws the king of the gods into an amorous tryst after devising a ploy to subtract from Aphrodite the faculty for arousing such emotions. She then corrupts Morpheus by promising him the favors of one of the Graces and thus obtains his help in putting Zeus to sleep.[41] There seem to be no moral commitments, neither towards other gods nor to men, that the gods are expected to respect. At times, it can even appear that the individual heroes protected by the two camps of celestial opponents are little more than extensions of a god in which he can narcissistically mirror himself, rather than individuals whom he in any way loves. The authority of Zeus himself over the gods and men is often in fact non-existent. Menelaus vigorously denounces this fact to the king of Olympus, declaring that no punishment seems to be destined to the Trojans who, after stealing his wife and his treasures, have also given proof of *hýbris* [42] in their conduct during the war.

The behavior of the gods in the *Odyssey* is considerably different and begins to show aspects of equity and almost of providence. Odysseus can count on the protection of Athena and on an incipient concern for justice on the part of Zeus himself. Attention is drawn to these new orientations at the very beginning of the poem: Zeus initiates a discourse on the problem of responsibility, inveighing against the presumption of men who attribute their misadventures to the gods, whereas they ought to understand that the roots of their misfortunes are to be found in their own misdeeds.[43]

The gods are still untouched by the fates of men, but they begin for the very first time to think about men in terms of justice rather than of personal vanity. One begins to glimpse the possibility of the alliance that was only later to qualify, in any strict sense, as religious "faith," since the notion of faith implies fidelity, or that men trust God. This improvement in the relationship between men and the gods also contained the germ of the gods' demise or loss of viability. Human beings would claim ever more space for themselves. The *Odyssey* begins with the word "man" – *ándra* – and thereby seems to announce that the road lay open for the development of the kind of active individual who was later to assert themselves as protagonist of western culture. And in the *Odyssey*, unlike the *Iliad*, the efforts of a single protagonist run uninterrupted throughout the poem, allowing us to study the nature of the route that leads the individual psyche through the process of gestation and finally to birth.

One also notes that the thinkers of Ionia began for the very first time to attempt to explain the world without making mention of myth. Courageous spirits began to question traditional morals well before the flourishing of the Athenian enlightenment. Xenophanes criticized the official mythology, saying that "Both Homer and Hesiod have attributed to the gods all things that are shameful and a reproach among mankind: theft, adultery, and mutual deception."[44] Xenophanes also suggested that man can travel a road that leads towards "progress": "Truly the gods have not revealed to mortals all things from the beginning; but mortals by long seeking discover what is better."[45]

Intercourse between men and the gods was slowly undergoing a change, even if love could not be said to have become a part of the relationship.[46] But the gods – following the path that the *Odyssey* had opened – began to act more fairly, even while remaining at a distance. Zeus' distance is no longer equivalent to indifference. Starting from the moment in which human actions began to have good or evil consequences, that distance itself began to make room for the assumption of moral responsibilities. Some observers have turned to the terms of cultural anthropology[47] and maintained that the Greeks of this period were passing from a civilization of shame to a civilization of guilt,[48] inverting their values (or, better, their sense of limits) in the space of no more than a few generations; but to say that values ceased to be imposed from the outside and instead arose from interior experience is to adopt too modern a point of view. The pressures that the Greeks had to neutralize were far less social than divine.

But surely the question of freedom of action began to constitute a problem for the Greeks, or at least to be experienced as a source of personal torment. Reflections of such a development can be seen in their lyric poetry,[49] which spoke a new language, constructed around a narrative "I."

Taboos, in any case, survive the disappearance of the convictions that originally motivate them.[50] The Greeks attained a higher level of freedom through a process that enlarged and enriched their field of cultural inquiry and that made their religion more rational, but the energies they managed to re-appropriate now came to be directed to another cult: to the new cult of the state. This is a subject to which we will shortly return. People were unable to take true advantage of the new moral spaces in which they were free to move. Like animals confined too long in a cage, they made no immediate exit through the newly opened door. They remained behind and avidly continued to observe their fellows. Plagued by the feeling that destiny could never be channeled into a definitively positive course, they did not do away with the harshness of the gods. Instead they endowed it with meaning and attempted to explain it. The gods ceased to be seen as capricious and their actions came to be understood as the manifestation of a stable principle: the gods were jealous of men who succeeded in being happy, and such men were therefore punished. What came to be affirmed was the rule of *phthónos theôn*.[51]

Homer's use of this notion was sporadic and he never saw it as central.[52] But within the space of no more than a few generations, it assumed the status of a law. It was the law to which Aeschylus subjected both men and the gods, and Herodotus described its sway over history. Morals construed the foundations that sustained the great events of the fifth century.

5

THE GREEK SENSE OF LIMITS

NOTHING TOO MUCH

Happiness achieved: you make one walk
on the edge of the blade.
You appear to the eyes as wavering flame,
to the foot as a span of splintering ice:
whoever loves you will not touch you.

(Eugenio Montale, *Ossi di Seppia*)

The notion of the envy of the gods asserted itself at the close of the Archaic period of Greek civilization. It constituted a profound and radical innovation but can hardly be said to have gone unannounced, since its birth had in fact been preceded by a period of gestation in various areas of literary, political and religious thought. Even the Archaic gods had been prone to act in terms of machineries of justice that in some ways harbingered the notion of *phthónos*. Each of them was jealous of the faculties and qualities that he or she represented, and though willing to share these treasures with mortal men, they would do so only to a certain degree, or in respect of certain limits. Men who transgressed those limits, threatening the primacy and privilege of a deity, thus abandoning that deity as a point of reference, could expect a rash reaction. Aphrodite was the goddess of love and womanly seduction. But she bore no resemblance to what we would think of as a provident deity who distributed her qualities to mankind; her faculties were wholly her own preserve. Women were well advised to be careful not to rival her beauty; and Anchises, whom she disguised herself to seduce, despaired of all salvation when he learned that he had trysted with a goddess.

But the modes of thought that prevailed in Archaic Greece contained no norm of justice that accounted in general for the jealousies of the individual gods. Rather than an instance of the workings of a higher, all-governing principle, the jealousy of each of them was an absolute fact in its very own right.

The establishment of *phthónos* as a central rule marked the birth of a

46

more abstract and evenly applicable principle. But even though wider in range than the sum of the egoistic jealousies of the individual gods, it still primarily assumed the form of a kind of surveillance on the part of the whole community of gods. *Phthónos theôn* – the envy of *the gods* – in fact contains a plural term. The generalization of the concept can also be seen as primarily an expedient for protecting the continuity of the religious creed of the Greeks. The true and final source of *phthónos* lay no longer in the egoism of the gods – an egoism which made them in no way superior to men – but rather in a principle of distributive justice, which by now had also established itself as the distinguishing mark of the functions of the state.

The term, of course, is not to be understood from a modern point of view. Justice was not distributive in the sense of giving every man his due, as demanded by more highly developed codes of morals. Justice found its goal, much more simply, in preventing mortals from taking possession of anything that ought to belong to the gods alone; and it was also a question of prohibiting shifts in the ways in which a meager prosperity had been portioned out among men. But an innovation had none the less taken place. The decline of a panoply of emotional gods, often at war the one with the other, signaled the affirmation of a single principle of divine jealousy as the only form of justice. The code of morality evolved and found a unification that would later facilitate the affirmation of monotheism.

Phthónos was a principle that governed both gods and men, and the deities were gradually called upon to mitigate their egoism and to take up their place within the framework of the new law. The consolidation of the law required that Zeus be conferred with clearer and greater authority; the need for order demanded that he finally hold a position as truly the king of the gods.[1] And the law was further accompanied by general regulatory principles, such as destiny and necessity, to which even Olympus owed obedience.[2]

Medén ágan, nothing too much: this maxim, attributed to Solon, was inscribed on the oracle at Delphi, which was the center of religious life throughout the whole of Greece. Its importance for the conduct of private life in Athens at the time of the city's greatest achievements can seem paradoxical, and yet finds confirmation in one of the stories of Thucydides: the Athenians had been the first of the Greeks to amass considerable wealth, and already in the past they had adopted an easier mode of life and allowed themselves a certain degree of luxury; but then – at a time still previous to the writing of Thucydides – the wealthier men of Athens had returned to more simple forms of life, following the example of the Spartans.[3] In his description of the Athens of the fifth century, Thucydides reports these words to have been spoken by Pericles:

47

For we are lovers of beauty yet with no extravagance and lovers of wisdom yet without weakness. Wealth we employ rather as an opportunity for action than as a subject for boasting; and with us it is not a shame for a man to acknowledge poverty, but the greater shame is for him not to do his best to avoid it.[4]

We are not, however, to imagine that the envy of the gods worked in opposition to every form of excess. *Phthónos*, in fact, struck down excessive fortune but did nothing to mitigate excessive misery. The Greeks were a pessimistic people and knew no god who set limits to the intensity of suffering. The jealousy of the gods, moreover, dealt out punishment for purely factual manifestations of excess, and remained unconcerned with questions of individual responsibility.

When we look, a bit further on, at the writings of Herodotus, we will see quite clearly that his accounts of the interventions of the gods present them in fact as specific expressions of a general principle of *phthónos*. We can limit ourselves for the moment to a single example.

The story of Polycrates, the tyrant of Samos, is a particularly telling illustration of the way in which divine justice cruelly strikes down the objectively excessive, entirely heedless of men's intentions, and thus preventing human beings from assuming a status as agents or protagonists of historical event.[5] Polycrates was very rich, powerful and fortunate. Not even his conscious desire to avoid excessive prosperity, and with it the envy of the gods, was able to ensure his safety. He accepted the advice of his friend Amasis, the king of Egypt, and decided to free himself of the most precious of all his possessions: he ordered a ship to be readied, set out to sea and threw the finest of his rings into the waves. A few days later, a fisherman arrived at his palace and made him a gift of a particularly large fish, and when the servants slit its belly, they rediscovered the ring. Amasis then perceived "that no man could save another from his destiny,"[6] and sent a herald to Samos to renounce his friendship with Polycrates, so as not to have to grieve his heart for a friend on the occasion of the terrible mishaps that now were sure to strike him. A short time later, Polycrates fell victim to a ruse, and was taken prisoner and crucified.[7]

Herodotus' account of the story expresses sincere compassion for Polycrates, and yet the historian also makes it clear that he considers the tale to be exemplary proof of the workings of a superior justice. He never reflects at all on the fact that Polycrates had attempted to live in accordance with the principles of distributive justice by spontaneously relinquishing what he saw as "too much." Much like king Amasis, the historian too abandons the man who is about to be stricken by the gods.

The story's true protagonist is the superior principle that maintains its watch over all the forms of excess. It sees the jealousy of the gods no longer as an expression of their egoism, but rather as a form of vigilance.[8] The complementary law, from the human point of view, is the law of moderation.[9]

Seen in terms of this complementary law, and in terms as well of its meaning within the context of the relationship between man and the gods, the notion of the jealousy of the gods seemed finally somewhat inadequate. Its point of view was restricted and unilateral, since it exclusively expressed the gods' point of view, and as such it was clearly in conflict with the growing self-awareness that the Greeks were in the course of acquiring. The narratives of the time thus began gradually to flank the concept of *phthónos* with the already extant notion of *némesis*,[10] using it nearly as a synonym for *phthónos*. But *némesis* was in fact a more advanced concept since its power derived from the realm of morals rather than from notions of jealousy. It could also be rendered more specific, as indicated by the contrasting notions of *hýbris-némesis* and *aidós-némesis*, which inserted the question of human conduct into the law. The growing parallelism between the world of men and the world of the gods is reflected in these couplings of words. The first pair of words – *hýbris-némesis* – establishes a relationship between human transgression, *hýbris*, and the divine punishment that answers it. The second pair – *aidós-némesis*[11] – indicates the powers that discourage immoral action: shame before other men, *aidós*, and the indignation of the gods. These pairs of concepts were to play a fundamental role in the passage from myth to history.

NÉMESIS

One should quench arrogance [*hýbris*] rather than a conflagration.
(Heracleitus)

The notion of *hýbris* is found already in Homer, and always at decisive moments. Achilles, and Athena as she comforts him, applies it to the unjust arrogance of Agamemnon when he robbed the hero of Briseis, thus giving rise to his ire and to all the events of the *Iliad*.[12]

The *Odyssey* refers to the chieftains of Ithaca who asked for the hand of Penelope as having been overwhelmed by *hýbris*. Antinoos, the most unruly among them, at one point mistreats a beggar who has asked for hospitality, and another of the suitors reproves him, warning him that gods in disguise frequently walk the earth so as to learn who is just and who is arrogant.[13] These are very wise words, and they anticipate the story's dramatic and final outcome. (Similar devices were frequently employed in the tragedies as well.) Hidden beneath the rags of the beggar we in fact will find Odysseus, and the chieftains of Ithaca are to feel the brunt of his arrows as the agent of their final *némesis*.[14]

49

For Hesiod, the constant degeneration of the successive epochs of human life was likewise due to the ways in which men give themselves over to *hýbris*.[15] But Homer and Hesiod had not yet elevated *hýbris* to the status of a guiding principle. Its course of activity had barely begun, and *hýbris* was still nothing more than one among a panoply of mythic abstractions. But when the marriage of myth and real events was celebrated by the thinkers of the fifth century, it was *hýbris* that governed its meaning.

Pindar, even while writing Odes in praise of victorious competitors at the games, never ceased to exhort his heroes to modesty.

In Herodotus' *History*, the whole of the story of the Persian Wars – the substance of books V–IX – was to constitute a mammoth effort to understand an epoch-making event from precisely such a point of view. *Hýbris* and *némesis* are mentioned no more than is necessary, and yet the way in which events are presented and articulated makes it clear that *hýbris* and *némesis* are the story's true protagonists.

In his only historical tragedy, *Persians*, Aeschylus too concerns himself with a superior principle that regulates events – not by means of specific interventions on the part of the gods, but through the insistent presence of an *álastor*[16] or a *daímon*[17] that beguiles the barbarians and causes them to fall into *hýbris*[18] and expose themselves to *phthónos*.[19]

Now we can turn our attention to the pairing of *aidós* and *némesis*.

These two terms are already found in the Archaic period, sometimes appearing as moral precepts and at others as deities. *Aidós* and the verb *aidéomai* indicate the shame that the Greeks experienced on confronting their fellow citizens after committing an act of injustice. We have already noted that the gods of this period were highly unpredictable and of little service as models for human action. Honor and its opposite, shame, were on the other hand such sure and palpable experiences as to lead modern thinkers to speak of the Archaic epoch as a "civilization of shame." The Greeks found it difficult to articulate a notion of justice in terms of the vertical relationship of men to the gods, and their clearest norms of behavior were structured horizontally, in terms of the relationship of people to other people.

In ancient Greece, or at least in Archaic Greece, the relationship between the gods and their worshippers was entirely the opposite of what one finds in later religions: mankind was on the whole more moral than their deities. *Némesis* was divine justice, and *aidós* was justice as practiced by society. And if the gods of Olympus can be said to have found their birth in an upwards projection of the psychopathology of everyday life, one would likewise have to assert that individual inhibitions, ambitions and everything else now referred to as the super-ego, found their origins in an introjection of social pressures, even if mediated by family and education. But the importance of the family as an hierarchical organization should not be overestimated. In the various epochs and cities of ancient Greece, fathers had very little relationship with their children, and almost no direct role in their education.[20] The image of the father in an ancient Greek family was of less importance for the formation of a principle of interior authority than what Freud hypothesized for the modern family in the context of a monotheistic society. Boys were in direct and constant contact with the society around them and learned to bend themselves to its moral pressures. The development of the personality of the individual in modern society depends upon the presence of a father, since the father serves as the voice of its individualistic ideals. In ancient Greece, the ideal had more to do with the *pólis* than with individual values, and the group was therefore the model that functioned as the individual's point of reference.

The verb *aidéomai* (to feel shame) is one of the most powerful terms that come to be employed in the *Iliad*. There are two separate occasions on which Hector speaks the phrase, *Aidéomai Trôas kai Trôadas elkesipéplous*, "I have shame of the Trojans, and the Trojans' wives with trailing robes," addressing it once to Andromache, and once to his own heart.[21] Andromache and his heart were afraid, and begged him not to enter combat. We can be certain, moreover, that so important an emotion was not felt by the Trojans alone. Homer would not insist upon it, if it were not a part of the Greek experience as well, and he customarily attributed these two peoples with similar modes of behavior and similar spiritual attitudes. Hector knows that he is going to his death, having clearly predicted it on both of the occasions when he speaks this phrase, but his respect for his fellow citizens is a deeper obligation than the command of a god.

Aidós and *némesis* were often invoked at one and the same time. They were complements the one of the other, and together they formed a notion of full and complete justice.[22]

The divine personifications of *aidós* and *némesis* were also paired by Hesiod when he recounted the succession of the epochs through which the human race had passed in the course of its constant degeneration. At the end of the fifth and lowest epoch, the age of iron, *Aidós* and *Némesis* took flight and abandoned the earth,[23] choosing instead to live on Olympus and leave men defenseless in the face of evil. This ascent is the allegorical expression of a transformation: human *némesis* (*némesis anthrópon*)[24] was superseded by divine *némesis* (*némesis theôn*).[25] Distributive ethics was losing the aspect of a human feeling and undergoing a transformation into a religious theme that contained the very essence of justice. *Aidós*, on the other hand, gradually faded away, since it neither developed into a personification nor discovered a clearly defined place in the codes of social behavior.[26]

Aristotle was once again to deal with *aidós* and *némesis* together. But rather than as qualities that lead to moderation, he saw them as emotions in which the individual should be careful to indulge with moderation, always maintaining the "proper mean."[27] As societies evolve, they tend to substitute norms for what was previously entrusted to the feelings.[28] Their tendency to rely on abstractions reveals the extent to which the Greeks anticipated modern thought; they progressively diminished the importance of the heroic figures that had formerly embodied their world of ideals.[29]

Of the two ethical principles that the Greeks originally associated with one another, we see that only *némesis* was to survive and develop.

But what does this word mean?

All of the various words that derive from *nemes* – indicate a wrath – usually a just wrath – "provoked by the person whom it strikes." *Némesis* "arises as an automatic punishment that the gods or human beings set into motion, entirely involuntarily. It is presumed, both logically and linguistically, to be *something that already exists in the world.*"[30] The gradual transformation of *némesis* into a principle of justice stronger than the traditional deities was thus foreseen by the very linguistic root of the world. *Némesis* was perceived as something that had always existed from the time of the very beginning of things, or as a component of nature itself and not as a human code of behavior. This would explain why Hesiod presents it at the very beginning of the family tree of the gods, as we now will see.

Other scholars have suggested that *némesis* relates to *nómos*,[31] a word that designates the law. *Némesis* would indicate an attitude of resentment for any lack of respect for the law, and would derive from the same root. With the passage of time, the meaning of the word tended to include an opposition to all the forms of excess, which the gods find offensive. *Némesis* was thus a no less supernatural force than the jealousy of the gods, but it served a different purpose since there was nothing it aspired to return to the gods. It was exclusively concerned with dealing out justice to mortals. The egoism of the gods was replaced by a moral law.

Here is what Hesiod had to say about the origins of the goddess Nemesis.

Nemesis, "the affliction of mortal men," was born from "deadly Night,"[32] who in turn was the daughter of Chaos. Night, without having lain with any other creature, also gave birth to "hateful Doom and black Fate," Death, Sleep or Morpheus and the whole tribe of Dreams, and then Blame and Woe, the Hesperides, the Moire or Destinies and the "ruthless avenging Fates," or Keres. Nemesis afterwards gave birth to Deceit and Friendship, hateful Age and Strife.

Nemesis stands nearly at the head of the genealogy of the gods. She was the daughter of Night, who was not so much a traditional god as a still dark and shapeless element; and the only thing precedent to Night was the primal disorder of Chaos. What we find to the rear of Nemesis amounts in fact to two absences: the absence of light and the absence of order. Her brothers too are fearsome. Sleep and Dream allude, like Night, to the lack of consciousness, whereas Death is the lack of life itself.

What were Hesiod and the Greeks of the Archaic age attempting to express through the creation of such a myth? What was their unconscious fantasy of justice (*némesis*) if they personified it in such a way? Listed as it was amongst siblings that correspond to dramatic experiences that no human life can avoid, *némesis* too would belong to the class of events that all human beings must necessarily encounter. Such things are imposed upon human experience, whether we like it or not, and their influence is constantly felt. All pre-modern peoples gave a great deal of attention to dreams. To say that Nemesis is the sister of dreams is also to speak of the quality of justice that she represented, and we have to conclude that the nature of justice was experienced as very much similar to the nature of dreams; justice, like dreams, was non-reflective, deeply rooted and a presence in the life of everyone. The modern mind would expect a principle of justice to be connected to a process of evaluation, as conscious and rational as possible. But the Greeks experienced justice as an un-conscious drive, or as a passion that rose from the viscera and refused to be questioned. *Némesis* was the name of that emotion. As a feeling, it was justified ire, and as a deity it was soon to dubbed "irate."[33] Under ideal conditions, our individual acts of ethical judgment may well be ex-perienced as conscious and rational events, but to search out the roots of the need for justice is to rediscover the passion of a primal drive.

But the myth offers yet another detail on the nature of the impulse to ethics, and this detail is quite important. Nemesis is a female deity: in statues and engravings she is often represented as accompanied by a wheel (the cycle of good and bad fortune as well as an image of the passing of time?), and she lifts to her face a corner of the hem of her dress, both modestly to hide her features and to form in its hollow a measure used for grain – a "just measure."

Archaic Greek society had elaborated a structure in which males were entrusted with the task of furthering the development of civilization and they enjoyed the rights that ensued. And from Homeric times to the fifth century, women had to accept an even further restriction of their roles.

In all epochs, and especially in ancient Greece, actions oriented to conquest or to the creation of new forms of enterprise have mainly belonged to the masculine sphere of activity. It thus seems reasonable for the correction of excesses in thought and initiative to have been seen as the province of women, since in fact they were allowed to take no part in them. Such an inevitable compensation might itself be seen as an ex-pression of *némesis*.

There are no historical records of the primordial Mediterranean civil-izations, but they are generally presumed to have been close to the state of nature and to have observed a cult of the Great Mother, or Mother Earth, within the context of a matriarchal or at least matrilineal form of social organization. The Greeks appear to have been among the very first peoples to have overthrown such forms for the structuring of society, and their achievement resulted in a more efficient control of the outside world and as well in a convention of strong paternal authority. The Hellenes who descended from the north crushed the matriarchal peoples and imposed the laws of their own warrior communities. Traces of the subjugation of a more woman-centered society are to be found in the process in which the Erinnyes (or Furies) were tamed and transformed into the Eumenides (the Kind Ones), as described in the tragedy of the same title by Aeschylus. The *hýbris* for which the Greeks predicted inevitable punishment – and to which they replied by shaping the figure of *némesis* – was the sin of a society in which all excess bore the imprint of the male; and the first of its excesses had lain in the subjugation of woman.

Némesis represented a return to a more natural state; and as such it was also a return to a world in which masculine and feminine were more evenly balanced. Women, in fact, had not grown as distant from nature as men had.

But these are not the only reasons for which Nemesis was a goddess rather than a god. And in order to understand them, we have to turn back to a few of the elements of the myth as told in the *Kýpria*, the great epic poem of the seventh century of which our knowledge is unfortunately no more than partial.[34] Nemesis was the object of the sexual desires of Zeus. In the grips of shame and justified ire – attributes with which she is connected – she transformed herself into innumerable animals as a way of escaping from the king of the gods. Her flight continued across land and sea. Nemesis then finally transformed herself into a goose, and Zeus, having assumed the form of a swan, was able to capture her and to satisfy his lust. Nemesis then gave birth to an egg that contained Helen, the most beautiful and fatal of women.

Kerényi,[35] referring in turn to Leo Frobenius, reminds us that the theme of the coupling of gods who have taken the form of birds and then of the birth of a daughter who hatches from an egg is to be found in numerous myths from various parts of Europe, Asia, Africa and even North America. In other and probably previous versions of the Greek myth, the female personage is Leda rather than Nemesis; and one presumes such versions to be earlier since Leda is not a Greek name, and comes instead from older Asiatic cultures in which it simply means "woman." The vast diffusion of the myth and its relationship with woman in the absolute connect Nemesis to a kind of original sin committed by the male in his lust for possession, and to its necessary castigation. Archaically, punishment and woman are linked to one another.[36] Hesiod's tale of Pandora, which appears in both *Theogony* and *Works and Days*, can be seen, for example, as the punishment, of which the agent is inevitably female, inflicted on the human race for the sin of Prometheus.

The daughter of Nemesis/Leda, the gorgeous Helen, was the cause of the death of enormous numbers of men, both Trojan and Greek. The meaning of such a fact could lie hidden in a popular conviction, recounted by Homer, that the city of Troy and all of its enormous power had become an example of constant *hýbris* and thus an intolerable challenge to natural limits. For the fall and destruction of Troy to have been caused by the daughter of Nemesis would have been absolutely logical. And yet Homer – an expert genealogist, like every ancient Greek – makes no mention of Nemesis as the mother of Helen. Kerényi maintains that Homer intended to rescue Helen from her destiny as a destructive and vindictive woman by suppressing all reference to her mother and by underscoring instead that she was guided and protected by Aphrodite, who, even despite her irascible egoism, represented a further and higher evolution of the image of femininity.[37]

This interpretation can perhaps be improved by recalling that Nemesis and Aphrodite were linked quite intimately the one with the other;[38] and we have already seen that Nemesis was, yes, a primordial goddess but was also quite advanced as a regulatory principle. Homer knew from tradition that *hýbris* comes to expression in men, or in the leaders of men, and not in weak women. He knew and employed the concept of *némesis*, but he made no mention of the connection between Helen and Nemesis since that would have raised the problem of a female arrogance, in connection with the excessive power of seduction with which Helen was endowed. Epic tradition – or at least the profound sensibility of Homer – thought of female fascination as a natural fact. It was something quite different from the strength of a hero. Masculine strength brought merit or demerit – though always within the limits strictly established by destiny – on the basis of the hero's use of it. The spaces in which woman moved allowed for far less autonomy. Homer felt great pity and sympathy for the defeated: for Hector, first of all, and for Priamus as well. But the women were even more thoroughly defeated, by society no less than by fate: Andromacha shares the destiny of Hector, but without glory. And this is why Helen bears no responsibility. *"Ou némesis,"* declare the elders of Troy. "Small blame that Trojans and well-greaved Achaeans should for such a woman long time suffer woes; wondrously like is she to the immortal goddesses to look upon."[39] The companions of the aged Priamus clearly imply that the Trojans and the Greeks – the men – act; Helen is passive. She is nothing more than the object, the *sine qua non*, required to unleash their strife. How without her could they have given themselves to action and glory? Helen's fascination is fatal: rather than the will of a seductress, it represents the work of the goddesses and of fate. The words *ou némesis* have several meanings: "it is no shame," "it is no cause for ire and punishment," and simply "it is not Nemesis." Helen's beauty is in no way subject to the chastisement of Nemesis, and so much so that the very presence of the mother of justice is excluded. In a world such as Homer's, the extension to women of concepts that concern the male, such as *hýbris* and its punishment by *némesis*, is highly unlikely.[40] The excesses of women come to expression in beauty and women make use of their beauty; but there is no violation of natural limits, since nature created that beauty. Women remain a part of the realm of nature and they follow the laws of nature; and nature can include the marvelous, which is not a form of excess. In the Homeric world, the division between male and female is infinitely more radical than in our own. The male is the dynamic principle and produces civilization. Woman, who like nature brings forth children and nourishment, represents a homeostatic principle of reproduction and preservation. This is her paradoxical privilege: excluded from political and cultural life, she knows the pains and anxieties of biological life, but is exempt from those of guilt.

DIVINE JEALOUSY AND ATHENIAN POLITICS

The human side of *phthónos* and the crusade against *hýbris* can be seen in a series of profound reforms in the political life of the city of Athens, since the form of the state, like the principles of ethics, was also in the midst of a process of rationalization. The notion of *phthónos* most probably reached maturity as the Greeks were attempting to organize their lives in terms of a system of clearly defined limits. The new moral ideal became widespread in the fifth century. But Athens, the city that piloted the changes that swept through Greece, had previously prepared the institutions that were destined to embody it.

The roots of politics lay in religion, already in the Archaic period. Politics, as is clear from the word itself, foresaw a commitment on the part of every individual to the life of the *pólis* (the city-state). Active participation was required of everyone. At the close of the seventh and the beginning of the sixth century, Solon was responsible in Athens for a series of juridic reforms and also for a revision of theology, fusing the two and thus making himself the continuator of an almost mythic idea of the law, inherited from Hesiod.[41] The cosmic world and the political world had to be reflections of one another. This fusion of religion and jurisprudence was deeply accepted by the citizens of Athens, and it elevated the *pólis* to the status of a deity, absolute and unquestionable, and much more worthy of devotion than the gods of Olympus. It was the source and focus of all law. History, surely, has known other states that asserted their own divinity and advanced a claim to the absolute, but they rank as totalitarian tyrannies that surrounded their leaders with idolatry. In Athens, quite to the contrary, the "political" universe was itself the great new message –

an all-embracing faith that the great reformer founded on the rejection of *hýbris* in social behavior and in all of society's institutions.

At the juridic level, Solon developed the first democracy, in an almost modern sense, in which everyone, with the exception of foreigners, women and slaves, enjoyed a reasonable level of participation. A form of *hýbris* was implicit in the notion of aristocracy,[42] and Solon therefore dismantled the hegemony of the ruling class. He achieved this goal quite gradually and without the use of violence, and he was also careful to prevent the common people from assuming definitive supremacy. He was guided not by personal goals, but by a very deep faith, convinced that avoiding the primacy of the few, and also of the many, was a way of forestalling the ascent of arrogance. He hoped to imbue society with a proper sense of divine order, and thus to make it self-protective. Solon can nearly be said to have intuited the future course of western history, with its lust for the unlimited: "And as for wealth, there's no end set clearly down; for such as have today the greatest riches among us, these have twice the eagerness that others have, and who can satisfy all?"[43] Solon's desire to institute socio-political limits was a facet of his sense of limits as the universal source of morality:

> For I gave the common folk such privilege as is sufficient for them, neither adding nor taking away; and such as had power and were admired for their riches, I provided that they too should not suffer undue wrong. Nay I stood with a strong shield thrown before the both sorts, and would have neither to prevail unrighteously over the other.[44]

Solon's description of Zeus hinges quite clearly on the very same principles.

> For the works of man's wanton violence [*hýbris*] endure not for long, but Zeus surveyeth the end of every matter, and suddenly, even as the clouds in Spring are quickly scattered by a wind that stirreth the depths of the billowy unharvested sea, layeth waste the fair fields o'er the wheat-bearing land, and reaching even to the high heaven where the Gods sit, maketh the sky clear again to view, till the strength of the Sun shineth fair over the fat land, and no cloud is to be seen any more, – even such is the vengeance of Zeus; He is not quick to wrath, like us, over each and every thing, yet of him that hath a wicked heart is He aware alway unceasing, and such an one surely cometh out plain at the last.[45]

Beneath the sign of distributive justice, the unjust gods of the Archaic period – gods who had been consistent with the old aristocratic regimes – were beginning to coalesce and to take on a form that brought them into line with the needs and aspirations of the *pólis*.

The premise for such a notion of divine order was found in the postulation of Zeus as the absolute ethical authority, and was thus an anticipation of the Greeks' acceptance of monotheism. Zeus was not to be equally cruel and capricious with everyone, but justly severe with those who soiled themselves with evil. Evil, in turn, was found in *hýbris*. The idea of justice thus found a center that had previously been prepared for it. And since the deification of the *pólis* was underway, the spirit that regulated justice could lie in the bosom of a renovated god. Law was divinely inspired, and whoever obeyed the law was safe from guilt, since observance of the law was much the same thing as respect for the limits that the gods imposed on man. But such perfect intentions found realization in ways that contradicted them. The new institutions – which descended from men and not from the gods – stood at the side of Athens' greatest achievements, yet everyone found themselves spurred to precisely the pride that all commonly held principles condemned.

Everything we know about Solon corroborates the image of a man who was wholly committed to countering *hýbris*, in himself no less than in others: "For had another than I won such an honour, he had not restrained nor checked the commons till his churning were done and the richness taken from the milk, whereas I, I stood as a mark in the midway betwixt the two hosts of them."[46]

And he truly personified that mark, imposing limits even on himself. He might easily have turned into a tyrant since both of the two contending parties courted his favor; but after completing his compilation of the laws, Solon chose a voluntary exile that lasted for many years, declaring that their application was now not up to him but to the citizens of Athens.

Solon was surely no ordinary man; he had any number of talents and may perhaps have been aware of having been tempted by the infinite. He was a moralist, thinker, legislator, and theologian, and he is also the only surviving lyric poet of the Athens of his period. The melancholy soul of the introspective poet probably gave him a safeguard against the temptations of politics. His friendship with Mimnermus is perhaps significant; Mimnermus composed verses where life is presented as dark and gloomy, if not for the briefest instants of love.

The reforms of Cleisthenes were enacted at the end of the sixth and the beginning of the fifth century and completed the foundations of Athenian democracy.

Cleisthenes also introduced the practice of ostracism, for the purpose of preventing the return of the tyrants who had recently threatened the continued existence of democracy. By means of a procedure that guaranteed secrecy (writing on *óstraka*, or fragments of pottery) the people were invited to indicate the names of the persons whom they wanted to see banished from the city. What makes this institution seem so anomalous is that it had nothing to do with the punishment of crimes already committed, but aimed – with abundant prudence and excessive imagination – to prevent the possibility of future crimes. Ostracism was inflicted on persons who were simply presumed to have the intention of rising to power, and it ranks as an institutional form of that attitude of aggressive diffidence that today we refer to as paranoia. The *phthónos* shown by the gods towards those who excel was introjected into civil law.[47]

For the Athens of that period, and thus for the origins of the whole of western democracy, religious impulses can probably be seen as having been much more important than political or social ideals. The new and arrogant practice of ostracism was a replacement for divine punishment, and as such it potentially branded itself with *hýbris*. The epoch that preceded the achievements of the century of Pericles witnessed a process of evolution where developments in politics, religion and morals were intimately intertwined with one another. And they likewise meshed with the process of psychological maturation that attempted to give stability to the consciousness of the individual. A struggle was in course for the gradual re-appropriation of forces that had formerly been attributed to the gods, and such forces were progressively rationalized and given the form of norms. In terms of the individual, any number of unconscious processes grew available to consciousness; and in terms of the collective, the arbitrary powers of the gods were transformed into laws. Democracy was born as an attempt to restrain superstition but still continued to feed on it.

Athens' political institutions can offer examples of the complicated ways in which the city attempted to pursue its goal. To avoid the possibility of public careers that led to a permanent acquisition of power, power was to be exercised by everyone. Most forms of public office were assigned by lot and rapidly rotated among quite high numbers of equally ranking functionaries.

All of the citizens of fifth-century Athens were members of the *ecclesía* (the general assembly) which was responsible for every major decision. Archons and members of the Boule (*bulé*, the council) were chosen by lot. The former, of whom there were nine plus a secretary, kept watch over the ten Athenian tribes and supervised the various functions of the state (juridic, religious, military, and so forth); the members of the Boule were the representatives of some forty thousand citizens who were franchised to vote and numbered all of five hundred. At any given time, fifty of the members of the Boule functioned as its pritanes or presidents for the term of one-tenth of the year; and these fifty pritanes were guided by an epistate or supreme president who was chosen by lot every day. Most court proceedings were entrusted to the six thousand eliasts. In the course of the century all of these offices also came to be remunerated, even though state expenditures were already far too high; and the size of this remuneration was significant at least for the poorer citizens, who otherwise would have found it impossible to set aside their ordinary activities. With so dispersive and splintered a structure, it is surprising that the democracy could function at all. The Athenians must have been truly terrified by the thought of giving legitimacy to any stable form of individual power, and clearly they were much concerned with avoiding both divine and human envy.

The world's first democracy was born from moral needs that can best be described as negative, and not from any clear commitment to a positive notion of justice; and that first democracy is history's only example of a total democracy. Prohibitions were numerous, but the time was not yet ripe for moral injunctions that prescribed what was proper to do. Solon's purpose in reducing the debts of the common people and in abolishing slavery for insolvency had nothing to do with giving justice to the poor; he simply intended to curb the ascendency of the powerful. Democracy was not created for the good of the humble, which might perhaps have led to reflections on the rights of foreigners, women and slaves,[48] but rather for the purpose of limiting the evil that was seen as inherent in affording power to the more fortunate. Athens can thus be seen to have had no functionaries or politicians who represented the state: everyone, by turns, *was* the state. Rotation was equally rapid in the field of creative activities, and equally inspired by the thought of discouraging pride. We have only to remember that the tragedies were written with only a single performance in mind. Repeated performances were an invention of later centuries and countless numbers of masterpieces had forever disappeared in the meanwhile. There was a long period of time in which even the figurative artists remained anonymous.

This extremely rigorous need for limits, which undermined any and all pre-eminence, unfortunately found its affirmation in an Athens that was already vast and complex; the dimensions of the city were quite unusual and essentially undesired. The need for direct democracy was a reflection of a nostalgia for a lost sense of measure and as well of a feeling of mistrust for a level of social complexity that already had come to exist and that no sense of measure might any longer exorcise. *Phthónos* was something that the *pólis* as a whole had reason to fear, and cities aspired to an abstract ideal of modest and pre-established proportions.[49] Aristotle's distrust of an over populous state rested on the need for the citizens to be able to gather together in a single place, and to hear each others' voices in the public square.[50] But his point of view presumed the existence of a direct parliamentary democracy of the Athenian type, which already was the fruit and not the cause of a faith in limits. That faith was indeed quite radical and came to expression not only in politics, but in social customs in general. The *póleis* paid no heed to their interests as political powers and bridled the growth of their populations. At the cost of creating great discontent, Athens was to issue restrictive laws that deprived many people of citizenship. When the number of a city's citizens grew too vigorously, no thought was given to any expansion of the original state; the solution was found in detaching a part of it, founding a colony separate from the mother *pólis* (*apoikía*). "Colony," moreover, is a modern term and here can be deceptive. We have to remember that the community of a new Greek colony was an entirely independent state from its very first day of existence and that colonies often transferred themselves to territories so distant from the mother *pólis* as to make it extremely difficult to maintain cultural or commercial ties with the original community. Greece has fertile agricultural lands, but always of limited extent, and increases in population are surely quite likely to have suggested the notion of finding some other place for those whom it became difficult to feed. And yet the practice of founding new colonies cannot be entirely explained by demographic pressures;[51] otherwise there might have been a tendency to colonize nearby territories, or even immediately adjacent territories, and the independence of the new state would not have had to be automatic. Even while creating true and proper empires, the Greeks never broke the taboo that demanded that every single *pólis* be an entity in its own right – its citizens' only source of law and the center of all their obligations.[52] At the time of its greatest expansion, Athens exercised a power of life and death over its various satellite cities but they were never forced into any officially subservient status. Like Athens itself, they were simply members of the League of Delos.

6

HISTORY BEGINS TO MOVE

THE CONCEPTS OF HISTORY AND PROGRESS

During the period of their greatest power, that small, well-known people of a not too distant past, the Greeks, remained quite tenaciously committed to an anti-historical spirit.
(Friedrich Nietzsche, *Unzeitgemäße Betrachtungen. Zweites Stück: vom Nutzen und Nachteil der Historie für das Leben*)

A well-known passage in Aristotle[1] describes the poet as superior to the historian since the poet speaks of things that the future could bring whereas the historian talks of things that already have happened; the poet speaks of the universal, the historian of the particular.

These words hold the essence of the Greek sense of becoming. The perception of historical change, and even more so of progress, was considered an illusion. Today we might say that the Hellenic peoples denied the existence of history. But any such statement would be based on the use of a concept that was not to appear until later, and in the vocabularies of other languages. *Istoría*, for the Greeks, was a word that simply meant "observation," or "inquiry." An *ístor* was a witness and his only duty was to report precisely on what he had seen. These words were exclusively concerned with the viewer and the viewer's particular point of view, and they tell us nothing at all about the nature of the objects that any such a viewer was involved in observing. History, in modern usage, is the movement of the world through time, and we presume that the existence of history predates all human attempts to make it an object of study. Things stood quite differently for the Greeks. Before Herodotus' decision in the fifth century to turn himself into an historian, history did not exist at all. In this sense, no difference can be drawn between history and philosophy; surely we accept the notion that philosophy began with the philosophers and found its birth as the child of their minds.

The modern world makes use of dynamic equilibriums. It is rather like a two-wheeled vehicle that keeps itself upright only by remaining in a state of motion. Older civilizations were based primarily on principles of static equilibrium. Rather than resembling bicycles, they were more like chairs. We have nearly lost all conception of such static modes of life. We are so thoroughly accustomed to rapid successions in every facet of life that surrounds us as now to find it difficult to understand cultures that were populated by objects, institutions and attitudes that were always the same, and utterly indifferent to notions of progress.

While observing the lives and affairs of other peoples, we automatically – sometimes consciously and sometimes not – see them in terms of the concepts of history that have shaped our own sense of culture. Most of us have been taught to spy the workings of the hand of God (or of History with a capital "H," which is His heir in not quite convincingly secular form) in the expansion of Rome, or in the discovery of America, or in the decline of dictatorships. The inevitability of past events is connected with the need to justify the shape that things have taken while leading up to ourselves. At every moment of the present, we ourselves are history's point of arrival, and it is from precisely this position that we see ourselves as participants in the flow of history, and as capable of contributing to its meaning. Such a vision seems to descend quite directly from the traditions of the Bible. The pact that we unconsciously presume to hold between ourselves and history seems to reflect the special relationship between God and His chosen people.

An ancient Greek, on the other hand, might have been able, as Herodotus made the effort to do, to reconstruct a continuity of facts that led back from himself to the events recounted by Homer. But the construction of such a relationship would at most have offered a kind of aesthetic satisfaction, rather than any perception of a chain of necessarily linked events.[2] The relationship between the two epochs would have testified to no necessary connections, nor to any concatenation of meaningful purposes, and surely not to any course of evolution. The great Homeric texts had themselves created a tradition of thought that flattened out temporal distances and rendered them insignificant. Homer describes events that happened at least four or five centuries before his time, and he supplies us with lists of customs and objects, but only on the basis of an oral tradition. He thus created a mixture of things that had truly belonged to Mycaenean civilization in the second millennium BC and of others that dated from later epochs. And the Hellenic peoples experienced this as raising no problems of truth, in any modern sense. Homer was the first true written source, and nothing of what he said could have been verified or questioned on the basis of earlier documents. The truth was Homer's truth. Homer himself was the line that delimited the horizon of time, and everything behind it – as with the edges of a pre-Copernican Earth – was indescribable emptiness. In relief against that background, the figures of the past stood flat; and they were all contemporaneous.

This was the feeling felt by the Greeks whenever they looked backwards.

And even though able, naturally enough, to wonder about the future, they seem to have done really very little with a view to shaping the course of events. Surely some of the cities were more conservative, like Sparta, and others, like Athens, were more open; and some social classes, like the aristocracy, held more narrow views, whereas the common people were desirous of change. It is possible to discover any number of different attitudes to novelty, and differences will even be found in the thoughts expressed by single authors. Plato's *Politics* looks favorably on the creation of new forms of art and endeavor; but the *Republic* and *Laws* insist on the banning of innovations, with a view to maintaining the strength and stability of the state. On the whole, however, interest in change and novelty was of an infinitely lower order than what is to be found in modern societies.

Up until the fifth century, there was truly no perception of the existence of civilization as a series of transformations rather than as a fixed and stable condition. It is quite normal, moreover, at least to a certain degree, for every epoch to see itself as the most complete, as the age to which all previous transformations have led, and that requires no further transformations. Greece as yet had no access to the revealed monotheism that has accustomed us to accepting the duty of continuing to perfect the world. We have already seen that the religious and ethical system of the Greeks was capable of prohibitions, but in no way ready to work for the advancement of a good, and thus for improvements and innovations. Technical expertise was accepted, but only to the extent that it presented itself as a continuation of nature,[3] in accord with the modes of nature. A stick for shaking olives from the trees was an extension of the arm. The same applied to the spear. But things stood differently with the bow and arrow. The legends of Odysseus and Philoctetes imply that the use of the bow and arrow had been fairly widespread in the Archaic period, but this art had fallen into nearly total disregard by the fifth century, and the initial superiority of the Persian invaders was partly due to their numerous ranks of archers.

Hesiod had told the tale of mankind's constant and progressive deterioration, and the ancient Greeks were essentially quite satisfied to be able to remark that they had maintained the same conditions that their fathers had passed on to them; and they were capable of imagining, in the lack of proof to the contrary, that they continued to live in the original conditions with which their age had begun.[4]

Even if sharper observers could not help seeing a slow accumulation of new conditions and new possibilities, it would surely have been difficult to think of any important change as having made itself definitive. Any such possible *hýbris* would have made itself subject to violent *némesis*. The Greeks believed that entire civilizations had previously disappeared in precisely such a way, and we know today that events of that order in fact had taken place.

How, moreover, might the Greeks have imagined things differently? They could hardly, after all, have foreseen the continuity that in fact began with themselves and with the world in which they lived. It is only with the Greeks as our starting point that we can think of questions of language, art, science and philosophy as having developed through the centuries – in spite of periods of highs and lows – and as having been passed on finally to us. It is only as a result of this singular and complex form of the survival of the Greeks – which makes them seem closer to us than to the barbarians who were their contemporaries – that an idea of history as a continuous movement was able to be born.

Non-history appeared to be a great deal stronger than history, as in fact it formerly had been; and mythical, repetitive time seemed much more impelling than progressive time. Non-history – which is where all of us live as children – is the experience of the absence of change in the human condition. As such it ranks as a very generic place, but the idea can help us grasp the quality shared by true pre-history, by the Greeks' devaluation of history, and by the a-historical attitudes that are still today to be found in agrarian societies. The simple addition of one of a series of adjectives to the notion of history – "ancient history," "mythic history," and so forth – hinders the understanding of the past since it contains what might be described as a "modern-centered" point of view. The idea of non-history, on the other hand, abandons the modern point of view. It contains a notion of homeostasis. Nature itself was thought to be self-regulating; it was a place without temporal or territorial borders, and it happened for brief intervals to offer hospitality to human civilizations.

Yet the Greeks were different from various other peoples since they raised the problem of change, and from a number of points of view: ethical, technological and religious. Most of their answers to the questions they raised were fairly dismal. Hesiod recounts that human life had passed through a series of five eras, from the golden age to the age of iron.[5] This lack of faith in the development of the life of the collective was very much in line with the fatalistic attitudes that marked the Greeks' assessment of the destinies of individuals.

If these were the dominant attitudes, what can be imagined so suddenly to have formed the fulcrum that would stand at the center of the movement of western civilization? We can only imagine that the spirit of change was coming to maturity and indeed already active beneath the rigidity of traditional convictions.

To explain the plethora of cultural, artistic and political innovations that arrived with such intensity in the course of a single century, and mostly in the city of Athens, we have to imagine a process of enantiodromia: a passage from one extreme to its opposite suddenly took place after a period of long preparation in the unconscious spaces of a previously dominant Weltanschauung.[6]

The principal characteristic of modern society is its infinite complexity, but the world of the ancient Greeks was highly different. Compensatory processes surely took place with greater ease in a world of strong, asymmetrical and elementary contrasts where the gods distrusted mortals, where men were wary of women, and where the Greeks looked askance at the barbarians.

We have to remember that the Greek frame of mind saw reversals and compensations as one of the basic expressions of natural and social law; its superstitious expectations in fact encouraged them. The moral concept of *némesis* pointed after all to a process that was not very different from what modern Jungian psychodynamics refers to as enantiodromia, or from what history speaks of as revolution. We can imagine that a compensatory flow of enlightening optimism had till then been repressed by the unilateral pessimism of the Greeks; but it accumulated in the soul, reached the point of overflowing and finally found release. A new self-confidence spread with the speed of an epidemic; a courage that allowed the thinking of what had never been thought before, and that likewise allowed a confrontation with enemies who were thought to be invincible. It found its authorization in a faith in a natural distributive justice, and that faith in turn was reinforced by the quick sequence of achievements that this flood of optimism in fact made possible.

This enantiodromia first found expression in the workings of a few extraordinary minds that had new ideas to offer, in addition to serving as spokesmen for a general need for fresh departures. The changes that were underway in Athens must quickly have accelerated to tremendous speeds, and one imagines them as well to have been self-nourishing. Thanks to the high average level of education, and also to the way in which the the active members of the *pólis* were in direct and constant contact with one another, the thinking of new thoughts was by no means limited to the few who had the genius to promote them; a considerable part of the populace came in fact to be involved in a wide-ranging public debate. This is not, however, to say that the new ideas were able to surge triumphantly forward; we see them derided in the popular comedies of Aristophanes, and clearly they belonged to a process that excited suspicion and a chain of counter-reactions. As innovative thinking grew bolder and escaped the under-standing of the majority, the reaction against it grew likewise more conspicuous. Every epoch that has avant-gardes is also acquainted with retroguards and their attempts to make use of legalistic artifice to shore up systems of values that would otherwise collapse beneath their own weight. And the Athenians – who precisely while becoming less religious gave themselves over for the very first time to the persecution of those who questioned faith in the gods – were in this respect no better or worse than others, even if they assured their immortality in the history of fanaticism by condemning Socrates to death.

It should also be remembered that the new spiritual condition and the novel attitudes that made their appearance in Greece did not at first take shape as a part of the interior dynamics of Athenian life; they were promoted, quite to the contrary, by powerful external pressures.

THE ROUT OF THE PERSIANS

There are three things for which I give thanks to destiny: for having been born a man and not an animal, male and not female, a Greek and not a barbarian.

(Thales)

History set itself in motion, dragging Greece behind it, and slowly converting Greek culture to a new belief. Change took the form not only of cultural innovations, but also of political and military events. Asia had begun to march against the west and threatened to trample the Hellenes. To speak of Asia is not, however, to speak of the continent to which we now refer as such; Asia, for the Greeks, consisted of that continent's vast west-central regions which were ruled by the king of the Medes and the Persians, and also of ample tracts of Africa. Greece, on the other hand, was less than half the size of modern-day Greece, and at certain decisive moments it consisted of only the city of Athens. But we are dealing none the less with what can count as the first world-scale war, and it saw the participation of any number of the peoples of three continents, including the Carthaginians and Phoenicians.

The language of the Oriental invaders was incomprehensible to the Greeks, to whom it sounded like a labial babbling. Attempting to imitate its frequently recurring "b" sounds, they invented the term *barbarian* applying it both to the language and to the people who spoke it. We use the word *barbarian* as a synonym for "uncivilized," but its philological roots are exclusively onomatopoeic.

The Greeks considered the barbarians to be different from themselves, since the barbarians knew no moderation. Everything about them was excessive. They were alien to the uses of the Greek symposium, where drink and dialog tempered one another, and gave themselves over instead to rowdy noise and drunkenness. Rather than sobriety in clothing and furnishings, they loved flowing, brightly colored robes and objects that shone and sparkled. The very structure of their society was different. It had no basis in norms that related equal citizens each to the other, fixing their reciprocal limits and turning them into individuals. The barbarians were an indistinct horde. Rather than count their subjects one by one, barbarian rulers would mass successive groups into a kind of corral that served as a unit of measure, since there was an approximate idea of the number of people it could hold.[7] Rather than citizens of a society, the barbarians were a despot's subjects; there were no such things as lateral social relationships. No one was anything more than an object in the hands of a chief, and everyone was controlled from above. And the only purpose of chiefdom lay in the continual pursuit of new conquests, without regard to any real need for them.[8]

The troops of the king of Persia thus began to advance towards the west. The movement was gradual, since years were required to assemble armies, and still more years to displace them. But it was likewise relentless, since the conquest of new lands was one of the ordinary occupations in the life of the king of Persia rather than a specific task that belonged to any particular phase of it.

The two great campaigns against Greece were realized by Darius (in 490) and his son Xerxes (480–479). If the first was grandiose, the second was immense: a true mobilization of the world against Greece. If the first can be seen as an imperial enterprise, the second was intended to restore a fundamental justice on earth. Xerxes had to right the offense that the Greeks had dealt to his father by repelling him. The barbarians felt mortally insulted by what the Greeks had considered to be a just and proper exercise of the right to self-defense.

The interval between the wars was dedicated, for the Persians, to the logistic problems of organization and displacement to which we have just referred; and the Athenians spent that period investing all of their resources into preparation for the second wave of invasion. But there was never a real interruption of activity on the two opposing fronts, and the Greeks remembered the whole experience as a single event.

Contacts with the barbarians had been limited up until the turn of the century when a few Greek colonies in Asia Minor rebelled against the Persian empire. As the Persian forces expanded towards the Aegean, the Greek colonies had found themselves on the verge of being subjected to vassalage. Frightened by the far greater number of the Persian invaders, they had asked for help from their mother country, but none the less had been crushed. Athens, however, had answered their appeal, and was therefore scheduled for punishment. The war would now be fought to the death, and the invasion of Greece was inevitable.

Greece and the world of the Hellenes presented the great Persian king with a revolutionary surprise. The Greeks had the custom of refusing to bend in the face of a stronger enemy, and they even went so far as to argue in defense of their refusal, insisting that excessive power could only be rewarded by the punishment of the gods. The messengers of the Persian king demanded that the Greeks send a tribute of earth and water to Darius as a symbolic recognition of his dominion on both land and sea.[9] They were told, however, to help themselves to whatever quantity of water and earth they wanted: the Athenians threw the Persian ambassadors into a gully, and the Spartans tumbled them into a well.[10]

A Persian army landed near Athens in the summer of 490, only a few years after the revolt of the Greeks in Asia Minor. Athens asked for assistance from the other *póleis*, but the only help received was a small contingent from Plataea. The Greeks could not yet see that the shape of their world had changed: it was no longer a place of immobility and all of them had come to be enrolled in it.

To close off the road between Athens and the northern coast of Attica, all the available forces – in the order of ten thousand hoplites – took up position near Marathon, at the edges of the narrow plain where the barbarians would have had to camp in order to prepare the deployment of their massive strength and to organize their numerical superiority to full advantage. The size of the advancing Persian army has been greatly overestimated, but still it vastly outnumbered the Greeks. Even after the Persians divided their troops into two separate task forces, the number of soldiers that remained in Marathon was at least twice as many as the Greeks. The Persian army, moreover, had the additional advantage of the fear inspired by its traditional invincibility. It also included large numbers of professional soldiers and ranks of specialized brigades, of which the most fearsome were the corps of archers and cavalry. The Greeks had no archers or cavalry at all. The Athenian hoplites were a heavy infantry composed of simple citizens in an improvised role as soldiers, each of whom had procured his own arms. The armies faced and observed one another for several days without engaging battle. The barbarians were waiting for the signal with which traitors and opportunists were expected to invite them to enter Athens. The Athenians waited in a state of great anxiety. To defend themselves from siege was an act of heroism; but to enter into battle at so great a distance from home[11] was an act of possible *hýbris* that no Greek could have been anxious to undertake. The Spartans – the best of all the Greek fighters – were supposed to join them, but presented a series of religious excuses for delaying to do so. The truth was somewhat different: the Spartans, by tradition, were even more reluctant than the Athenians to leave their city.

The rules of Athenian society allowed for no office of permanent command, and command of the troops was in fact assigned by rotation. While Miltiades was holding the post, he observed that the Persians were embarking a part of their troops and apparently preparing to take Athens by sea. The remaining land troops, moreover, were closing ranks and advancing. Having learned that the Athenians were awaiting the arrival of the Spartans, the Persians had decided that the time had come to strike simultaneously on two fronts, and thus to take advantage of their full numerical superiority. Miltiades quickly decided to attack. He ordered his army to abandon its trenches and to make a compact running charge. The small Marathon Plain must have trembled beneath the feet of the hoplites.[12] They reached the barbarians before they had time to recover from the surprise. No army of foot soldiers had ever before been known to make a running attack or not to have flagged at the sight of the Persians in full military dress.[13]

By swiftly attacking the enemy, the Greeks avoided the brunt of a Persian cavalry charge and they also neutralized the advantage of the archers, who could have struck them down at a distance. As in other realms of knowledge, Athenian intuition grasped the essence of things. Maneuvers would have been a question of superfluous *hýbris*; the important thing was to charge against the wall of the barbarian troops or to die on the spot. There was no defense behind them to protect their families from the attacking empire.

The world was to remain amazed when it learned that these few city dwellers, educated in dialog and the arts more than in military skills, had reversed the hierarchy of the continents for centuries to come. Six thousand four hundred Asians remained dead on the field, as compared to only 192 losses among the Europeans.[14]

But other enemies were sailing towards Athens, and Miltiades had performed only half of his task. Allowing no pause along the way, he relentlessly marched his hoplites along the craggy road that led back to the city. Once again, the barbarians were too ambitious. Their boats had taken the time to embark the numerous prisoners captured at Eretria, intending to take them back to Persia. When they arrived in Athens, Miltiades was waiting for them. His second victory cost not so much as a single drop of blood. Faced with that second surprise, the Persians decided not to disembark.

The story of the victory at Marathon is of course well known, but it has to be completed by recalling an episode with which fewer are acquainted – an episode that sums it up in an allegory of the punishment of *hýbris*.

Various sources[15] recount that the Persians were so certain of victory as to have brought along a block of marble from Paros, intending to use it for a monument to their glory. Their unexpected defeat was attributed by the Greeks to the intervention of Nemesis, a deity till then of little importance but none the less entrusted with the punishment of excess. A sanctuary was erected at Ramnos, on the northern coast of Attica, facing Eubea and not too far from Marathon. Phidias used the barbarians' marble for a statue of Nemesis,[16] to whom the site was thereafter consecrated.[17]

The descriptions of the second Persian campaign against Greece are even more dramatic, and often so exaggerated as to be hardly at all reliable.[18]

Xerxes announced his intention to take revenge and restore the honor of his father. But if such a declaration was in line with the moral principles of the epoch, the terms of his proclamation were nothing less than impious and thus an anticipation of further tragedy: "We shall make the borders of Persian territory and of the firmament of heaven to be the same; for no land that the sun beholds will lie on our borders, but I will make all to be one country, when I have passed over the whole of Europe."[19]

The morality of the Greeks speaks to us through the voice of the historian; and Herodotus, so as to express his point of view without drawing attention to himself, confronts the king with the warnings of his uncle Artabanus, the brother of Darius.

> You see how the god smites with his thunderbolt creatures of greatness more than common, nor suffers them to display their pride, but such as are little move him not to anger; and see how it is ever on the tallest building and trees that his bolts fall. For it is heaven's way to bring low all things of surpassing bigness. Thus a numerous host is destroyed by one that is lesser, the god of his jealousy [*phthonésas*] sending panic, fear or thunderbolt among them.

He then concludes, "for the god suffers pride in none but himself."[20]

But Xerxes continued to follow his road, and the dimensions of his sin of pride are gradually revealed.

In an age when the crossing of a river was a difficult enterprise, Xerxes ordered that Asia and Europe be tied together with ropes that traversed the Hellespont, and thus to proceed to the building of a bridge that the whole of an army could cross.[21] A great storm canceled out his efforts. But rather than see this as a sign of a higher will, the king of the Persians grew furious and added still further allegorical arrogance to an already arrogant undertaking. He attempted to impose his dominion on the waters of the sea itself, commanding the Hellespont to be "scourged with three hundred lashes" and branded by fire as chains were meanwhile thrown into its waves. Those who whipped the Hellespont were also ordered to accompany their blasphemy with "words outlandish and presumptuous" (*bárbará te kai atásthala*): "Thou bitter water ... our master thus punishes thee, because thou didst him wrong albeit he had done thee none."[22]

Two bridges were finally constructed, one by tying 360 ships together, the other with 314 ships.[23] Xerxes thus took another step towards his own ruin.

Artabanus was alarmed and repeated his invitation to moderation, couching the principle of divine jealousy into a convincing logical argumentation on the facts of geography. He saw the land and the sea as the true enemies of so vast an army. He insisted that precisely the unrivaled size of the fleet was what most endangered it. There was no place in the world – and surely no place along the route that the fleet would follow – that offered a port sufficiently large to give it protection in the case of a storm. And with respect to the army, it was again its invincibility that placed it in danger. Since no one could stop its advance, it would forever continue to push forward, since no measure of success is ever considered sufficient for a man. And finally, ever more distant from its base, the army would encounter and succumb to hunger.[24]

Xerxes responded to his uncle by saying that if the kings of Persia had shared such prudence, their country would never have achieved greatness. He therefore crossed the Hellespont, accompanied by soldiers of every nationality and with endless lines of baggage trains.

Tradition insists that the passage of Xerxes' army across the Hellespont continued without interruption for seven days and seven nights.[25] And the overall count of Xerxes' fighters is said to have amounted to 2,640,000 men – a number that would have to be more than doubled to take account as well of the workers required for seeing to provisions and transport. Such figures are clearly absurd. Even without ceding to the prudence of Artabanus, Xerxes would have found himself faced with the insurmountable problem of feeding such a horde.[26]

Modern calculations suggest that Xerxes counted on an army of from 200,000[27] to 360,000[28] soldiers. His fleet probably amounted to about a thousand ships. Such numbers were in any case imposing for his day, if only in consideration of the enormity of the distances that had to be crossed, demanding still further multitudes of animals and men for purposes of logistics and communications.[29]

Xerxes' army can be seen, in short, to have been fearful not only from a military point of view; it also unleashed a visionary panic, exciting the powers of the Greek imagination to unprecedented levels of effort.

If we think about the dimensions of the world of that time, it is clear that – in addition to the military threat that they knew to be extremely grave – the Greeks had never before laid eyes on a gathering of a similar multitude of men, no matter whether soldiers or civilians. And their minds can hardly be imagined to have been prepared to host an idea that corresponded to such a sight. This, precisely, was the period in which the Greeks were gradually developing the ability to think in conceptual terms. Certainly they were capable of calculations that estimated the size of the enemy forces, but the vision with which they found themselves faced was surely more terrifying than any abstract idea that they may actually have been able to formulate. Eidetic thought, or thinking by way of images, precedes conceptual thought in the life of the species no less than in the life of the individual; and in addition to remaining the psychic activity to which we abandon ourselves when we regress to states of consciousness such as reverie or sleep, it is also the form of thought that asserts itself when we find ourselves in the grips of violent emotions. The great black blot of the Persian army that spread across the mountains and the fields triggered a return to that infancy of the mind and to all its terrors as well. When Xerxes' troops had completed their passage across those two long bridges, one of the inhabitants of the Hellespont is reported to have exclaimed, "Oh Zeus, why hast thou taken the likeness of a Persian man and changed thy name to Xerxes, leading the whole world with thee to remove Hellas from its place? For that thou mightest have done without these means."[30]

Continuing along his road, Xerxes – according to reports that ought not to surprise us, since we have already seen his propensity to deal with the features of geography as though they were persons subject to his will – is said even to have written a letter to Mount Athos, threatening to cast it into the sea.[31]

The fleet too traveled at maximum speed, halting as little as possible, and darkness overtook it one evening before Mount Pelios, in an area that offered no ports. Anchored close together on the open sea, the Persian boats were surprised at dawn by a hurricane. It was to blow for three whole days, at the end of which four hundred ships and thousands of men were missing.[32] The summer weather of that part of the world is notoriously stable, and that was a fact on which both the Greeks and their enemies had counted: it was difficult not to read this event as a sign.

While the Persians were descending from the north, the Spartan king Leonidas was marching at the head of a small and partly traitorous army to meet them. He pitched his camp at Thermopolae, where the narrowness of the gorge and an already extant wall offered some chance of stopping them. The days continued to pass, and wave after wave of Persian soldiers continued to shatter in defeat against that meager barrier. A traitor, however, was finally to lead the finest of Xerxes' troops to the rear of the Greek position.

Leonidas, who was forbidden by Spartan custom to retreat, dismissed the majority of his allies – many of whom were then quick to become traitors in their own right[33] – and prepared to die in the company of three hundred of his fellow citizens.

As a way of persuading them to beat a retreat, the Greeks were warned by a Trachinian that the arrows of the barbarians would soon fly so fitly as to block out the light of the sun. It was in the midst of the summer and the Spartan Dieneces raised his eyes to the torrid skies of Thessaly: "Our friend from Trachis brings us right good news," he replied, " . . . we shall fight them in the shade."[34]

Herodotus' reason for recording these words had less to do with their heroism than with the homage they pay to phthónos. Divine justice was tallying the measure of the Persians' hýbris. That roof of flying arrows was soon to be transformed into a shield. The will of the arrogant counts for nothing, and the protection of the gods lay everywhere.

Having shattered their spears and then their swords, the Greeks fought on with their hands and teeth.[35] They died one by one beneath the crush of the arrows and the corpses of the Persian soldiers. Leonidas' body was beheaded and crucified.[36]

But would it not bring misfortune for the larger army to heap such insult on a smaller foe? Were they fighting out of military necessity, or to give fulfillment to a prophecy?

The Asiatic forces now flooded south and met with no further obstacles. Faced with their advance, the whole of Attica was evacuated. The Spartans walled themselves in behind the isthmus that separates the Peleponnesus from the continent, and refugees from Athens scattered among the islands.

Xerxes put Athens to the torch and devastated Attica. Acclaimed as triumphant by his troops and also by a growing crowd of opportunists, he then deployed his ships for the final blow. Most of the Greek sailors were by now in a mood to take flight. Themistocles therefore contrived to spread false rumors[37] that informed the enemy that the Greeks had already broken ranks and irremediably deserted, thus inducing the Persians to launch an immediate attack and thereby forcing his own men to fight before actually having time to flee. Xerxes ordered a throne to be taken to the top of a hill, and then took up his place on it to observe his triumph from above.

But now, for a moment, we should attempt to reconstruct the moods and states of mind that must have prevailed among the barbarians in the course of their campaign.

Given the extent of the Persian empire, its armies were composed of any number of peoples, and we can assume them to have been at least as superstitious as the Greeks. These masses of people were certainly not indifferent to the widespread Greek predictions of their imminent misfortune, and in the course of a campaign that had lasted for years they had surely been exposed to countless dire murmurings. Trapped, at such great distance from their homes, in an adventure of which the only visible meaning lay in Xerxes' megalomania, they were likewise unable to extract themselves from the effects of unfamiliar circumstances that aroused and nourished their doubts. Collective anxiety, or a panic that was always ready to burst to the surface of the feelings of a great mass of uprooted and ill-assorted people, is a term that a modern interpreter might apply to the workings of the divine jealousy to which the Greeks attributed the defeat of so powerful an army. If jealous gods are born in the minds of men, then surely they lived as well in the souls of the barbarians; and the barbarians' secret fears were sure to abet their possible defeat.

The final battle[38] took place in the narrow strait that separates Salamis from the coast. Measureless strength was once again to turn against those who deployed it. Confined to these restricted waters, the maneuvers of the enormous Persian fleet were hopelessly encumbered. The ships rammed one against the other while the Greeks never ceased to pursue them. Just as at Thermopolis, the barbarians once again lacked an ample front on which to deploy the whole of their strength. By nightfall, the waves were covered with bobbing corpses that knocked against the hulls of the triremes.

Twenty-five centuries later, the Persian campaigns still manage to amaze us; we discount the contemporary exaggerations and still it truly seems that the armies were guided not by generals but by jealous gods. To explain these events, we have to conclude that the Greek belief in Nemesis was very deeply seated, and that it led the faithful into the fray of battle with high expectations. The Greeks were certain of enjoying the collaboration of revengeful gods; and precisely the opposite feeling, a latent and superstitious fear, grew ever more diffuse among the barbarians, preparing them for mass panic and defeat.

Within the space of a year, the Persians were definitively to withdraw from Greece. The enantiodromia became visible in the behavior of the two armies. Caught in a tide of events that had begun in Marathon and that was destined to last for decades, the Athenians pursued the barbarians all the way to the coasts of Asia. The last of the Greeks' efforts to defend themselves slipped seamlessly over into the first of their acts of conquest.

THE DIN OF HISTORY

Education certainly gives victory, although victory sometimes produces forgetfulness of education; for many have grown insolent from victory in war, and this insolence has engendered in them innumerable evils.
(Plato, *Laws*)

In his account of the Battle of Marathon, Herodotus reports an episode that makes no apparent sense.[39] He tells the story of a valiant Athenian named Epizelus who fought quite bravely and in the course of the battle lost his sight, yet without having ever been wounded. He was blind for the rest of his life, and those who questioned him were always rewarded with the same explanation: in the midst of the fray, an enormous hoplite had appeared before him, his likewise enormous beard casting its shadow over his shield. The giant had then passed on and had killed the comrade who fought at Epizelus' side.

Such an episode was hardly a real event, and it shows no resemblance to the tales and fancies that Herodotus frequently includes in his narrative for the purpose of the moral they prove. Such tales, in fact, embellish the story of the Persian wars with evil forebodings for the barbarian invaders or with accounts of fruitful covenants that come to be stipulated between the Greeks and their gods,[40] thus skewing the reading of history towards an act of acknowledgment of the workings of heavenly justice.

Herodotus would not have included this "prodigy" (*thaûma*) in his *History* if it had not already been famous, or if it did not already have a hold on the collective imagination. It is an entirely imaginary episode, but its inclusion in the story can be seen as legitimate on the basis of its correspondence to a widespread unconscious representation. We can therefore attempt to interpret it in much the same way that we interpret fables and legends, which we know to be capable of describing significant unconscious elements of collective psychology, just as dreams are illustrations of unconscious elements in the life of the individual. The episode tells the tale of a man who was suddenly blinded. To be blinded implies a loss of direct contact with the world of daily life, and studies of the symbolism of dreams can reveal it to be a true and proper representation of such a process: a weakening of the relationship with the real, of which the final extreme is the loss of the power of reason. (A person described, for example, as "blind with rage" or "blinded by love" is considered incapable of reasoning.)

According to the story, Epizelus was fighting quite admirably. He is described with the adjective *agathós*, which means "virtuous" or "valorous." There is no reason to think of his affliction as a divine punishment. Quite to the contrary: listeners who heard this story should in fact have experienced the pleasure of being able to identify with one of the heroes of the Battle of Marathon. This supposition is confirmed by the name: "Epizelus" means "the envied one," or "the man much to be envied." Though sometimes associated with *phthónos*, *zélos*[41] is a positive form of "envy" between men, corresponding most closely to the notions of "emulation" and "admiration." ("Epizelus" might also be translated as "he who is imitated.") We can therefore dispense with the thought that the story might illustrate the punishment of an evil man and turn our attention to further elements that might more clearly delineate its meaning. Epizelus is dazzled by a vision, blinded by a phantom, without the occurrence of any physical contact. We are dealing here with a spiritual force, or with a psychic rather than a physical enemy. We know only that this enemy is colossal in size, and that the same holds true for his beard, which is one of the most frequent attributes of strength and virility. Who can he be? He is described as a hoplite, which is the standard designation for a Greek foot-soldier. And yet he threatens Epizelus, causes the loss of his sight, and strikes down one of his companions. Quite surely he is an enemy of the Greeks, and yet he would not appear to come from the ranks of the Persians.

We can briefly recapitulate by saying that Herodotus has recounted a fable-like episode of which the moral is anomalous, since the usual moral insists on the punishment of Persian pride. Here, quite to the contrary, the victim of the story is a Greek. There are two possibilities: either we are faced with a story that has no moral – as would clearly be appropriate to a more mature notion of the writing of history, but not to the canons of Herodotus – or the moral of the story, rather than absent, is in largely unconscious form. In this latter case, the psychological structure of the episode would be the same as what one finds in a fable, and we know that the new-born discipline of history leaned quite radically in the direction of fable and moral sentence. So the second possibility is by far the more likely. I would not in fact give so much attention to a minor narrative incident if its interpretation as fable did not align with my principal thesis.

When we look at this episode as fable, it allows for only a single interpretation: it embodies a nightmare on the part of the victors at Marathon. It reveals their intuition of possibly being blinded by an aggressive, invincible enemy who roamed among their very own ranks and not among those of their foes. The unconscious fears that here reach expression most probably arose quite gradually in the years that followed the Persian Wars, and tales such as this one would have come along with them. Herodotus, who himself was quite gradual in assembling his enormous stock of material, would perhaps have embraced it as a result of having perceived its power, even while remaining unaware of its full meaning.

This enemy's identity can be clarified by the course of events themselves. A radical division had made its appearance and was growing constantly more evident in Greek culture. The call to moderation, for the purpose of forestalling *phthónos* and *némesis*, was always sharper and of greater insistence, but intellect and material prosperity had likewise embarked on a course of expansion of previously unknown proportions. The contrast between these two tendencies – between austere morality, on the one hand, and, on the other, the lust for knowledge that gave a new and wholly unprecedented shape to the Athenian mind of the fifth century – is of a nature and intensity that makes one suspect that the execration of pride already included a perception of the general burgeoning of aspirations; and it thus gave voice to the need to oppose them with all the vigor required to prevent a degeneration of customs and mores. It is hardly coincidental that the city of Athens after the Battle of Marathon began to make use of the practice of ostracism. Aristotle had perfectly good reasons for connecting this institution to the new spirit of collective audacity that the victory brought in its wake.[42] Yet collective audacity, no matter how conspicuous, was no more than a single facet of a series of motivations that may well, in addition, have concealed unconscious fears and feelings of guilt. The most usual way of finding liberation from incipient feelings of guilt consists of projecting them, and thus of seeing others as bearing responsibility for whatever might be their cause. As the temptations of *hýbris* became an ever more general experience, the people of Athens sought out a mode of self-purification; they denied their ever more frequent infraction of the commandment "nothing too much" by attributing all such behavior to political personalities whose star was on the rise. Ostracism made it possible to expel such persons before they had the chance to triumph. But precisely the champions of ostracism revealed the truest extent of arrogance, since they appropriated the administration of divine justice. *Phthónos* was taken into human hands that asserted their own omnipotence, supplanting the gods and striking down in their stead whomever was suspected of *hýbris*. *Hýbris* itself was the final victor.

The sudden spread of the practice of ostracism corresponds to a superstitious fear of watching the further advance, in emblematic persons, of the taste for success; ostracism was an attempt to make use of political means to drive that vision out of view. The era of non-history was perishing, and the less cultured strata of society attempted an act of nostalgic self-mummification, hoping to be able to continue to live in a previous condition of eternal stability. The people were full of fear and diffidence in the face of new ideas and attitudes that were beginning to influence their world, and they demanded a return to the traditional virtues. But at one and the same time they were carried along by the stream of new events that imposed a rupture of tradition and in fact that came from outside of it. The world, which the Greeks had believed to be non-historical, had set itself in motion. The notion of the insignificance of human individuals as determinants of political and military events – the events we describe as historical in the simplest sense – became less credible in the light of grandiose facts like the winning of the Persian Wars. Such facts were rapidly broadcast by the first exercises in the writing of history; and even while continuing, like Herodotus himself, to praise and render homage to the justice of the gods, the Greeks ended up by employing such facts for their own glorification, finally appropriating them as national history. These entirely new ways of thinking were gradually prettified, but they exuded the same self-inflation that the Greeks maintained to have vanquished forever in the person of the Persian barbarians.[43]

Since these barbarians sought out and cultivated excess, the Greeks considered the Persians' moral status to be the opposite of their own. But the victory over the Persians, no less grandiose than the number of their soldiers, already held the germ of another reversal and also of another *némesis*. Since Marathon and Salamis were magnificent victories, they implicitly signaled a victory of the very idea of magnificence. Unhoped-for victory stimulated pride and haughty self-satisfaction (*kóros*), and *kóros* in turn excited the taste for conquest, and the taste for conquest encouraged the arrogance of unlimited expansion. The charge at Marathon was to remain emblematic: the disruption of the Persian lines gave birth to new attitudes that see limits as always to be shattered. The grandiosity of the Persian empire was battled against and defeated; but it exerted a secret fascination.

From a military point of view, this tiny people had defeated an enormous empire. But from a cultural point of view, the notion of empire had begun to enter the thinking and actions of this tiny people. The war had marked the advent of a sudden enantiodromia.

The notion of immensity asserted itself as the center of a different way of looking at the world. The jealousy of the gods was of ever less importance, and a principle of human imitation was fired into life. *Zélos* superseded *phthónos*.

It is said that the losers write no history. But the losers are absorbed into the spirit of the victors and thus become a part of the culture that writes it.[44] The movements that now had begun were never to come to a halt. Having abandoned the sphere of relatively local rivalries, they in fact had donned the solemn apparel of a conflict between continents, and they have continued to wear it ever since: Greece against Asia; Rome against Carthage, and then once again against barbarian peoples; Christianity against Islam, and then against the whole of the globe, since all of it was to be evangelized and colonized; and on and on.

History was the place where novelty was possible, if human beings had the courage to create it. This was implied even by the pious Herodotus in his description of the overwhelming assault at Marathon. He tells us that the Athenians "were the first Greeks, within my knowledge, who charged their enemies at a run, and the first who endured the sight of Median garments and men clad therein; till then the Greeks were affrighted by the very name of the Medes."[45]

But if novel events can freely unfold, history ceases to be circular and monotonously repetitive. Instead, it has beginnings. And if it is acquainted with beginnings, and thus also with ends, that is all the more reason for it to dwell among men, whose lives have likewise beginnings and ends, and not amongst the gods, who are eternal and unmoving, and who thus preside over a sphere of motionless non-history.[46]

Insistence on heavenly intervention in the Persian Wars ended up – as so often occurs when religious messages are still in a state of active evolution – by nourishing a greater knowledge of self than of any deity. If a superior destiny had defeated the Persians, the Athenians, who had borne that destiny on the points of their lances, could identify with it.[47] Shortly after, they were able to suggest, using these words to demand the submission of a defenseless people, "that we hold sway justly because we overthrew the Persians."[48]

That was the moment, as never before, in which *némesis* most truly asserted itself as the root of all justice. The Greeks were convinced that justice had completed its course by castigating the barbarians. But now that justice was to turn its attentions to them.

Greek creativity reached its highest mark in the fifth century, and that century saw the decline of a religion made of gods who did not know how to create. The lords of Olympus, capable of self-exertion only for the purpose of maintaining their eternal privileges, had now to bow down to man, whose sweat could generate novelty.

The redimensioning of polytheism was something, however, that the Greeks had to pay for; they suffered a loss of psychological agility. Their constant respect for the complexities and conflicting points of view of the gods had led them to develop an ability to see the relativity of their own points of view; they could likewise use their hearts to accept realities that reason was unable to deal with. Many of their gods were enemies of others; and many stood on the side of their earthly enemies. So rather than simply and only evil, enemies too had links with something divine.

This profound capacity for accepting the other, even the adversary,[49] comes to expression in the Greeks' epic poetry, and it turns the *Iliad* into a song of intense fellow-feeling for the Trojans. One can point just as easily to Aeschylus' *Persians*; its very title pays homage to the vanquished and not to the victors. Still another example can be found in the work of Herodotus himself; Plutarch was in fact to scold the father of history by dubbing him a *philobárbaros*, a friend of the barbarians. The Greeks – and thus the whole of the western world – were to lose this sense of symbolic complementarities and this capacity to identify with enemies. Our minds were to turn to the use and creation of strong and clearly delimited categories, seeing an always greater and less reconcilable contrast between good and evil, life and death, consciousness and unconsciousness, science and superstition, truth and falsehood. As had already happened in Judaism, the God of Christianity took up the sword of His people and deserted the skies of the others. Incomprehension fermented in hate is the feeling that guides the description of the enemy in a masterwork of Christian epic poetry such as the *Chanson de Roland*, where the Saracens turn into grotesque marionettes without so much as a trace of psychological depth. The ability to see one's reflection in a *tu* (and a *vos*) was trameled and dispersed by the new and emerging need to nourish the expansion of the *ego* (and the *nos*) in every possible way; and the affirmation of the *ego* was seen in turn to take place beneath the aegis of a destiny that not only is powerful and just, but that more than all else is an ally rather than an envious judge.

When the Greeks began to feel that justice and the forces of heaven were on their side, they were no longer very different from the Hebrews. And when they felt that history could give issue to growth and conquest, they were no longer very distant from the Crusaders and the other heroes of Christendom. And Christianity, when it reached them, had nothing more to do than to stride across the threshold of an already open door.

7

NEW HORIZONS

THE REVERSAL OF POLITICAL, ECONOMIC AND MILITARY PERSPECTIVES

After the victories over the Persians, Greek commerce expanded, and Athens here again knew no rivals. During the age of Pericles, the city's already consolidated economic supremacy shifted into a different and more aggressive register; it combined with new military policies to form a clear and coherent imperial design and thus became an integral part, along with advances in the arts, sciences and culture, of a general movement of expansion.

From modern points of view, the population of fifth-century Attica may appear to have been rather modest,[1] but the area in fact was already overpopulated in relation to the poverty of its soil and to the period's agricultural techniques. No part of Greece enjoyed the favorable relationship between population and resources that was typical of the enormous open spaces inhabited by the barbarians, but Athens was particularly crowded, and Attica was especially arid.

Since the climate was in any case mild, and since ports and winds (and thus the trade routes in an era in which the only true means of transport was by sea) were excellent, that difficulty proved finally to be of relative importance. In fact it made the Athenians a more enterprising people, turning them in the course of time into better navigators, craftsmen and tradesmen, and as tradesmen they were capable of a certain degree of surplus accumulation. The supremacy of Athens might thus be said to have derived from an additional measure of culture that special but not insurmountable difficulties had spurred the city to create.[2]

Athens developed quite quickly in any number of directions. The city became more open, cultured and intellectually curious than others, attracting both wealth and human talents, and as such it excited a spiral in the growth of population and the scarcity of resources. The city grew more rapidly than any other, and its greater size favored still more growth, since it reduced the risk of enemy attacks, which at the time was one of the most significant factors that limited the growth of population. Local resources grew ever less sufficient. We lack precise statistics, but we know that Attica was deforested earlier than other regions of Greece; wood was cut in order to build boats and for the purpose of clearing new farmlands. We also know that Athens was the first Greek city to lose the ability to feed itself; but at the time of that development it already possessed a pool of intellectual resources that was large enough to permit it to undertake a new experiment: the development of a rudimentary industry and the beginning of regular commerce with other states.[3] Athens' total democracy was the most revolutionary of all its resources; unlike the other *póleis*, Athens offered equal rights and opportunities to persons involved in occupations that tradition considered to be less noble, such as merchants and craftsmen.[4] This direction of development did not, however, represent, as today we might imagine, a system of rigid specializations and thus a loss of versatility. Quite to the contrary: it stimulated a continual invention of arts and professions, which was also favored by the lack of them in other regions.

Wine and oil were exported in ever greater quantities, and grain was imported on a similar scale. Expert ship builders were needed for the construction of boats of all kinds, and navigators were needed to pilot them; the making of vases likewise flourished, since they were the very first form of transport packaging, especially for liquids. The development of commerce also required a medium of exchange, which led to the coining of money and to the mining and refining of silver. The laws of economics had to be studied, and the customs of other peoples had to be understood, and of course their languages as well. And finally, the complexity of this new society required an ever greater number of politicians and intellectuals to whom to entrust its administration. After losing the ability to feed itself, Athens proceeded to invent a new and definitive situation in which the city was no longer an appendage to the rural areas around it. The city itself became a stable and constant source of material and spiritual wealth.[5] Pericles remarked:

> We have games and sacrifices regularly throughout the year and homes fitted out with good taste and elegance; and the delight we each day find in these things drives away sadness. And our city is so great that all the products of the earth flow in upon us, and ours is the happy lot to gather in the good fruits of our own soil with no more home-felt security of enjoyment than we do those of other lands.[6]

This combination of individual inventiveness and social complexity was destined to become typical of the daily lives of all city-dwellers, but at the time it was totally new and utterly surprising. So the feelings it excited can be easily imagined to have been both deep and ambivalent. On the one hand, there was the pride of witnessing the flowering of a prosperous and enjoyable condition of human life such as had never been experienced before. On the other hand, the fear of *phthónos* grew ever more intense; it was imagined that the gods might have no liking for the things that were rapidly assuming the status of the greatest of the pleasures of mortals.

This was the state of mind in which Athens had confronted the Persian Wars. The city's course of economic expansion had already begun, and it was already accompanied by unconscious fears of the totally new developments that had come in its wake. Our hypothesis, as stated before, is that the Athenian victory in the Persian Wars was experienced as an equally unconscious but absolutely persuasive invitation to embark on a further course of imperial expansion, trusting in a military strength that already had been tried in the greatest test imaginable and then exaggerated by the widespread tales that sprang from the collective imagination.

The Athenians' audacity, their love of the new[7] and their constant acts of *hýbris*[8] seemed now to find more rewards than had ever been gleaned by modesty and the fear of *phthónos*. The versatility, articulation and hierarchicization of roles that had accompanied the growth of internal prosperity was soon to find further expression in external affairs as well, or in Athens' relationships with the other *póleis*. The League of Delos (477–404) thus came to be formed, initially for the purpose of acting in the interests of all of its members and of safeguarding Greek superiority over the barbarians. Athens was of course at the head of the League. The other city-states at first furnished ships or tribute for the League's common defense. But the Athenians, as years went by, adopted severe reprisals against the minor cities that attempted to withdraw from the League, and the payment of tribute was imposed as the norm, so that Athens might maintain direct control of the fleet and also have access to a growing supply of money. Finally, in 453, the treasury of the League was transferred from the sacred island of Delos to Athens, thus doing away with the last pretense of equality in what was now its empire. All of that wealth was turned to the benefit of the city, unjustly financing works of art that today we justly admire.

Unlike the conquests of the barbarian kings, who declared their wars for personal pleasure and personal glory, the conquests of Athens were part of an expansionistic project that involved the city's social and economic structure. This shift of perspectives – even though it represents the least radiant or even at times the most perverse of the qualities of its civilization – once again gives evidence of Athens' propensity to anticipate the future. Athens' project seems more similar to present-day forms of expansionism than to that of the Persians with which it was contemporary.

An almost modern network of commercial exchanges grew up, accompanied by the first banking institutions. Athens practiced regular trade throughout the Mediterranean, and also with the lands that are now the Ukraine and southern Russia, which were the source of the enormous quantities of grain that the city's populace required. The political achievements of Pericles and the cultural achievements of the city as a whole walked on the robust legs of the world's earliest example of a regularly replenished and rationally administered treasury. The "owl" – the coin that pictured this bird on one side and the goddess Athena on the other – was everywhere accepted and everywhere desired. It never varied in weight and its percentage of silver was always the same, even in moments of utmost monetary difficulty; such wisdom seems barely credible in terms of the era's knowledge of economics and was probably based, once again, on motives that largely amounted to pride. Athenian finance was even to practise the budgeting of future expenses and income, thus making use of an administrative tool that others were not to discover for millennia. In spite of reversals and growing expenditures, the system was able for three-quarters of a century to organize trade and military expeditions all throughout the Mediterranean, issuing and circulating an unprecedented quantity of coins and decreeing the end of natural economy.

The League of Delos marked the birth in Greece of a source of uninterrupted financing; and a quantity of money that grew at fabulous paces financed Athens' political expansion while also, however, creating inflation.[9] The new financial policies were once again a question of going too far too fast, or of courting an uncertain future. As though to close a vicious circle, they were based on the same psychological attitude that underlay the wars of conquest, which in turn were the primary reason for the city's ever growing need for money.

In spite of various attempts to restore it, the world of tradition was definitely a thing of the past.

THE GOLDEN AGE OF ATHENIAN CULTURE

Athens' golden age was a veritable explosion of novelties; but it also represents the implosion of Hellenic psychology. Much as with the charge at Marathon, Athens attempted to crash through limits that superstition or simple inertia had never before allowed to be touched. The barriers charged lay both outwards and inwards: the Greeks proceeded to the conquest of the physical world, and also to the discovery of the soul. They created radical novelties of three different kinds: as philosophers, tragedians and historians. A brief account of each of these fields of activity, which till now have been considered together to the extent that they concern our theme, can illustrate the disappearance of *phthónos*. Each of these three forms of knowledge can be seen to have abandoned the vision of human life as exclusively subject to destiny, and all of them came to adopt a new point of view that makes man the protagonist of events and that directs him towards ever greater knowledge.

Religious feeling was still quite strong in this period. So the extraordinary fact in the context of such an epoch – and the fact that most typifies the Greeks – is that the new teachers who appeared on the scene presented themselves not as prophets, but as independent figures who spoke in their own names.

Philosophy

The very notion of philosophy calls up the vision of a world that is no longer closed, mythic and regulated by tradition. It implies a world that is free from all forms of prejudice and always on the search for new and ever greater understanding.

Philosophy, moreover, cannot be thought of as having always been a part of the human condition. It was invented by the Greeks, and above all by Plato.

Speculative thought was typical of the Greeks, already in fairly remote times. But the pre-Socratic thinkers cannot truly be considered to have practiced philosophy, or not at least in terms of the modern view of philosophy as a systematic and unconditional availability to new ideas.[10] They were sages. And the source of their wisdom lay less in conceptual thinking than in their moral attitudes. Their wisdom was a part of their personal substance. Though it came to expression in thoughts, the meaning of all such thoughts lay in the lives of the sages who thought them, rather than in principles of logical necessity. Their wisdom in no way conflicted with the gods of Olympus, but developed in spaces that the egoism of the gods ignored: in the field of morals. These sages still had a great deal in common with the teachers of the Orient, who even today think of their messages as more connected to a style of life than to any system of abstract thought.

But life is limited, whereas it seemed to the Greeks that thought encounters no limits at all, and thus stands apart or branches away from the life of the individual. Gradually, in the era before Socrates, and much more radically in the period that followed him, the mind pushed out to beyond the frontiers of personal experience. The Greeks were no longer satisfied with simple wisdom (*sophía*). It was no longer enough to experience it as a part of life; it was something to be observed, studied and understood. Gradually they created the notion of *philo-sophía*: which is to speak of an attitude of benevolence, of love (*philía*) towards wisdom, with which it stands in relationship, but with which it is not identical. *Sophía* was a quality that belonged to an individual; *philo-sophía* exists in its own right, and is self-sufficient. Yet *sophía* was virtue: philosophy, when compared to it, is already a form of decadence.

Rational thought began gradually to battle against subjectivism, which came, like too powerful emotions, to be seen in a more negative light. It is likely moreover that the Persian Wars accentuated these attitudes. The Greeks were long since accustomed to associating the Asiatic peoples with emotional instability, and Heracleitus had already remarked, "The eyes and ears are bad witnesses for men if they have barbarian souls."[11] Subjectivity and excessive emotion came to be seen as typical qualities of the enemy and inferiors; and objectivity became an essential line of defense for the Greeks: in society, from the anomalous; in the self, from the uncontrollability of the unconscious. Abstract reason gradually began to take the place of first-person affirmations. Heracleitus had also remarked, "When you have listened not to me, but to the Law [Lógos] . . . "[12] We cannot be absolutely certain of what he meant by lógos, but it must have been something that was still at that time somewhat difficult to define, and certainly not identical with the rational mind: "You could not in your going find the ends of the soul, though you traveled the whole way: so deep is its Law [Lógos]."[13]

Socrates[14] marked the beginning of a new tradition in which abstract thought took control of the field of knowledge, drawing all attention to itself while the thinker withdrew into the background. Socrates knew that he did not know.[15] Concepts were born and functioned as general forms or molds that could be pressed into service again and again, like mental machines for the standard production of no longer personal knowledge.

"The courageous man" ceased to be a subject of discussion; thinkers chose instead to analyze "courage." There was no longer any need to consider the object in which a quality appears; the quality itself could be seen as an absolute. The death of a sage likewise marked the death of his wisdom. Conceptual knowledge, on the other hand, can be accumulated, quite independently of the knower. Socratic philosophy is a universal heritage that remains independent of Socrates, and so much so that we do not even know if he was actually responsible for inventing it.

No matter how long ago it happened, the birth of lógos contained the whole of the future course of western culture: monotheism, scientific theory, the legal definition of the powers of the state and the accumulability of knowledge all require it as a premise. This new mode of thought created the possibility of points of reference that offer explanations of everything while requiring none of their own. It created the possibility of impersonal institutions that have nothing to do with the oscillations of subjectivity.

Concepts (from the Latin cum-capere, to take together) allow us to grasp reality in terms of something more than single objects that stand before our eyes. We can extract an essential quality from an object and place it on a loom of theory that then can weave it back into numberless versions of its source. This is rather like the leap we make when we cease to count things and pass on to abstract mathematics, doing sums that make no reference to objects. When we limit ourselves to counting things, we can count no more of them than actually stand before us; but when we abandon material objects and play with the pure order of numbers, we discover the possibility of counting to infinity. We likewise discover the vertigo of infinity, with all its ambivalent fascination. Infinity is a locus of discovery and conquest, but also a fearsome unknown and a bottomless abyss.

This way of thought that was finding affirmation in Athens did not belong to the philosophers alone. Quite to the contrary: it was a concrete and inseparable part of the whole new way of life that was developing in the city. Abstract thought – directed to agricultural produce independently of its consumption, or to a tool independently of its use – was the premise for abandoning a closed and self-sufficient economy, and for the organization of a new economy based on commerce and the exchange of surplus goods. Rather than things to be utilized, surplus goods are numbers in an operation of which the goal is profit. Things for actual utilization are necessarily finite; one's hope with numbers in profit equations is to watch them grow to infinity.[16]

The new form of philosophical thought was closely connected with the first achievements of science, and especially with the science of medicine, as elaborated in precisely this period by Hippocrates. Socratic thought in fact found its model in medicine and saw it as the source of a mode of cognition that could be universally extended; it was the medical model that furnished the groundwork for all the new attitudes, allowing them truly to take flight and to supersede the irrationality of myth, which stood behind the barricades of a different world.[17] Hippocrates considered the past to distill into an anamnesis that could then form a basis for prognosis. It could hardly have been otherwise, since he insisted – even while admitting individual variations (an idea that once again became a part of philosophical thought)[18] – on the principle that sees a law as remaining always and necessarily constant in the course of time. For a law to do anything else would contradict its very nature as a law. "[Laches] and I have a notion that there is not one knowledge or science of the past, another of the present, a third of what is likely to be best and what will be best in the future; but that of all three there is one science only."[19] This observation, moreover, was pertinent to all of the branches of knowledge, since, starting from the natural sciences, the idea was extended to the whole new mode of cognition that was championed by philosophy.

For the individual no less than for society, and for the natural no less than the humanistic sciences, the past was to lose the last of the mythic tonalities that allowed it laws of its own, inscrutable and separate from those of the present. Philosophy was concerned with certain knowledge, no longer variable in the course of time or in the contexts of different disciplines; it was searching for a stable terrain on which to construct the whole of knowledge, both scientific and historical. The unification of the model of knowledge was one of the constant principles of the thought of Plato and Aristotle, who developed more general and abstract applications of procedures that had already proven their worth not only in medicine, but also in the science of navigation, in commerce and in husbandry.[20]

What Socrates set into motion was a mode of rationality and a notion of truth that ran, as it were, both horizontally, traversing all the forms of knowledge, and vertically, up through the whole of the genealogy of knowledge. These qualities laid the groundwork for a kind of knowledge that – unlike mythical and religious knowledge – could accumulate in the course of time. Advances in knowledge were no longer a question of breaking taboos, or of the theft of things reserved for the gods, like Prometheus' fire. They were lawful attainments, and were subject as such to no punishment by *phthónos*. The growth of knowledge was indirectly the source of our most profound revolution in the formulation of moral precepts.

The limits of the growth of knowledge, and of the actions that it authorized, were no longer seen to lie outside of the human being, in the form of divine presences; they lay instead within the human interior, in that faculty of rationality that only a few, it is true, can fully develop, but which many can to some extent deploy without disrupting any pre-established order. Philosophy entered human life as a source of assistance in moments of wonder and uncertainty,[21] and without promoting any form of arrogance. Socrates (and Plato, through whom he speaks) seems still to reflect a spirit of respect for the jealousy of the gods. He knew quite clearly that too great a longing for wealth is a cause of discord and war.[22] Both Plato and Aristotle were still well aware of the importance of limits. They insisted, in fact, as we have already seen, on notions of limits as criteria for the organization of the *pólis*. Leaders had to be in a position that allowed them to be acquainted with the city's citizens, and actually to reach them with their eyes and voices.[23] But this still remains the very first period in which such forms of direct contact might have been superseded, and precisely by means of the use of abstract concepts that do not depend on facts of material presence or directly perceived images. The continued appeal to mechanisms that found their inspiration in previous moral precepts must not disguise the fact that the commandment to the observation of limits had been overturned. In terms of its notions of will and knowledge, philosophy was pursuing an openness that in the centuries to come was to direct itself towards the infinite and to attempt to embrace it. Tradition had taught that mortals were to search out the meaning of their suffering and to place no faith in human will. Socrates assumed the enormous responsibility of reversing such attitudes; he cast aside pessimism and replaced it with optimism by declaring that the will of a man can only desire the Good,[24] whereas evil could only derive from ignorance.[25] No more blasphemous idea might have been imagined; it virtually amounted to a beatification of *hýbris*. Our Socrates was indeed an enemy of morality, and the mind of those times had no other choice than to sentence him to death.

It was not the intention of philosophy to place itself in conflict with the traditional faith, but it opened the soul to an unprecedented course of research that relegated religion to a minor position; it suggested, covertly, that religion belonged to a realm of fixity and boredom. Scientific and philosophical knowledge, which initially were unified, created for the very first time a notion of truth and a mode of knowledge that were inherently in expansion. Additions and modifications to a religious creed count as heresy; the continuing development of science and philosophy, quite to the contrary, expresses the very meaning of the questions they pose. Though the common people remained attached to the gods, the philosophers, even when they affirmed the existence of the gods, gave them a place in an optimistic and anti-tragic ideology;[26] and then they gradually reduced them to objects of rational analysis.[27] Truth no longer found a habitat in religious myth, which philosophy transformed into a story that found ever fewer listeners.

The soul (the psyche) was coming to be perceived as an independent entity in no way limited by the finitude and fragility of the body. It was finally superior even to the gods, since it was capable of creativity.[28] By the fourth century, religious feeling would seem to have waned considerably among the educated classes, and the fervor aroused by scientific and philosophical studies was so great as even to allow Aristotle to exhort that one pay no heed to persons who insisted that men should restrict themselves to the tasks assigned to mortals. He tells us that the human being contains something that itself is divine and immortal, and that we have to dedicate all our efforts to its further development.[29] Is it possible to imagine a clearer example of *hýbris*? Could there exist a more thorough reversal of the law that invited mortals to exercise moderation and to keep their distance from the prerogatives of the gods? Might any affirmation have contrasted more thoroughly with the notions of submission to destiny that were promoted by the tragedians of only a few generations previously? The philosopher's mind proceeds along the road that had been opened in the fifth century: the road towards the interiorization and assimilation of everything that had previously been perceived as lying outside of the human individual. Just as grandiosity, observed with such wonder in the barbarians, ended up by amazing, tempting and seducing the observers, immortality, adored in the gods, was psychically metabolized and then rediscovered as a potential quality of the thinking of the subject.

Both of these developments brought something else in their wake: the first was to lead to the loss of the traditional ability to empathize and identify with the enemy; the second led to a substantial diminution of the feeling of fearful communion with the divine. The human gaze was ever more insistently to center on man himself, and man became its object of wonder and contemplation. The philosopher attempted to achieve a clarity of vision that not even the gods had claimed to possess. Man grew drunk with his own independence and self-sufficiency. He had no further need to seek out dialog and identification with other human beings whose nature and culture were different from his own; and he likewise found it superfluous to prostrate himself before any metaphysical interlocutor. Instead, he could cultivate the psyche. He saw it, after all, to contain a potentially endless otherness towards which he might develop; and he also experienced it as a metaphysical territory that lay open for exploration. On the cognitive plane, he had discovered that knowledge could be infinite; on the social plane, he had crossed the threshold of individualism.

The orderly thinking of Socrates bristled with a power that had never been known before; and as he shifted the center and limits of action into man himself, the gods found no place in his discourse. While attempting to grasp them as a stimulus to progress, he reshaped them into forms that were wholly free of *phthónos*: "[The creator] was good, and the good can never have any jealousy of anything."[30] Aristotle was to remark, "Indeed if the poets are right and the Deity is by nature jealous, it is probable that in this case He would be particularly jealous. . . . But it is impossible for the Deity to be jealous."[31] Such words reveal an attempt to give the deity a new place within the context of the logic of a philosophical system, seeing him as the guarantor of an optimistic ethic. After the demise of the emotional gods, jealous divine justice was likewise to disappear. When Aristotle speaks of *phthónos*, he refers to nothing more than that singular human misery that arises at the sight of the happiness of other men.[32]

The coupling of an elevated and abstract concept of the deity with the criteria of philosophy was not, however, to lead to a synthesis of thought and faith, but rather to their final separation; they were vertically split apart in a way that ran parallel to the division between the intellectuals and the common people. Among the cultivated classes, it destroyed the traditional capricious gods, allowing the survival of truth and justice only within the vessel of a non-theistic philosophy. If even the gods become reasonable, reason without gods will be sufficient for men. *Lógos* had sometimes formerly been known to speak, but within the context of a universe ordered by the gods. The gods could now continue to speak, but found themselves compressed into a universe ordered by *lógos*. Science and abstract reason are able to delegitimize faith, even without proclaiming themselves to have done so; they do so by implication, since their creations, unlike those of the religious cosmogony, make themselves manifest every day.

The consistency of philosophical *lógos* seems to have established a unity and continuity of criteria that were much more powerful than the forms of tragic and mythico-religious knowledge that had formerly held sway. But this consistency was respected only by the vertex of society, just as it functions only at the vertex of the psychological organization of the individual. Greek society and the mind of the Greek individual were both divided by the very same fissure. That fissure was their weakness, and it constituted the void that Christianity was soon to rush to fill. The philosophers and scientists obeyed the dictates of the rationality that consciousness had acquired, but the mass of common people stood apart from it and followed the needs of the unconscious. The point, however, does not reduce to any question of a power of logic that the philosophers possessed and that the common people lacked. It was a question, rather, of the emotional power that lived in the archaic religious mind and that was lacking in philosophical thought. That power was the object for which the masses felt nostalgia. Logical truths are consistent, but shallow. Religious truths are irrational, but deep. The Ego commands thought to take place, to flow and to halt. But it can give no orders to tragic and religious feelings, which are rather like waves that hold the will in their power. We can philosophize one day, and stop on the next. We cannot be religious on one day, and not on the next. Philosophy is an attitude to life that can partly be controlled and directed; things stand differently with wisdom, which presents itself as a quality or integral component of life. "The love of wisdom (*philo-sophía*) stands lower than wisdom (*sophía*)."[33]

History

There is a particularly important moment in the life of the individual, and presumably of peoples as well, in which we first begin to exist as conscious subjects. And the extent to which that moment is an actual occurrence is of no real importance, since the way in which we remember it in any case turns it into myth. Its value is not as factual truth, but rather as revealed symbolic truth, and as such it stands at the origin of all self-awareness – the self-awareness of the individual no less than of a community. We do not question the existence of the Jews because of the lack of historical evidence for the meeting between Moses and Jehovah for the consignment of the tables of the law. God in any case gave self-awareness to His chosen people.

Such self-awareness was revealed to the Hellenic peoples by the Persian Wars. Homer's Greeks already realized that they largely shared a common culture. But that was not enough to unify them. Self-awareness was to come only with the Persian Wars, and the history of these wars became an attempt to create unity by means of force. This revelation was no gift of the Greek gods, who were in no way provident gods. The truth of national selfhood was self-revealed. Almost suddenly, the qualities that the Greeks had attributed to their gods were restored to them as they turned their indubitable strength to the affirmation of their collective power and identity.

The Greeks gave birth to the myth of their national origins, and to do so was to assume a debt to themselves rather than to their gods. Historical time erupted into human life and destroyed the older order of mythic time. When faced with the self-assured divinity of the mortals, the gods disappeared like so many noisy insects. The Greeks, unlike the Jews, possessed a body of knowledge of an already secular nature, and as such it was destined to be an early experience of many of the crises of identity that would come to afflict modern secular thinking. A more rapid course of evolution has never been witnessed, which is also to say, in spite of the progress involved, that we have never yet witnessed a more rapid generation of emptiness. Herodotus invented history so as to offer support to this course of evolution, but also with a view to bridling it, so as to hold it still close to the gods. Thucydides, however, was to follow him in less than the space of a generation, and we see him in the attempt to apply a secular and scientific model to events, from which he attempted to extract a natural law by means of impersonal diagnoses.

> What Herodotus the Halicarnassian has learnt by inquiry (*istoría*) is here set forth: in order that so the memory of the past may not be blotted out from men by time, and that great and marvellous deeds done by Greeks and foreigners and especially the reason why they warred against each other may not lack renown.[34]

These are the opening words of the work of the first historian.

The conjunction of myth and history establishes a connection between two different ways of living – between a way of holding oneself outside of time and a way of flowing along with it. Herodotus is the hinge that connects these two contrasting modes of experience. No one can say if he was fully aware of it, but the scope of his innovation is already to be found in his opening words. Rather than accept a purely passive role as the voice of the Muse, who made use of the poet as though he were one of her limbs,[35] Herodotus throws himself into the effort of constructing something: he conducts an *inquiry*. Rather than the deeds of the gods, he presents the deeds *of men*. Herodotus sings no liturgy, and instead offers testimony (in addition to "observer," "inquirer" or "researcher," *ístor*, as we have seen already,[36] also means "witness"). Instead of accepting the immobile perpetuation of myth alone, he challenges forgetfulness, writing "in order that so the memory of the past may not be blotted out from men by time," and recording events that have taken place in time. Previous to Herodotus – and for thousands of following years, in other cultures – events were recorded only for particular purposes: a report for the prince, the celebration of a funeral. He was the first to understand the importance of such a form of memory and the responsibilities involved in working in its service, on commission from no one. But this is also tantamount to saying that he was first to perceive the flow of historical time and the importance of what comes to completion inside of it.

Herodotus did not conceive of historical time as profane; he was, however, even willing to attribute a date to the formation of the images of the gods.

> But whence each of the gods came into being, or whether they had all for ever existed, and what outward forms they had, the Greeks knew not till (so they say) a very little while ago; for I suppose that the time of Hesiod and Homer was not more than four hundred years before my own; and these are they who taught the Greeks of the descent of the gods, and gave to all their several names, and honours, and arts, and declared their outward forms.[37]

This novel point of view is indeed surprising and revolutionary. Does he mean to imply that the truth has not always existed? Is he suggesting that time and men have created the gods, and not vice versa?

In the era before Herodotus, the epics had offered certain items of information on real events that had taken place at some indistinct time previous to their compilation but that none the less had not been forgotten. But the credibility of such stories depended exclusively on the Greeks' respect for tradition, and never on any form of research. And whenever the poet felt called upon to peer farther back than such events themselves, he recited a genealogy that quickly scudded off into the supernatural. Such reconstructions – no less irrational than the gods to whom they were dedicated – were entirely devoid of logical and chronological consistency.[38]

But even when Herodotus set real research to the task of transforming mythical tales into true events, the will of the gods continued imperceptibly to organize his narrative. We no longer find the ingenuous anthropomorphic causalism of gods who descend to the earth, but we are always made aware of the presence of a superior, impersonal wisdom – an inexorability, revealed by developments in human life but not determined by men.

The weakness of the scholarly foundations of history as recounted by Herodotus finds compensation in a narrative force that inherits the energy of myth (*mýthos*, we remember, is the most essential form of narrative), transferring it directly into reality according to a constant model of *phthónos*.

While turning his gaze to the earth, Herodotus was nevertheless capable of avoiding all ideological heresy. It was finally the heavens that authorized the birth of history, not in antithesis to themselves but almost as their epiphany. If history as the force that governs events replaces the gods, it had to be endowed with a metaphysical authority that was equal or superior to that of the gods.

Even if man is at the center of his interests, Herodotus always examined events with a view to the constant rediscovery of a supernatural presence that guided their motions. His stories, in fact, first of all confirm an ethical rather than historical hypothesis: he constantly offers proof that excess is destined to encounter catastrophe (*némesis*). Herodotus' men are described with sympathy and compassion, but they are not true protagonists. From this point of view, he was deceiving himself when he asserted that he wanted to write in their service. Rather than a witness of human affairs, he is the witness of the workings of *phthónos*. Men are expected not to be good, but to show moderation, and they count as no more than the earthly appendages of a deity who, rather than benevolent, is jealous and disruptive.[39]

To grasp the morality and consistency of this point of view and to see them as superior to anything to be found in the Archaic period, we have to perceive that its central perspective is that of the gods, in the hands of whom man is not a creature they love, but the instrument[40] of a justice that lies within events themselves. This is something that Herodotus' characters never forget, and when Themistocles recalls the great victory of Salamis, he is not so ingenuous as to attribute it to himself.

> For it is not we that have won this victory, but the gods and the heroes who deemed (*ephthónesan*, to forbid through *phthónos*) Asia and Europe too great a realm for one man to rule, and that a wicked man and an impious . . . that scourged the sea and threw fetters thereinto.[41]

The simple, monolithic law that here finds expression has nothing to do with the realization of human intentions, but restores the great to smallness and raises the small to greatness. It allows no rewards for arrogance and rejects disorder. This first, weak attempt at the writing of history relies on the strength of the structure of Greek ethics that lies beneath it. The weakness of the one and the strength of the other are linked and preordained, since a justice that always intervenes in favor of equilibrium and moderation calls for a vision of history as static, and of human possibilities as limited. So severe a sense of order strikes us today as ingenuous. Heavy with its carnage of defeated peoples and shattered cultures, the history of the west fits Shakespeare's description of the life of the individual: "it is a tale told by an idiot, full of sound and fury but signifying nothing."[42] But its inadequacy, today so evident, began to grow clear already in the course of the century in which Herodotus wrote. He had wanted to aggrandize the gods by making them responsible for something that only very recently had come into the range of human knowledge: the movement of history. But this knowledge would finally succeed in detaching man from the heavens and making him autonomous; in the course of creating history, man would discover that he himself was divine.

Thucydides, the other great witness of this period, describes the Peloponnesian Wars that, after the era of the Persian Wars, set Sparta and Athens against one another for hegemony over Greece. He followed Herodotus by barely a generation. One calculates that the difference in their ages was twenty-four years. But those twenty-four years are of much more weight that the twenty-four centuries that lie between them and us. Thucydides' history is already our own.[43] By extending the procedures for the study of the laws of human nature, he sought out the norms that regulate great historical events. Rationality and a commitment to secular thinking already imbue his analyses, which address themselves exclusively to clearly defined facts of the recent past. His extremely rigorous procedures can even be seen, paradoxically enough, to have led on to a somewhat precarious path for an historian who hopes to achieve objectivity. As he collected his source materials, Thucydides accepted only information that was thoroughly unquestionable, or that he personally had verified. Given the scarcity, in his times, of unquestionable sources, he was therefore obliged him to limit himself to dealing with very recent events, and thus with that sphere of contemporary history that a writer is unable to judge with serene detachment.

Herodotus' belabored nexus of myth and history, theology and anthropology, was swept away by a great new hypothesis: that the past and the present are a continuity, and always governed by the very same laws. Homer may have given pleasure, but at the expense of truth, which for Thucydides was too high a price.[44] This proto-scientific turn in his methods of research reflects the more general new departures in the speculative thought of Socrates. We have seen that Socrates' procedures were based on those of medicine, and the very same model was now to be applied to history,[45] thus further affirming the sudden unification of the model of knowledge. All knowledge now had to be a question of secular truth (*epistéme*) and no longer of religious doctrine. Thucydides studied his materials with a view to constructing diagnoses and prognoses. The very notion of cause (*próphasis*) was borrowed directly from medicine. He saw history to be edified by the power of competing states, and not by transcendent principles. The forces involved in the struggle pursue ends of pure dominion and encounter no obstacles other than those connected with their own particular magnitude and their abilities of foresightful calculation. These too, of course, have a limit, as Athens was to prove in paradoxical ways: the city burgeoned with intelligence and had great capacities for organization, but its foresight was sorely limited. Athens' policy of expansion seems constantly to offer the surprise of having survived so many reversals, but it was headed for disaster. Thucydides saw such an outcome as almost mathematically predictable: it was utterly rational. It was no longer seen as the manifestation of a transcendent justice that held watch over certain limits. In accordance with this new logic, Polycrates, whom Herodotus had taken as an emblem of divine justice, is remembered only in the context of a few annotations on political economy.

The contrast between morality and power was summed up for Thucydides in the debate between the representatives of the small state of Melos and those of Athens.[46] The ambassadors from Melos placed their faith in the abstract concept of justice and believed in a divine plan that in the long run would preserve and restore it. The Athenians, on the other hand, endorsed principles of *Realpolitik* that were entirely based on military power, and they evaluated the situation on the basis of immediate factual data. The ambassadors from Melos offered their neutrality, and, recognizing the utilitarianism of the Athenians as the final criterion,[47] presented it as convenient to both parties. They remarked that the states that till then had remained neutral would band together against Athens if Athens were to give proof of not respecting those who presented a threat to no one.[48] The Athenians, on the other hand, demanded the submission of Melos; otherwise they intended to take it by force, so that the states already vanquished would understand the fate of the disobedient.[49]

The outcome was bitter. The Archaic mind had shaped its thoughts in the universal terms of myth and religion, but all such terms had since been shattered. The new secular attitudes permitted recourse to rational concepts, and yet could do nothing to assure that the concepts called into play would not be so highly at variance with one another as to generate dialogs that led to no results. War was the only remaining solution. The Athenian siege was lengthy and concluded with the slaughter of all the adult men of Melos, whereas the women and children were sold into slavery.[50] Athens' expansionistic policies – free of all the limits previously imposed by myth – forced the city into ever more precarious positions from which to pursue the power that might finally assure its dominion.

It would be difficult to imagine a clearer contrast between an ethics of the real and an ethics of the ideal. The Athenians seem to have calculated short-term benefits but to have remained short-sighted with respect to the longer view. We have every good reason to remember that the Athenians themselves addressed the following words to the ambassadors from Melos: "you are the only men who regard future events as more certain than what lies before your eyes."[51] Yet our point of view rests precisely on our having accepted the story that Thucydides has left to us; and it is a story that proceeds by way of peaks and abysses, demonstrating the impracticability of a culture of uninterrupted expansion.

Even though it does not include the final fall of Athens, Thucydides' work makes no omission of a horrified account of the disasters to which the city-state was gradually conducted by its pursuit of an empire.[52] He recounts the story with compassion, but his compassion is a secular rather than religious emotion, and he never gives rein to the moralizations that one would surely have expected from Herodotus. Thucydides allows us to look at the outcome of events in any way we choose, and we can see them as the expression of a justice that perhaps derives from chance, or perhaps from a god; but we do so entirely at our own discretion. His entirely rational exposition in no way suggests the existence of any higher power that shapes the course of history, and the only limits to action are determined by the meeting of concrete circumstances and the will to power. If the small and the great come into contact with one another, the expansion of the latter remains uncontained. The laws that organize events are statistic rather than moral. We find these words in the mouth of his Athenians: "of the gods we hold the belief, and of men we know, that by a necessity of their nature wherever they have power they always rule."[53] We might speak of this concept as a kind of "historic liberalism" and see it as an early anticipation of some of the typical thinking of our own times. It harbingers those areas of study that see their objects of observation as independent of all external laws, presuming them instead to be self-regulated expressions of dynamics that are already active within them. We find such a vision in the radical independence of scientific thought, and it demands that the writing of history be free of ethical or religious presuppositions.

Thucydides' very mode of thinking, and not only the events he narrates, thus seem to obey a rule of limitless rationality that displaces all laws of transcendent and absolute limits; no such things control the human mind or constitute the loom on which history comes to be woven.

This is not, however, equivalent to any nascent enlightened optimism on the part of Thucydides. He simply reached the conclusion that the mixing of history and religion is superstitious and insincere. Truth is a question of looking at events as manifestations of political forces, and not as theophany. This is far from any assurance – and the lesson can be found in the conduct of the Athenians – that the rational thinking of politicians is always a source of progress.

In this sense, Thucydides is still a voice of the traditional Greek fatalism. Choosing to imbue his work with a tone of sobriety, he adhered to a notion of limits as a question of style. His rationality announces no program of enlightened self-confidence on the part of the human mind and simply expresses the disenchantment of an act of observation that remains independent of any and all creed. Thucydides seems to be aware that his task as a witness is different from the task of an innovator: he has to eliminate untrustworthy attitudes rather than to furnish new ones. But his faith in objective reporting is itself a radical innovation.

He questioned himself on the possible drawbacks of his way of freeing history from myth. But he answered – and here he perhaps anticipates a *hýbris* on the part of later enlightened thinkers – that objective truth, unlike myth, lasts forever:

> And it may well be that the absence of the fabulous from my narrative will seem less pleasing to the ear; but whoever shall wish to have a clear view both of the events which have happened and of those which will some day, in all human probability, happen again in the same or a similar way – for these to adjudge my history profitable will be enough for me. And, indeed, it has been composed, not as a prize-essay to be heard for the moment, but as a possession for all time.[54]

The tragic sentiment

Aeschylus, Sophocles, Euripides: we are accustomed to speaking these names in a single breath, and we know that the greatness of classical tragedy resides entirely within them. We never cease to be amazed at the thought that a creation certainly in no way inferior to the modern novel, to ancient epic or to any of the world's lyric poetry could have found its affirmation and then its extinction in the space of a generation and a half,[55] and all within the walls of the city of Athens – an almost invisible splinter of the history and geography of the world. But Greek tragedy was a great deal more than a literary genre. It was a form of the since vanished cult of Dionysus and no one managed to keep it alive outside of this religious tradition. Not included among the gods of Olympus and ignored by Homer, Dionysus was none the less the son of Zeus, and he was a very popular god. Since it authorized various forms of frenzy, his cult gave satisfaction to more instinctive needs and thus enjoyed more followers than others. At the other extreme, he was also a god of artistic creation. Their course of development has stimulated a variety of hypotheses, but we know that these Athenian dramas in honor of Dionysus found their roots in a pre-history of choruses and processions (tragedy means "song of the goats," *trágon odé*) that gradually absorbed a series of themes drawn from myth and epic and finally became an all-comprehensive voice that uttered religious, moral, political and philosophical truth, all at the same time.

Our interest in the tragedians centers not on the notion of tragedy itself, but on the subject of limits, and we will concentrate on Aeschylus and Euripides. This juxtaposition of extremes immediately brings to light the changes with which we are concerned.

Aeschylus was in every way a nobleman; he was a continuator of the ideals of Solon and aware of living in exceptional times. He took direct part in the Persian Wars, and the way in which he deals with them[56] contains a great innovation. His account of the clash with Xerxes' troops makes no mention of the triumph of the Greeks and concentrates entirely on a description of the sufferings of the barbarians. In his drama, the great king is overwhelmed by tears, aware of having been ruined by *hýbris*.

This inversion of points of view was more than a narrative technique. It expresses the author's deeply felt religious conviction that the sufferings of the Greeks, having been caused by the arrogance of the Persians, were transformed into their opposite, and that a similar reversal might again take place.[57] This sense of the mutability of human triumphs is the essence of the myth that controlled the way in which Aeschylus, like Herodotus, wrote history. History had the right to be born only by virtue of finding its flow within the stream-bed of metaphysics.[58]

Aeschylus, however, could not be said to have confused historical event with mythic event, as had happened in previous centuries. He both recognizes and respects the objective autonomy of historical event, no longer in the sway of pre-established models. This explains why *Persians* was only a single drama, though written by an author whose dramas on mythical themes continued to be cast in the traditional form of the trilogy. Myth created tales that were circular and repetitive, forming complete and perfect cycles; an episode from history, on the other hand, had the character of a fully unique event that reaches forward to the present and that always continues to await fulfillment.

Aeschylus' mythical tragedies articulate a vision in which the individual is still of slight importance with respect to the laws imposed by myth and the life of the tribe, and the individual tragedy is therefore of little meaning outside of the context of its trilogy. The trilogy is the locus in which three events are bonded together to form a single story and where individuals present themselves as links that chain the generations to the workings of justice, or to the *némesis* that has to follow *hýbris*. This is quite clear in the *Oresteia*, which is the only one of Aeschylus' trilogies – *Agamemnon*, *Choephoroi* (*The Libation Bearers*) and *Eumenides* (*The Furies*) – to have survived complete. The destinies with which it presents us are not personal destinies, just as there is nothing personal about the morality of distributive justice that seethes within them. The characters can be seen as whole individuals, but their meaning is incomplete outside of the context that they form as a group. Agamemnon dies in the course of the first drama, but he continues to be a presence in those that follow since the sufferings and reparations of his son Orestes refer constantly back to him. And the moral condition of Agamemnon was firmly connected to that of his father Atreus.

A tragic destiny condemns everyone in its range to bear some kind of guilt. Clytemnestra murders her husband Agamemnon when he returns from Troy. Orestes, then, must either commit the heinous crime of matricide or assume the guilt of not having rendered justice to his father and his people. It is not that he has no choice or possibility of personal action, and in fact he reaches a decision. But his culture's moral code had no true place for the individual and there is no way of evaluating the act he performs, since the repercussions of decisions made by individuals never fall on themselves alone. The family bond is a limit that totally circumscribes the individual. The symbiosis of father and son, and finally of the whole of the folk, has not yet been dissolved. We are likely now to see Orestes' sufferings as unjust, since he attempted after all to perform the proper action; but our point of view is a reflection of essentially ungrounded assumptions on the part of the modern world. Orestes is only a hand that performs an action; the moral responsibilities of an active subject simply have nothing to do with him. The active force that sets all events into motion is the chain of fathers and sons, the myth of the Atrides. Individual conscience is a non-existent quantity that Orestes cannot possess, even though it seems to us, in part, that he makes use of such a thing. The limits imposed upon action lie first of all in the impossibility of the individual's freeing himself from the ways in which destinies intertwine.

Limits are everywhere present in the work of Aeschylus. His Agamemnon – quite different from the arrogant king to whom Homer introduces us – is constantly obsessed by the thought that he must not enjoy too many pleasures; he wants to contract no excessive debts with fortune, and he is anxious to show no taint of the pride and grandiosity of the barbarians.[59] The chorus, moreover, reminds us that the only happiness is the happiness that excites no jealousy.[60] Clytemnestra, on the other hand – the action of the drama finds its focus in her punishment – seems to merit death not for having murdered her husband, but because she is dominated by the *hýbris* of her masculine heart.[61]

Aeschylus sees Zeus as the force that maintains the balance between *hýbris* and *némesis*, and he thus reinforces the vertical thrust towards the monotheism that Solon, for reasons of social order, had already proclaimed.

The force that guides events lies ever less in the will of the gods, and ever more in law. Having contributed to the linkage and unification of myth and history, seeing them to obey a single group of criteria, Aeschylus too stood at the highest point of tradition; but in doing so, he already encountered the need to supersede it. He had seen that destiny was dark and immobile, and he was then to decry the dawn of a form of justice that was active and generous. *Eumenides* recounts how Athena and Apollo bring the Furies to silence and effect Orestes' definitive release from the chain of suffering and vengeance. But the passing of darkness shed light on the future weight of responsibility. Clytemnestra gives voice to traditional attitudes when she screams out her innocence, saying that what was acting within her when she killed was not the spirit of the wife of

Agamemnon but the impersonal demon of revenge.[62] But the chorus, which only just earlier had likewise echoed traditional attitudes, declaring that everything is the work of Zeus,[63] covers her with all of its scorn: "That thou art guiltless of this murder – who will bear thee witness? Nay, nay! And yet the evil genius of his sire might well be thine abettor."[64]

Aeschylus truly believed in the vanity of arrogance and in the passing of all human glory. When he dictated the inscription for his tomb, he made no mention of having been a tragedian; he wanted to be remembered only as a hoplite who had fulfilled his duties while combatting at Marathon.

The works of Euripides formulate their principal innovation by moving in a direction quite different from the religious piety of Aeschylus. Even though Euripides' characters are dragged along by the uncontrollable forces of tragic destiny, they here and there speak words that show a spark of the beginnings of an autonomous mode of reason. It in no way resounds with the voices of the gods and sometimes raises radical doubt about all previous certainties; it sometimes opposes destiny itself, and sometimes, as a way of bearing it, sees it as glimmering with a solitary revelation of which the nature is existential rather than religious.

These were precisely the years in which the critical thinking of Socrates was opening a new dimension. Socratic thought was beginning to question the passivity, or even the serenity, with which the tragedies traditionally accepted the catastrophes that derived from unbridled passions. Socrates insisted on the viability of human will, which was seen to be capable of desiring only the Good.[65]

Euripides did not reject the notion that limits are imposed by the gods.[66] But if he did not yet have the courage to lower their rank and assign first place to human will, he can none the less be seen to have hollowed out within the human being an interior space that belongs to man alone. Rather than posture as the moralist who agrees with the dictates of destiny, Euripides frequently prefers to retreat into this new dimension where men struggle to understand and guide their fates. The new attitudes that his generation brought to manifestation had an effect on the writing of tragedy no less than on the thinking of philosophers and historians. *Hýbris* in the work of Euripides has largely ceased to function as a collective principle that controls and regulates events; he sees it instead as a feature of personal psychology. Still another of his innovations is that *hýbris* is often found in women.[67]

For the very first time, the jealousy of the gods, as the factor that preserves equilibrium and guides events, was challenged by the passionate rationality of men. In *Heracles*, the hero, condemned by the power of tradition and according to the will of the gods, declaims a law of his own that makes them more lofty and noble than tradition itself would have demanded. But by doing so, he also empties them, since his deity, purified of jealousy and egoism, though not yet endowed with Christian love, shrivels up into an abstraction that has no connection with human life: "I deem not that the Gods for spousals crave / Unhallowed: tales of Gods' hands manacled / Ever I scorned, nor ever will believe, / Nor that one God is born another's lord. / For God hath need, if God indeed he be, / Of naught: these be minstrels' sorry tales."[68] The birth of interior dialog – which is also the birth of psychology – thus went hand in hand with the weakening of exterior dialog with a divine interlocutor. And just as the spiritual presence of the gods had grown less impelling, the threats of hostile earthly enemies had also waned. Aeschylus at Marathon had taken part in a battle for his culture's survival; Euripides' generation experienced a certain ease in its confrontations with natural and military obstacles, in much the same way that it found little difficulty in dismantling religious taboos. Psychic forces that before had been absorbed by a struggle for survival now found release in feelings of pride and a general sense of disquietude.[69] One of Euripides' heroines expresses the epoch's state of mind when she declares: "Right is it that Hellenes rule barbarians, not that alien yoke rest on Hellenes. . . . They be bondmen, we be freeborn folk."[70]

The period between the end of the Persian menace and the birth of a proto-psychology, primarily visible in the works of Euripides, was marked by a rapid interiorization of energies. The Greeks now felt secure from external threats, and the confidence unleashed by those grandiose events could now be invested in themselves.

From current points of view, many of the novelties of fifth-century Greece present themselves as extraordinary anticipations of modern rationality. The distance between the new-born philosophy and the previous *sophía*, or the similar distance between Euripides and Aeschylus, seems greater than the distance between ourselves and Socrates. It is as though that brief generation intuited all the possibilities of subsequent human development, suddenly but once and for all. It is as though the gods, inclusive of the stable and monotheistic gods that were later to assert themselves in the west, fully endorsed the newly found optimism of human will and happily accepted themselves as man's heavenly extensions.

Aeschylus had seen the throne of Zeus as the locus of the tragic gaze, and from there he trained it down onto human life. Euripides places the tragedy's point of view in man himself, who still looks up towards the heavens, but above all into himself. Socrates and Euripides both became objects of public scorn, and we see them ridiculed in the comedies of Aristophanes. Euripides' greatness was not recognized until after his death. Socrates and Euripides – and Thucydides as well, to a certain extent – initiated a mode of thought that has always continued to expand, and they were thus to find their interlocutors less among their contemporaries[71] than in modern culture.

But Euripides did not share the optimism of Socrates, of whom he is said to have been a friend. Rather than a philosopher, he was a true psychologist; he could not believe that ignorance was a sufficient explanation for the existence of evil, or that consciousness was the arbiter of what was good. He voiced that conviction in the words of the terrible Medea as she prepared to murder her children: "Now, now, I learn what horrors I intend, but passion (*thymós*) overmastereth sober thought; and this is the cause of direst ills to men."[72] Euripides' already secular notions of psychology could find no expression in a correspondingly secular setting, since that would have meant abandoning the very locus of tragedy. Everything remained suspended in a state of pained ambivalence. The Dionysian rites that were voted to the sense of pain had promoted a profound critical reflection that now began to travel a road that no longer depended on religion and the gods.

Tragedy abandoned the vessel that contained the whole of Greek society – its ever present sense of limits. The intensity of the emotions that the tragedies transmitted was rendered absolute by the fact that any particular play was performed only once. Each of the annual Dionysian festivals presented new cycles of tragedies. But as time went by, a certain lack of imagination led to repetitions of the performance of the plays, and the sense of identification that they aroused in the public thus began to wane. Nietzsche was convinced that the tragedies committed suicide, and they were to find no subsequent rebirth. And two thousand years were to pass before Europe returned to the writing of history according to the canons proposed by Thucydides,[73] or to the reading of Plato, Aristotle and the Greek language in general. Only the Arabs kept a part of Greek culture alive.

A proverb tells us that no man is a prophet in his own country. And the word *pro-phet* (he who speaks first, or in anticipation) tells us that he does not speak of the present, but of things that are still to come. These innovators were secular prophets and had spoken of things that lay in a too distant future.

An overview

> Aristocratic nations show a natural tendency too highly to narrow the limits of the notion of human perfectibility, whereas democratic nations sometimes excessively dilate them.
>
> (Alexis de Tocqueville, *De la démocratie en Amérique*)

Greek civilization was most visibly characterized by forms that attest to stability: sculptures and works of architecture that expressed a sense of perfect balance; non-expansionist political systems that had permitted the flourishing of an elevated number of city-states; epic and lyrical poetry imbued with a sense of tough and refined resignation; intensely moving tragedies that dealt with perennial and already well-known themes and that insisted on the impossibility of change. (When Euripides found it necessary somewhat to alter the plot of a myth, he was careful at the start of the play to declare that he had done so, almost as though to excuse himself.)

In the course of the fifth century, this sense of equilibrium rapidly declined. In addition to expanding in any number of directions, Greek culture also invented the very notions of change and expansion. Myth, which had made all destinies fixed and immobile, was replaced by rationality, which spurred men on to progress.

Of the two commandments at the Delphic oracle, "Nothing too much" and "Know thyself," it was the second that flourished, forcing the former to invert itself into "No amount of knowledge is enough."

At various times in the course of history, shifts of epoch have been known to emerge from within a civilization. But in cases where such innovations offer no continuity with the previously dominant myths, and where they furnish no symbols that are equally rich and accessible as those of such myths, they can provoke a void of necessary collective images. Most of the members of such civilizations will find such a void intolerable, and the new ideas will find themselves thwarted. They can prove to be incapable of reforming the societies to which they owe their birth. Something on this order seems to have taken place with the extraordinary but premature monotheism of the Pharaoh Ekhnaton; one imagines the creed to have been adopted by only a few of his subjects. The Greek enlightenment of the fifth century was a far more vast and profound event, but not sufficiently so as to make itself irreversible.

A new way of thinking that brutally breaks with traditional symbology can formulate radical innovations but seldom is able to diffuse them. And since precisely the supersession of the controlling mythic language was one of the greatest of the novelties of the Athenian enlightenment, its novelties remained confined to the sphere of its intellectuals. The Greek world that immediately preceded the era of Christianity created a body of highly advanced intellectual achievements, but it was unable to organize them into a new, global myth that could serve as a model for a civilization devoted to progress.

What prevented the enlightened Hellenistic world – like the highly civilized China of the post-medieval period – from making a precocious and definitive leap towards modern civilization is less to be found in a lack of intellectual ardor than in the lack of a fantasy of growth and of an ideology of expansion that were rooted in a mythical system and organized as such. What they lacked were not the means of progress, but a cultural orientation towards progress that the majority might have been able to put into practice.

It was only after monotheism had rationalized the myth without abolishing it that the universality of Christianity and the Roman state was to furnish the foundation for such a global model; and that model was then to prove its ability to articulate the new discoveries into a coherent "civilization of growth." An unconscious myth of growth became the common denominator of every activity. It is true that technology and capital were not to become definitively available until a still later date, with the industrial revolution; but it is likewise true that neither the industrial revolution nor the previous mercantile-bourgeois revolution of the free communes can be fully explained without taking recourse to that latent myth.

Our analysis has suggested that the basic ideas, if not the means, for a culture based on growth and expansion can already be found in fifth-century Greece.

What we find before this period is a closed Archaic culture, fearful of the gods, ordered by myth into a stable unit, and alien to intellectual and geographic expansion; the successive culture is open, has lost forever the notion of limits, and is thus predisposed to continual conquest, both intellectual and material. It not only reaches down to us, but also seems prepared to continue endlessly into the future. With various accelerations and periods of stagnation, the reticence of the Middle Ages and the impulsiveness of the Renaissance, history was gradually to develop and promulgate a program of which the psychological nucleus was pre-announced over twenty-four centuries ago by a tiny part of the population of Greece.

The seeds of European expansionism can be rediscovered in the passage from tragic thought to scientific and philosophical thought, which is also, accepting the terms of Nietzsche, the passage from the world of pessimism to the world of optimism.[74]

What can the analysis that we have so far conducted tell us about this shift?

We have seen that the first world was religious, aristocratic and aesthetic. It was religious because it fed on the fear of the gods, and especially on the fear of their jealousy. Rather than any kind of exhortation, guide or example for mortal men, the presence of the gods was a limit, and the perception of this limit had the quality of a powerful emotional experience of the sphere of the divine itself. Religion here was the vehicle of a double negation – exterior and interior – of the Ego of the individual. From the external point of view, the individual lay always prostrate before fearsome and superior forces. In terms of interior experience, this poly-theistic religion was related to its mirror image in the psyche, where it corresponds not to the individuality (or indivisibility) of the Ego, but to

105

the polymorphism of the soul (love is Eros, aggression is Ares, etc.), or to an interior Olympus of separate and impersonal emotions.[75]

It was also an aristocratic world.[76] And again in two ways. First of all historically, since the values that guided it were primarily the values of the aristocracy. But also psychologically: it was immobile; it lacked all faith in progress; it was interested in the preservation of the era of non-history; it was committed to aesthetic rather than to ethical principles. The religion of the Greeks was a self-sufficient dimension little concerned with the lives of men, and its lack of ethical substance is something that it had in common with the religions of other "primitive" peoples; it belonged to that stage of civilization in which faith and morals have not yet grown the one into the other. But in the aesthetic dimension, the profound feelings of the Greeks found release from primitivity through the creation of unique artistic forms.

Finally, the former world had a tragic vision of itself, which is to say that it gave itself the task of grasping the lessons of suffering rather than the hope of redemption; it entrusted itself to wisdom rather than to knowledge.[77] This, still today, is the world to which we mainly refer when we speak of the Hellenic spirit. Nietzsche and Burckhardt, no matter how biased their views may have been, have embedded its sense of tragedy into our collective imagination.

The new world towards which the Hellenic spirit projected itself was, quite to the contrary, a world of ethics. It was opened up by philosophic thinking and its predilection for clear, consistent and unambiguous agents, which is an attitude that leads on the one hand to the scientific search for causes, and on the other to the sense of the essential that typifies the monotheistic religions.

Just as it began to believe in deterministic sequences of cause and effect, this world also became aware of a temporal sequence that lies within events, and of an accumulation of notions and improvements in its stock of knowledge. To speak of an accumulation of knowledge is not simply to make use of a mode of figurative expression that was later introduced by the study of history. The accumulation of knowledge was a concrete and visible phenomenon. Aristocratic culture came to expression and found its diffusion orally, in song: first in epic and later primarily in lyric poetry. This was a very great limitation. Only a very few people could be present at a recitation, and the number of songs of which a singer could adequately commit the words and music to memory was likewise restricted. But, starting with the end of the sixth century, texts began to be available in the form of written prose. The trend grew quite rapidly and scrolls[78] of writing were sold in the market place, avidly consumed by private citizens, and accumulated throughout the generations. The old aristocratic culture grew shrill and sterile in its attempts to discredit it; but then it was forced to decide to coexist with it and to resign itself to its far superior power to reach out to an audience.[79]

In the period that followed the Persian Wars, the new faith in the personal potential of the individual found further manifestation in the rapid development of education, for which interest in democratic Athens assumed the proportions of a kind of mass frenzy.[80] And yet the spread of education gave rise to one of the most conspicuous paradoxes of the new *hýbris*, which of course was exposed to *némesis*. The Sophists developed a science of complete education from which everyone could benefit; but this highly refined education was not actually available to everyone. It was offered only to those who looked forward to roles as helmsmen of the state.[81]

The new world was a world of the Ego. As a psychological parallel to the development of science and the beginnings of a monotheistic sense of the oneness of everything divine, it reinforced man's centers of will and reason (that Ego that psychoanalysis writes with a capital "E"). The unconscious and emotional components of the psyche (the partial personalities or complexes) were gradually displaced and repressed.[82]

This was also a democratic world, since its expansive and optimistic rationalism also found expression in the desire to include the whole of the *démos* – the people (even if the *démos* in fact consisted only of the free males who enjoyed the rights of full citizenship).[83] The previous period's aristocrats had developed closed economies that were based on the lands they owned, and the classes that were now on the rise were quite different. Their interests were primarily commercial and were based on the recent conquests, as well as on industry and craftsmanship, which is to speak of activities that were theoretically able, unlike agriculture, to expand without limitation. These expansionistic forms of enterprise were also accompanied by a new monetary economy that likewise worked on a model of infinite reproducibility, thus differentiating itself from the old agricultural systems which were based on barter. Once its value had been decided upon, money, unlike the produce of the fields, could be coined, which is to say that it could be identically and limitlessly reproduced. Since this world was in the midst of a process of change that gave it new dimensions, it had a need for more substantial rules with which to regulate itself, and it came gradually to find its guide in ethics. Emotion – which was the force in control of the previously tragic *Weltanschauung* – ceded primacy to a rationality that directed its attention to the problems of equitable distribution, and to the measurability and predictability of human behavior. The refined tensions that were called into play by the tragedies now came to be looked down upon, since they aimed to excite unnecessary popular passions, rather than to construct new truths in the service of the Good.[84]

This world of justice, virtue and rationality was the most revolutionary of all the creations of ancient Greece. So it now seems paradoxical that we moderns, who directly descend from that revolution, hardly ever refer to it when we talk of ancient Greece; instead we once again court nostalgia for the terrible gods, for the melancholy poetry, for the sublimated pain of the tragedies.

This rational, democratic world appeared too early on the scene of history; it was inhabited by a society that was still quite largely composed of uncultivated men, or of slaves, and where constant superstition was a part of daily life. The world of ethics, simply by virtue of its own existence, is optimistic, since it postulates the existence of a good; and in the attempt to reach that good, it believes in a "better." The very nature of the world of tragedy, myth and the maxim "Nothing too much" is to set up its own limits; as a world of aesthetics it loved the beautiful but hoped for no "better" and was therefore incapable of turning towards the future. The world of ethics, revealed by reason and philosophy, made itself available to possibility; it contained an optimism, if not quite a prophecy, that was not to reach maturity until the advent of the era of the Christian notion of redemption.

THE RELIGIOUS INVOLUTION

Part of Athens' population resisted the novel developments of the fifth century. It clung to the gods and attempted to forestall their jealous punishments by shoring up the limits that innovational modes of knowledge and an expansionistic course of political and military conquest were beginning in fact to annul.

A general regression and a fragile religious revival found their point of departure in the Battle of Marathon. In particular, a cult of just and severe destiny arose in connection with the legend of the block of Persian marble. As interest in the traditional emotional gods declined towards fable, far more emphasis came to be placed on deities that were not representations of primary qualities (beauty, strength, and so forth) but that instead, more psychologically, personified principles of justice: Tyche (fate, destiny), Dike (justice, law) and Nemesis. The ways in which these figures mesh with one another is quite obvious, and so much so that traditional tales often superimposed them or presented them as relatives. Dike is sometimes the mother of Nemesis or described as an analogous figure of justice[85] who, like the latter, indignantly abandoned the earth.[86] Like Nemesis, Dike too is a punishment for *hýbris*. This is found, for example, in the words of the oracle when it predicted the punishment that was dealt to Xerxes at Salamis.[87] And in a religion without a written tradition of revealed truth, the oracles were the voice of the gods. Tyche too is often associated with Nemesis, and, in time, came to be ever more superimposed upon her.[88] The goddess Nemesis was ever more intensely worshiped after the stunning victory over the Persians, which was the occasion on which her major sanctuary was constructed, at a short distance from Athens.

This was clearly an involution, and its goal was to rescue the principle of distributive justice, no less than its anthropomorphic representation as a god, from the decline of polytheism. And yet this movement was something more that a simple reaction. It was also a new event that concerned itself with historical time, and no longer with mythical time. We must not be misled by the fact that Nemesis was an already extant deity. The mythology and veneration that had previously surrounded her were fairly slight. The true myths of Nemesis arose with the perception of the novelties abroad in the world. The cult that developed and spread was not purely concerned with the narration of a myth; its purpose was to give these novelties an explanation, no matter how rudimentary it now may seem to have been. Rather than an emotional god, Nemesis was a normative or ethical god, even if she was not a true abstract principle like those that were then being introduced by philosophy.

The development of the cult of Nemesis was strictly related to the vigorous affirmation of a feeling – above all an Athenian feeling – of collective self-esteem, as witnessed by Thucydides' report of Pericles' praise of the city. And it was likewise related to the attempt to formulate a "national history" as the first perception of the general flow of events and as a prototype of justly conceived history.

Unlike the myth, however, the political policies that guided the nation were highly questionable; indeed in the course of the fifth century they proved to be disastrous.

Instead of finding inspiration in the moral lesson of the Persian Wars, the conduct that came in their wake on the part of the city of Athens was brutally expansionistic. An attempt was made within the city to promote distributive justice and social cohesion, as one sees from the detailed care and elaborate caution with which rights of citizenship and positions of public power were assigned. But with respect to the world outside of the city, Athens' democracy became an instrument of imperialistic egoism. On the one hand, the city of Athens used its power to condition the internal affairs of other states and to assure the victory of the democratic parties that were beginning to come into existence. On the other hand, it excited the ever greater aversion of the empire of which it was the capital since its democratic rights were a luxury conceded only to its own citizens. The enjoyment of this luxury was constantly denied to other centers, in spite of continual requests. Unlike Alexander the Great, who hastened to establish kinship with the defeated Persian king, and unlike Rome, which gradually extended citizenship to the peoples it defeated, the enlightened Athens lacked a whole and global vision of its empire, which remained a shaky construction that stood on too small a pedestal. In mortal contradiction with the greatness that its own intelligence had summoned into existence, Athens condemned itself to disappearance. Like Chronos, the god of the conservatives, she denied and devoured the progeny to which she herself had given birth.

The criterion of limits survived for the Greeks in an always more negative form, assuming the guise of a kind of mistrust on the part of provincials who had too rapidly opened up to the world, and who hungered simply to swallow as much of it as possible. This rigidity, moreover, is even more clearly visible if we shift our attention for a moment from the great and enlightened Athens to its rival Sparta. In the Archaic period, the city of Sparta had enjoyed a certain level of cultural life. But already in the fifth century, it conducted an essentially military existence in which all male citizens were forced to participate up until sixty years of age. Sparta thus provided itself with about 5,000 highly trained hoplites who kept the other populations of the Peloponnese in various degrees of subjection. Rights of citizenship were never extended to these dominated peoples, and the dominators lived ever more completely in a state of permanent siege, their numbers growing ever more restricted as they fought among themselves and with all of their various subjects, on whom they had come to be highly dependent for the performance of all basic tasks. In the fourth century, the power of Sparta was practically extinct and the city had no more than a thousand hoplites. The *hýbris* of the masters punished itself on its own. On the one hand, they were capable of relinquishing everything, leading a life that still today we speak of as "Spartan" – a life that consisted of marches, fasting, nights in encampments. On the other hand, they relinquished never a whit of their pride as lords whose only vocation was command.

The first war between Athens and Sparta (460–446) inevitably arrived. But in the midst of this conflict with a reputedly invincible adversary, the Athenians allowed themselves an orgy of audacity and also embarked a great fleet to combat the Persians in Egypt, which had rebelled against their dominion. The Athenians' temerity derived from the knowledge of having already defeated the Persians in the past. But that had been at Marathon and Salamis, and thus at the distance of only a day's march or a league across the sea from their families, whose very lives they had to defend. Could they repeat that miracle at enormous distances from their mother country and on the basis of a pure lust for conquest, while already at home in Greece they were at arms with so many enemies? And is it possible for miracles to be repeated at all, or is it already an act of *hýbris* to expect such a thing? Athens achieved none of its goals, and yet the city and its empire survived.

But the temerity that intoxicated the city in the second Peloponnesian War (431–404) was even more radical and finally fatal. Among any number of brutal episodes, the Athenians definitively made themselves the object of the hatred of the minor city-states by annihilating the population of the island of Melos,[89] which had committed the sin of refusing to ally itself with Athens in its war against Sparta.

During a fragile interlude in its struggle with Sparta, Athens also organized an expedition against Syracuse, a very distant and powerful city, the second center of the whole Hellenic world in terms of population and commerce. Athens dared too much. But it might have been able to continue the combat if the gods had not truly punished it, devastating the city with the plague, which consumed like dried grass that mass of refugees of which its population had come to be composed. The city collapsed from one reversal to another, and would never rise again.

To what degree was the populace in agreement with so much folly? As said before, Athens was the very first *pólis* to spare no effort to assure that all of its citizens took part in its government. Yet a quorum of 6,000 citizens was sufficient for important decisions in the assembly, and that was a very low percentage – no more than a sixth or even a seventh – of those who had the right to vote. It is even more significant that the Pnyx, the theater in which the assembly (*ecclesía*) met, could in fact hold no more than just about a maximum of 6,000 people. Six thousand was also the number of ballots required for an act of ostracism that banished a citizen from the city. We have to conclude that the citizens who actively participated in the life of the democracy always remained a clear minority which showed a propensity to precisely the *hýbris* that the complicated system of political participation had been designed to thwart.[90] This minority perhaps considered itself to be the protector of an ideal, and one remembers that it was roughly the size of the total population that Plato declared to be proper for a *pólis*. Athens, unfortunately, had long since shot beyond that mark. It had become a great mass of people, and as such was difficult to govern, and its ideal of direct democracy had degenerated into a form of political superstition. Pericles and his successors, who had increased the retributions for active political participation so as to make it possible even for the poorest, were even accused of purchasing popular support with public money. We can therefore imagine that the greater part of Athens' population, precociously inserted into an unprecedented mechanism of self-government, had no solid foundation of political ideas and fluidly adapted themselves to the proposals of their leaders. Surely the advantages that derived from the city's military victories and commercial expansion must have been persuasive, and the same would have to be said of the able orations of Pericles. Reason and self-evident fact are capable of giving rapid birth to new attitudes, but such new attitudes will seldom be seen to eliminate their predecessors; they are far more inclined to superimpose themselves upon former points of view and to relegate them to a place in the unconscious. So we can easily surmise that the fear of the jealousy of the gods, which had ceased to be active as a norm of conduct,

111

created an ever higher level of superstitious uneasiness. And this renewed fear of *phthónos* was destined to come to manifestation at the base of the social pyramid, in the strata of society that were culturally more vulnerable to superstition. Having benefitted less from the city's course of expansion, this stratum of the populace can also be imagined to have been more inclined to fear its arrogance. So when the city fell into the grips of afflictions that had never before been experienced – such as the great plague, from which Pericles too had died, or the disintegration of immense armies, or the new-born phenomenon of inflation (a strange new monster that annihilated the people's small savings in the course of an incomprehensible metastasis in which the mass of money both flourished and devoured itself) – such phenomena were most likely experienced as divine punishment for the expansionistic *hýbris* of the politicians, and also, perhaps, for the *hýbris* of the knowledge of the intellectuals. Such circumstances offer a clearer explanation for the fact that nearly all of the trials for atheism[91] took place during the period of the Peloponnesian wars and came to an end towards the close of the fifth century, but not before the crusade against the faithless had led to the death of Socrates in 399.

Athens had a guilty conscience. The expansion of the city-state had been accompanied by cruelties that could never have been accepted by a god who punishes the arrogant. One had witnessed an aggressive imperialism that exploited revolting pretexts. It was based on the conquest of its nearest neighbors, and on the denial of all their rights; its colonial policies aimed not to assimilate indigenous populations but to eliminate them and to consign their lands to Athenians; whole populations were expelled from their lands and sold into slavery; when other solutions seemed insufficient the military proceeded to genocide; Athens, moreover, was a racist city, and the civilized Pericles – who himself loved a foreign woman who bore him a son – issued laws in 451–450 that rigorously limited citizenship to persons who could claim Athenians as their parents on both sides; thousands of people were wiped off the list of the city's citizens. And yet these decades of horror that weigh on the shoulders of Athens now seem to be no more than so many pebbles on the ample back of history.

In the course of only a few generations, Athens had made the leap from static to expansive modes of life; and in the course of a brief span of time, it seemed first to have been rewarded for its courage, and then punished for excessive audacity.

But the amazement and disorientation of the populace were to increase still more, since the arrogance of Athens, and later of Sparta and Thebes, was to be followed by something unheard-of. First Macedonia and then Rome forced the free *póleis* into submission, not by virtue of any moral superiority, but simply by virtue of greater audacity and a higher level of organizational efficiency.

In the course of such cataclysmic reversals, the cult of Nemesis behaved differently from others: the cults of the traditional deities fell into decline, but the cult of Nemesis prospered. After the Roman conquest, the cult of Nemesis was to fuse with the cult of the goddess Fortune. Fate and the punishment of arrogance came together into a single figure that aroused considerable veneration, and most of all fear. The vigor of this cult seems even to have continued to grow during the period in which Christianity was definitively eliminating all of the other pagan gods.[92]

The populace was desperate and attempted an impossible return to the past, hoping somehow to subtract itself from the tidal wave of history. They hoped once again to be able to perceive events as lying within the control of a strong and inflexible deity. But the roots of such an idea lay by now in the ills of society, which is to say that it ranked as an expression of superstition rather than of orderly theological thought, and it was to make the religion of the Greeks even more fragile when it came into conflict with Christianity, where history and religion do not simply acknowledge one another when they meet among events, but instead are always parts of a single, well-ordered unit in the custody of God. The second upsurge of the cult of Nemesis and Fortune, in late Roman times, was no longer a reply to Persian invasions, but a resistance to the "invasion" of Christianity, which was a much more rational, democratic and finally a much less limited faith.

During the period of the Roman empire, the goddess Fortune degenerated into an ever more irrational figure[93] who struck out at chance rather than as an agent of justice. Her cult by then was no more than an excrescence of the history of religion: its only function was to attempt to exorcise the turmoil of social and economic changes that were already irreversible.

The commandment to self-limitation as expressed by Nemesis was doubly anachronistic. As a form of religion it was born too late. It was still grounded in an image that derived from the declining polytheism, but it was devoid of the wealth of myth that polytheism had previously contained. As a form of more highly evolved and rational ethics, it was born far too early. It was not until the over saturated times in which we currently live that the sense of limits was once again to impose itself as a concrete part of general experience.

We can sum up our thoughts with the statement that the ethics of limits – no less than philosophy, classical art, the writing of history and the tragedies – represents a Greek invention of meta-historical scope, and that it rises up through the whole of the genealogy of western culture. The goddess Nemesis – the religious metaphor that embodied the ethics of limits – was an anomaly and an anachronism among the deities of ancient Greece and she enjoyed great popularity in the period of their decline. Like the morality of limits, she was cultivated by Archaic Greece, but the solemn proclamation of her fundamental importance was not to come until the fifth century, which was already dedicated to denying her. As a theological figure, Nemesis is the way in which the antique tradition from which we stem effected the unification of religion and morality. And as a moral concept, Nemesis was the principal that both directed and weakened the writing of history on the part of Herodotus; it was the criterion that guided his sense of historical transformations while at the same time limiting its scope. History, for Herodotus, offered proof of the workings of Nemesis in much the same way that historians of a subsequent era were to examine events with a view to confirming the existence of redemption, justice and progress.

Nemesis stands at the line of demarcation that separates two western concepts of history: to the one side we have the Christian and modern concepts that attribute history with tasks of rebirth, growth, and improvement; to the other stands the Greek concept – closer to the typically Oriental attitude of detachment and mistrust with respect to epoch-making events, and yet already aware of their existence – that sees the finest realization of history as a return to the confines of proper limits and thus as a restoration of a natural order that has come to be disturbed. Various modern ideologies that attempt to restore morality to collective events by curbing the excesses of capitalism, of imperialism and of aggressive abuse of the environment can be understood as a re-evaluation of such a scheme; and in terms of the psychogenesis of symbols they represent a return of the repressed goddess Nemesis.

We should not find this surprising. As direct descendants of the Greeks, we proudly accept the heritage of their art, their philosophy and all of their other important contributions to culture. But ancient Greece was also governed by limits; it would be absurd to embrace its civilization with so much enthusiasm and yet to deny the law on which it attempted to nourish itself.

Part III

FROM THE GREEKS TO THE PRESENT

8

CONTINUITY AND TRANSFORMATION: FROM THE SENSE OF LIMITS TO THE HUNGER FOR INFINITY

Western civilization, taken as a whole, is a single, vast and continuous entity.[1] The course of its evolution from out of the ancient Greek and into the modern world may have turned it upside down, but it has suffered no interruption.

The unbroken line of the development and constant metamorphosis of western civilization is largely due to its predominant allegiance to Christianity. Christianity sinks its roots into the soil prepared by the innovational modes of thought of fifth-century Athens, which it both continued and opposed, and it likewise relates to the modern age as predecessor no less than as adversary. An unbroken thread leads from the Greeks to the western civilization of the present day. It has twisted and turned and found itself transformed in various ways, but its continuity has remained essentially intact. We will attempt to follow a few of its movements.

PROPHECY AND EPIPHECY

The Greeks were initially uninterested in large-scale transformations. Their modes of thought offered no place for such phenomena, and least of all for the transformations that the Greeks themselves were preparing to unleash. The religion of the ancient Greeks addressed itself to the past. The Old Testament and the religious creed of the Jews was something quite different. The Hebrew faith was prophetic. The pro-phet is the man who "speaks first," or in anticipation of events, and the religion of the Jews was forward-looking. Faith, for the ancient Hebrew peoples, was a question of faith in a future: in an advancement, in a possible form of evolution, in what we might currently refer to as pro-gress. This pro-gress, in turn, lies under the aegis of the pro-vidence ("looking forwards," etymologically speaking) of a benevolent God, who concerns Himself with the problems (pro-blems) that the future will present. The Bible directs its attention not only towards the past (the myth of the origins of things, as recounted in the book of Genesis) but also towards the future. It speaks to a chosen people and assigns them tasks that lead to their salvation. This may explain the ancestral creative spirit that has accompanied the Hebrew people throughout the millennia. "Truth" (*alétheia*) for the ancient Greeks had the nature of a conquest or an acquisition of knowledge (the word stems from *a* – signaling deprivation – and *lantháno*, to lie concealed or hidden, and thus refers to something that comes out of hiding). But rather than something that one can know, the Hebrew word for "truth" (*'emet*) is something to be constructed by living in accordance with the word of God.[2] The Greeks placed the accent on truth as something that is already extant, the Jews on truth as an action to be performed. Christianity branches off from the Jewish tradition, or is grafted onto the Jewish tradition, and sees itself as collaborating with God for the creation of a new and renovated world. Even while asserting that the messiah has already come, Christianity preserves the emphasis on activity and innovation that was typical of the Hebrew faith. The liturgy of Catholicism even allows for its own enrichment through the acceptance of new and additional saints. This forward-looking gaze and this openness to things to come is expressed by the prefix *pro-*, both in Greek and in Latin. This need for new revelations, or for new truths that require to be constructed, created a series of attitudes that prepared the road for scientific research and that finally found their coronation in the modern "cult" of such research. Progress and the acquisition of constantly new knowledge are the tables on which secular and scientific thought record their corpus of commandments.

The Greeks had no acquaintance with such a frame of mind. If Christianity and Judaism are to be thought of as "prophetic," the religion of the ancient Greeks would be best described as "epiphetic." It voiced a message that was wholly after the fact and that spoke of an already completed creation; this message was no less tragic than resigned and it functioned as a simple accessory to an already given cosmology that could be altered by neither men nor the gods. Its only pro-phetic, or pro-gressive personage was Pro-metheus, whom Zeus saw fit, significantly enough, to condemn to eternal punishment. No matter how creative it may in fact have been, Greek culture of the periods that preceded the shocks and enlightenment of the fifth century was primarily concerned with a sphere of events that had already taken place. It discovered the center of its tragic inspiration by bending constantly backwards towards the origins of a future that the past had already determined, and it thereby courted the demise that its vision would suffer on finding itself confronted with the patent existence of history and its states of constant movement. The Greeks did not believe that the personal experience of the human individual could be freely chosen, and they never imagined that the body of the truths and values that form the fabric of a people's common identity might be enriched or improved upon. Traditional Greek thought maintained that men consist of their destinies. Christianity introduced a new point of view, insisting that men consist of their possibilities. This is the vision that science was later to follow to its most extreme consequences. Two entirely different psychic economies are at work. The psychic economy of the Greeks found its apex in aesthetics (from *aisthánomai*, "to feel") since its every fiber was charged with emotion, and with emotions in no way directed to an unforeseeable future. The psychic economy of Judaism and Christianity (and not only of the former, as the stereotype would attempt to convince us) invented retention and accumulation, creating veritable stockpiles of emotions and enthusiasm (from *en-thoúsiasis*, the interior presence of a god) as a part of their project to heal the split between human and heavenly life. The disappearance of the gods had nothing to do with any depletion of the psychic energies that governed them; it was a question, rather, of the advance of rationality and of the ways in which men learned to control and direct the emotions to which the gods correspond as a part of the interior administration of the psyche.

The struggle to create a better future and to achieve the faculties of self-control that such a project requires had not, however, been wholly alien to the Greeks. From as early as the Archaic period, Odysseus had exemplified such an ideal. But in the process of defining its values in the course of successive ages, it was rather as though the Hellenic mind had set aside Odysseus' willful rationality, preferring to replace it with a code of honor and dignity that found their expression in immediate action and tragic emotion. According to the Archaic model supplied by Homer, Odysseus had been the complete hero, capable of doing battle even with himself. He passed victorious through the superhuman experience of facing the deadly song of the Sirens by having himself tied down; but unlike his companions he did not close his ears. He was capable of self-control until reaching the moment of truth, disguising himself and refusing to react to any and all provocations up until the time had come to deal out punishment to the chieftains of Ithaca.

Such a complete and foresightful heroic ideal was disparaged by the tragic code, which reached its apex in the fifth century, but in the form of a one-sided fatalism. The dramatic power with which Odysseus had come to terms with ambivalence was seen as no more than a form of utilitarian calculation that sought to take advantage of circumstances. Sophocles was fully convinced that this was the mortal flaw of heroism and he turned the ambiguous Odysseus into the emblematic enemy of the loyal but solitary Philoctetes.[3] Pindar too held a similar opinion, remarking that Homer had deceived the Greeks by singing the praises of the king of Ithaca, and that the Greeks bore the unpardonable guilt of having preferred him to Ajax.[4] The conflict between the two ideals of heroism – Odysseus on the side of individual foresight, allied with the gods, and Philoctetes and Ajax on the side of immediate feeling, conditioned by the codes of society – was insurmountable, and nobility had to prevail over the capacity for making calculations. But the person most persuaded that intelligence destroyed the heart's capacity for feeling was perhaps Euripides. His own Odysseus who vanquished the Trojans never appears on the scene, but when he speaks he leaves us aghast. Odysseus is the person who insists that Astianactes – Hector's son, almost still in swaddling clothes – be thrown from the walls of Troy.[5] The vanquished were to be taught that they would know no descendants and be deprived of all hope.

The classical age seems to have demoted Odysseus and to have seen him as perverse; but he found his revenge by surviving the advent of Christianity. He was far more in tune with the Christian spirit of self-discipline than might have been said of the traditional heroes.

THE REJECTION OF THE BODY

Plato unconsciously intuited the essence of the civilization of the future, and when he asserted the superiority of the soul over the body, he opened up the split that once and for all presents itself as its fundamental statute.

He declared the ideal of *kalokagathía* (the coupling of beauty and moral excellence) to be absurd. No one ever again was to commit himself to the notion of the complete and harmonious man in whom physical and spiritual development reciprocally reflect one another. Socrates had an ugly face and a prominent belly, and yet was the wisest of all men.

After the spectacular flowering of its youth, the body does not perfect itself in the years that follow, nor does it better itself from father to son in the course of the generations. The soul and its knowledge, on the other hand, march always forward. So it was better to establish once and for all the superior ideal of a culture of the spirit[6] and to abandon the culture of the body to the body's destiny of inevitable decline. The cultivation of the body was soon to reduce to a form of non-culture, or to a poor compensation for the spiritually poor who at best could seek refuge in beauty and physical prowess. The body – the divine forms of which revealed the virtuous man for the aristocratic tradition – totally respects the statute of limits, of which its very surface is an expression. There is no stature or musculature that does not rapidly reach its zenith, and age is the final undoing of even the most perfect of bodily forms.

The body is a chain that never grows longer, and to be unified with the body means to be linked to a static paradigm to which it corresponds. To set out on the road of what was later to be spoken of as progress, culture had to look at the body as dross and to lay it aside. It found itself forever expelled from the new ideal, since it was incapable of practicing the cult of the unlimited that came into existence with the great enantiodromia.

The rise of Christianity was greatly facilitated by its need to take up arms against nothing more than stubborn and stupid gods who strutted about in the limits of their perfect forms. The Christian commitment to the mortification of the flesh was to shape the moral cage that generalized and rendered obligatory the suppression of half of the human being. But its imprisonment had been ordained some five centuries earlier, not by a mind but by the graceless belly of Socrates.

THE DIVINIZATION OF THE HUMAN BEING

Though it rendered the heavens less anthropomorphic, Christianity was on the other hand to elevate the human world by setting up a bridge that connected it to the world of the divine. Christ, the "true man," established this connection, and thus stepped outside of the matrices of Judaism. It opened the road to the gradual introjection and humanization of the divine principle, and it prepared the way for total human responsibility, which was consigned to man by the rationality of secular and scientific thought.

Man is no longer so completely subject to destiny, nor so thoroughly cut off from the forces of the divine. A fundamental element of divinity in fact took human form and lived on the earth. Both man and his earthly habitat were thereby ennobled and rendered independent of principles that lay beyond them. The secular world became a viable world. Even human words and human reason were ennobled by this event. Whereas polytheism had been incapable of linking itself with philosophy, and had surely had no way of collaborating with philosophy, the new religion was prepared for a partial fusion with it.

The Gospel of Saint John, even in spite of preserving a good deal more of the former Greek culture than the others, expressed this new development as follows: "In the beginning was *Lógos* . . ." (*Lógos* as word, or reason, *verbum* in the interpretation of Saint Augustine, and "in the beginning" translates *en arché*, which is to say that *lógos* rather than myth lies at the origin of things, or at the roots of the world and of human life: the Christian revelation here anticipates the cognitive model of science) ". . . and *Lógos* (the Word) was with God, and *Lógos* was God."[7] "And *Lógos* was made flesh, and dwelt among us."[8]

With the deification of *lógos*, Christianity declared itself to be prepared for an alliance with reason – which would have been sacrilege for polytheism – and also for a collaboration with science and philosophy. Scientific and philosophical knowledge were no longer distinct from the knowledge acquired through faith. From a psychological point of view, the monotheistic god is a model for the workings of the rational ego, and not for the life of the emotions; and that allowed man to develop a theo-logy.

The humanization of God also presents itself as the line of demarcation that separates Christianity from its roots in Judaism. St Paul described Christianity as "unto the Jews a stumbling block, and unto the Greeks foolishness."[9] To understand the terrain on which the incarnation of the divine took place, we have to shift our attention from the theological continuity that ties Judaism to Christianity and to look instead at the geographical continuities involved in Christianity's superimposition of itself on the Greco-Roman civilization in which at first it lived, and which finally it inherited. Like the Roman world in which it spread, Christianity accepted the Hellenic influence, and it did so in various ways.

Unlike God the Father, the Son once again took on those human forms in which the Greek gods had customarily clothed themselves. But God made Himself flesh in another sense as well: the minds of many of the cultivated Greeks were accepted as an extension of divinity. Having invented philosophy, they had begun on earth to practise the wisdom that traditionally inhabited the heavens and belonged to the deity. The human-ization of God was also promoted by the diffusion, among the common people, of the cult of Zagreus (the Dionysus of Thrace), a god who like Christ suffered, died and was resurrected. Both Christianity and the cult of Zagreus were obstructed for quite some time by the authorities.

This slow but uninterrupted rapprochement between God and man prepared the way for a secular civilization in which man, by virtue of reabsorbing the "death" of God, holds total control and responsibility. If God could make Himself a man, the converse could also come about. Man transformed himself into a god, and thus destroyed the *raison d'être* of the deity.

This process came to completion with Nietzsche. He announced that "God is dead"[10] and he awaited the arrival of the *Übermensch* (the Over-man)[11] who contained the spark of divinity.[12] The disappearance of limits is implicit in the very notion of the *Übermensch*, who was destined "to go beyond." The German *über* and the English *over* are nothing more than modern versions of the Latin *super* and the Greek *hypér*, which has also been suggested as one of the possible origins of the word *hýbris*. The *Übermensch* is a *hýbris-mensch*.

GOD AS A MODEL FOR INFINITE CAUSES

Whereas polytheistic myth, with the irregularity and multiformity of the gods who were at work in it, contributed to the consolidation of modes of magical and superstitious thought, the Bible sees events as expressions of divine logic; events are guided by a principle of order and finally give voice to its purposes. With their absolute postulate of an always just and active God, the monotheistic religions anticipated the modern scientific attitude, which directs its attention to the discovery of regular, foreseeable and universally valid causes. Project and intention take the place of destiny; the administration of knowledge replaces the acceptance of the tragic and absurd; just, objective and impersonal cause replaces variable and anthropomorphic caprice. The monotheistic religions opened the road to the identification of causal agents. The Biblical God created things and events, and did not limit Himself, like the pagan gods, to interfering with them. Whereas "word" and "idea" come together in the Greek word *lógos*, Hebrew makes use of *davar* for both "word" and "thing."[13] The Greek word was concerned with cognitive potential, but such potential was reserved to the philosophers. The Hebrew word concerns itself with potential construction, and presumes such construction to be pertinent to the life of everyone, simply as a consequence of the existence of a God who by naming an object was able as well to create it.

God the Father does not go about doing things in the same ways that we do, as was true of the gods of classical polytheism, who resembled us in the lack of precision of their gestures and in the instability of their motivations. He is no longer a humanized figure. He is instead a superior, abstract principle, endowed with absolute power and unswerving determination; He is omnipresent, non-relative and unavoidably active, precisely like a scientific cause.

Such incorruptible self-consistency was an absolute novelty for the Hellenic world (with the exception of the noble message of Socrates, who found no following among the masses) and it accelerated the process of its modernization, drawing it towards forms of greater rationality, even if initially expressed through narrative and liturgy. On the trail that was blazed by the Hebrew God, the two later monotheistic religions were to continue to proceed towards modernity; as figures who give order and truth to the succession of the generations, Christ and Mohammed were rooted in a specifiable time that preceded and led up to them, thus reinforcing the consistency of theological logic with the new and additional authority of historical causality.

This new model could not in turn be dislodged by still more advanced religions, and instead gave way to a secular and definitively rational view of the world. What strikes us today as the secular antithesis of religious thought does not in fact derive from the intellectual conquests of reason, which to a large degree were already a part of the lives of the Greeks of the fifth century; it derives instead from thousands of years of the experience of monotheism itself.

CHRISTIANITY AS THE SEED OF THE ENLIGHTENMENT

The religion of the Greeks was acquainted only with evil, which came to manifestation as an experience of guilt that had to be expiated. But guilt was the abyss of an inescapable malediction rather than the mark of avoidable error. There was no such thing as good, and therefore no faculty of choice; there were only absurd dilemmas that raced towards catastrophe, only voices that screamed out pain, no minds that sought for solutions.

Judaism functions quite differently – even if Yahweh sometimes appears to be capricious and almost unjust – and the difference is even more marked in Christianity. Both of these religions anticipate the secular thinking of science and also apply it to the sphere of ethics, which comes to be ruled by clear and constant distinctions: good and evil, true and false. On their own these co-ordinates were not yet sufficient to create a world of science and technology, but they set up the categories, the mode of thought and the system of rational judgment that, when coupled with the notion of an improvable future, are the premises of a secular world view. The ethics of monotheism connect the assumption of cognitive responsibility to the search for progress, and thus present themselves as a remarkable anticipation of the Enlightenment thinking that was not to come to the fore until many centuries later, redeeming humanity from the darkness of evil by transforming it into the darkness of ignorance.

While forcing the godhead to behave with a level of consistency unknown to the pagan world, Christ could also demand of men "But let your communication be, Yea, yea; Nay, nay."[14] At the time of his expulsion from the Garden of Eden, man had already learned to savor the taste of knowledge. And the work of redemption undertaken by the Son of God was later to inspire the faithful to imitate Him. In sharp antithesis to the pessimism of the world of Greek myth, the follower of Christ has to take up the task of redeeming both himself and his neighbor, constantly working in the service of goodness. Faith in the possibility of improving the human condition draws Christianity and secular thinking together, involving them in a common effort to identify good and evil; they share an optimism that stands in stark contrast to the pessimism of the Greeks. Nietzsche, however, was also to see this development as the affirmation of a set of presuppositions that refuse to accept the conditions of human existence: destiny is forced to hide behind ideologies that formulate means for concealing its tragic ambiguities.[15]

THE ENTRANCE OF FAITH INTO HISTORY

The mission entrusted by God to the Hebrew people also charged Judaism and the two monotheistic religions that stem from its tradition – Christianity and Islam – with a strong sense of collective and historical responsibility. Peoples too, like individuals, have tasks that they have to perform. This anticipates our modern belief that we ourselves are the authors of history, which is a notion that antiquity's polytheism obscured beneath the omnipresence and constant immobility of myth.[16] Christianity here departs from the tradition of the Old Testament and expresses a new philosophy of history. Genesis still sited the origins of Judaism within the subjectivity of mythical time. Redemption, quite to the contrary, took place at a real and determined time and collocates the origins of Christianity in objectivity, drawing its truths into a more pragmatic configuration and bringing them closer to the sphere of events that we recognize as belonging to history.

History, unlike myth, can be redeemed. Christ assumes His status as the Savior on the basis of an actual life that is presented as historical fact, and He thus became the collective paradigm in which everyone discovers and realizes their personal identity. History is created day by day, for the early Christian no less than for the people of our modern secular societies. The only appreciable difference is that the modern secular person is trapped within the solitude of their own responsibility, whereas the people of earlier Christian cultures could feel themselves to experience the benefits of grace and divine providence.

The other side of the coin is to be found in the new burdens that man was to have to bear as a result of becoming the helmsman of history. The weight of these new responsibilities, and of the widespread feelings of guilt which came along with them during the first few centuries of the Christian era, was surely one of the principal factors that led to the pensive, isolationist, sometimes depressed and sometimes persecutory attitudes that were typical of the Middle Ages.

A burgeoning sense of responsibility made a potent contribution to the maturation of Christians and thus stimulated the spread of their faith, but it also obstructed its penetration into various social classes. Christianity initially found acceptance within the restricted circle of the common people of the cities, but found itself rejected by the rural population. Though Christianity today primarily survives among the remnants of what were once the masses of agrarian societies – in contrast to the ever greater atheism of metropolitan life – it started out as an urban faith that found rapid diffusion only in concomitance with an already notable level of civic evolution and economic comfort. The very word *pagan* expresses the contempt of more civilized and already Christianized city dwellers who associated the decaying polytheistic cults with the inhabitants of the rural village (*pagus*). The population of the countryside was not only reticent, as it generally is in every epoch, to lay itself open to novelties; it was also caught up in its day-to-day toils and found it difficult to make a space for tasks and responsibilities that dwelt outside of the area of simple survival activities. And it saw the concept of an historical time in linear development as depriving it of the reassuring repetitions of a circular form of chronology that was connected to the seasons and to the cycle of agricultural work, which in turn was scansioned by rituals that reasserted its continuity with the world of myth.[17] These difficulties were to be attenuated by the presence of numerous saints in the Roman Catholic faith: they frequently allude to pre-Christian figures and thus recuperate the rites with which they were formerly honored.[18] In other ways, and in terms of a greater attention to continuities, such obstacles were also confronted by the Orthodox church, which was partly imbued with an Oriental frame of mind that attributed time and history with a value less central than that which one finds in the attitudes of the Roman church. The eastern church conceived of itself as a repository of the atemporal values of stability and continuity, and it was clearly opposed to the mingling of the interests of religion and politics and also to the spirit of expansionism that it saw as prevailing in the west.[19]

There is a clear correspondence between the spread of the western notion of Christianity and of the idea of history as a process of development. And both found it difficult to capture the allegiance of the less prosperous strata of society.[20]

But resistances to the recognition of historical becoming, and of its ability to show us the way to radical new achievements, can also be discovered in some of the great modern schools of thought that seemed to find their very foundation in the notion of the movement of history. In hopes of appealing to a larger audience, both Christianity and Marxism (with Marxism the phenomenon is even more vigorous) have presented themselves not only as historically oriented but also, antithetically, as mythopoetic, or as fonts of immobile figures. Marxism proclaims the masses to be the very protagonists of political life, allowing them to exit still further from the sphere of the simple chronicle of customs and to assume a primary role within the philosophy of history. But to affirm the status of the masses as a fundamental agent of historical change requires a mythic restructuring of the system of historical thinking, burdening it with notions of models that demand to be imitated. Such models, moreover, are superimposed on former Christian paradigms with which they continue to share the taint of a slippage towards heroic stances.

ABSOLUTE GROWTH

Life in the city-states of ancient Greece was variegated, energetic, cantankerous and rewarding, and it required that those who lived it be consciously committed to its most specific characteristics; they had to look with ingrained and unshakable skepticism at every form of expansionism. Its theological counterpart lay in a plethora of multiform and capricious gods, which in turn went hand in hand with the commandment to self-limitation. The presuppositions of political and religious life coalesced in fact into a cult of limits and specificities that was not to be upset until the fifth century.

Polytheism was then to capitulate to the advent of Christianity and philosophy, but its decline was already well advanced and had gone hand in hand with the decline of the city-states themselves. The code that ruled their modes of civic and religious life had likewise ceased to be all-powerful. Once the emotional gods had fallen into discredit, notions of truth became more rigorous and rational. And when the equilibrium of the *pólis* was thrown awry by the need to come to terms with empires, "politics" itself collapsed and came to be replaced by imperialism.

Greek civilization turned gradually into Hellenism and coalesced with Rome to form the Mediterranean civilization of which the whole of the western world is the continuation, and in the course of this transformation from the particular to the universal it lost its moral foundations. And one of the necessary premises of Christianity was the growth of its size as an ecclesiastic community: evangelization and the constant spread of the faith to an ever greater number of believers count for the Christian as a duty and not an as act of *hýbris*.

The metamorphosis of Greek culture into Roman culture and of Judaism into Christianity widened horizons but entailed a loss of reference points. Rome denationalized Hellenism and turned it into the culture of an empire that embraced the whole of the then-known world. And Christianity denationalized Judaism: what before had been a message for a chosen people came to be conceived of as a universal or catholic (from *katholikés*, "for everyone") faith. The mind contrived its exit from the local and addressed itself to the infinite.

The notion of growth was called into existence by any number of factors and then became an absolute that functions as the pivot of all western activity. Geographic growth – on a Greek, Roman, European and finally on a world-wide scale – since European civilization, in spite of its recent rejection of the physical occupation of colonial empires, has spread to all of the continents of the globe and forced other cultures to adopt the habits of a technological and productivity-oriented civilization that they did not develop on their own. Growth throughout the course of time, since western civilization is the only civilization in which spatial and temporal expansion have uninterruptedly accompanied and reciprocally promoted one another. And this statement holds true even in spite of Europe's retreat before the advance of Islam, since Islam can also be seen as the eastern version of the new and refurbished idea of a monotheism that no longer belongs exclusively to a chosen people. The only societies to have saved themselves – and for a restricted period of time – are those that physically sealed their borders (such as the China and Japan of past centuries) or that recognize only cyclic and non-historical time. But western growth is also and primarily a question of cognitive growth, since the western world conceives of people as having been created in the image of an all-knowing God and further insists that their duty is to imitate God. People can and must expand the sphere of human knowledge since that is the ordained route to self-improvement.

The European mind has been thoroughly colonized by the notion of constant expansion, finally adopting it as an unconscious tenet of the philosophy of history.

Movement (understood in the most aggressive sense of expanding rather than cyclical motion) is so thoroughly a part of western civilization as to have made these terms unconsciously synonymous with one another; and on entering into movement, every other form of civilization factually throws itself open to a process of westernization.

Western or technological civilization seems today to be the only civilization that is destined to survive in the world, and it seems indeed to have furnished the world with a model of immortality. Experience had seemed formerly to indicate that civilizations too – like individuals, families, cities and states, as we ascend the scale of the organization of ever vaster groups of individuals – are born, grow and die. And Spengler, who had a great deal of impact on his generation,[21] considered the decline of western civilization already to be underway.

But do civilizations inevitably have to die? Or have they died till now because they thought that death was their destiny? We know that the members of pre-modern cultures easily came to terms with the notion of having to die and could second that thought with the whole of their being, actively consigning themselves to the moment of death's arrival.[22] There can be reason to wonder if similar phenomena do not perhaps assert themselves for entire communities and their forms of culture. We know, after all, that collective emotions reflect, reinforce and give orientation to the attitudes of individuals.

Something of the kind can surely be seen to have taken place in the pre-Columbian cultures of South and Central America at the time of the arrival of the Spanish.[23] The Teutonic gods likewise respected the myths that announced that they had to die, and with the advent of Christianity they relinquished all further existence.

But could it be, on the other hand, that our own civilization survives by virtue of being the first to believe in a process of uninterrupted development, in addition to creating technologies with which to effect its realization? If these are the terms in which we pose the question, we will have to wait for the future to give us its reply. But the question can also be phrased as a query about the present. Does western civilization differ from all other civilizations by virtue of conceiving its existence to be a course of unlimited development? Since the time of its birth in a polytheistic antiquity, and in the course of becoming what it is today, the creed in which the west believes has undergone a slow but profound transformation; and since that transformation was a process to which the west itself gave birth from out of its own interior, the west has managed to digest it much more thoroughly than might be the case for the non-European peoples who have since been overwhelmed by its culture. Christianity withdrew the more complex qualities of the psyche from the heavens and restored them to people, and the process was continued and brought nearer to completion by secular rationality. People moreover took possession of something more than the primary emotions of which the ancient gods had been the jealous custodians; they also learned to aspire to their perfection and immortality.

If the arguments till now presented are in fact correct, one should reply in the affirmative to the question that was raised a few lines back: western civilization would indeed seem to differ from all other civilizations by virtue of its having conceived its existence to be a course of unlimited development. Yet nothing allows us to exclude the possibility that the reaches of unconscious memory that lie behind the west's supposition of its own immortality contain a superstitious terror of precisely the opposite. Our status as the first human beings to believe their civilization to be of infinite duration condemns us as well to a deep-seated fear of the rancor of the gods from whom we have stolen infinity.

9

THE CONTINUITY OF
THE MYTH OF LIMITS:
GREEK STORIES

Any number of Greek tales recount the calamities of those who pay no heed to limits. Such stories appeared in various places and in the course of various epochs, and they reach us from a variety of sources. In spite of differences in plot and development, the moral they present is largely the same. We will discuss the three stories that are most widely known.

RECKLESS ICARUS

The myth of Icarus is quite famous. But it is better and more correctly described as the myth of Daedalus and Icarus, since these two symbolic figures are complements of one another, and their flight is a single mythic event.[1]

Daedalus, a craftsman and inventor of unsurpassed ability, lived with his son, Icarus, at the court of king Minos, and it was there that he practised his arts. He was actually an Athenian whose presence on Crete is explained by a previous incident that casts a shadow on his unmatched talents and that constitutes a prelude to his final act of *hýbris*. The apprentices he had instructed in Athens included Talos, the son of his sister Polycaste, and Talos while still very young had seemed to be on the verge of surpassing him. Daedalus murdered him, and when the crime was discovered he was banned from Athens. He returned to the practice of his arts at the court of Minos, and much to the king's delight. But there came a day when Daedalus committed the error of placing his gifts at the service of Minos' wife, Pasiphae, who had fallen hopelessly in love with a bull. He constructed a perfect replica of a cow, and the queen could hide within it and thus satisfy her lust for the bull. This monstrous coupling led to the conception of the Minotaur, who is the subject of other famous tales. One tradition informs us that Minos punished Daedalus by having him shut up along with his son Icarus in the Labyrinth that Daedalus himself had designed. The story in any case finds its conclusion in the escape of Daedalus and Icarus from Crete. Daedalus constructed two pairs of wings, one for himself and the other for Icarus, whom he warned: "Fly alongside of me. Do not descend too low, because the splashes of the waves could wet your wings and fatally weigh them down; and do not fly up too high towards the sun, since its heat could melt the wax that holds your wings together." But Icarus grew drunk with the joy of his flight and soon forgot his father's words; he flew ever higher and his disastrous fall was inevitable.

The principle that punishes excess – the *némesis* summoned by *hýbris* – runs throughout the tale. The need to follow a proper middle way is effectively couched in the warning to fly neither too high nor too low.

A psychopathologist could see the images of the legend of Icarus as a description of the manic-depressive states of which every human being is a potential victim. Our moods have the right to fluctuate through the various shadings of sadness and happiness, but an excessively low or depressed emotional tenor can set up a vicious circle that cuts us off from the natural variations of our moods and leaves us imprisoned. Flying too low would have wet the feathers of Icarus' wings, forcing him to fly still lower and to wet them even further until finally finding himself engulfed by the sea; those who allow themselves too "low" a level of vitality, passively accepting all momentary set-backs, can likewise promote a condition of still greater isolation. The refusal to accept or live up to commitments promotes a loss of self-esteem and thus still further with-drawal; the whole of the sphere of human relationships will finally collapse, and the psychic structure of the personality quickly follows suit.

The warning not to fly too high is open to a similar interpretation. The euphoria and hyperactivity that dominate manic states again set up a vicious circle that alters a person's sense of self-esteem, but in precisely the opposite way. If left unchecked, the fictitious sensations experienced in manic states develop into a progressive loss of contact with reality and an underestimation of risks; and the overestimation of personal capabilities exalts itself in an illusion of ever closer contact with an inexhaustible source of energy. That state of mind is nicely described by the image of flying always higher, directing oneself towards the sun.

Depression as symbolized by an approach to water, and manic states as symbolized by the proximity of fire still further coincide, respectively, with feelings of heaviness and lightness and also to the physical sensations – of cold in the first case, and of heat in the second – that frequently accompany this pair of pathologies, and for reasons that are far more symbolic than environmental.

The psychopathological interpretation of the tale offers a key to the cultural context in which these mythic figures emerged. Instead of concen-trating on the fall of Icarus, we have to widen our range of vision and consider the preceding events and the other persons involved, and Daedalus in particular. For if Icarus' specific excess lies in the exaggerated confidence with which he entrusts himself to the use of a technological invention, the myth refers not only to facts of individual psychology, but indeed to the whole of a civilization that feels tempted to steer its course on the basis of its technological expertise. So it is far from accidental for Daedalus to be the father of Icarus.

The reckless and self-destructive feeling of confidence in one's own capabilities is the "son" of a level of technical refinement that in itself is quite admirable; but former events have already warned us of its possible perversions.

In spite of his great nobility (royal blood was said to have flowed in his veins, and Athena herself was purported to have instructed him in his arts), Daedalus had committed the sin of pride; and his inability to accept that the skills of Talos might have been superior to his own had carried him even to the point of making himself guilty of murder. (But an attenuating circumstance should also be remembered: Daedalus suspected Talos of an incestuous relationship with his mother, Polycaste. This might perhaps suggest that technical skill does not necessarily encourage autonomy and can also correspond to a state of emotional immaturity that renders a person incapable of going beyond their origins.) Athens admired Daedalus, but then desired to punish him; and here the myth is a prophetic anticipation of the condemnations that were to fall on innovators such as Socrates. Finally, Daedalus' *hýbris* no longer respects natural limits and permits human technology to deceive and pervert nature, first by facilitating the monstrous coupling of the bull and the queen, and then by robbing the birds of their feathers so as to give them to man.

The story of Daedalus and Icarus follows the model of *némesis* while drawing attention to certain specific details. The rupture of limits is here a question of the excessive use of technology, and thus of abilities that in themselves are praiseworthy. And the whole course of events is represented through the use of two distinct persons who none the less share a single destiny. (We remember that the tragedies teach us that destiny involves the whole of a family.) A curse bears down on everything that is artificial, or on arti-facts. It seems that when we arrive at radical manipulations of nature, the mythic need for a punishment grows irrepressible. The purpose of such punishment is to restore an order that has been disturbed.

THE PRIDE AND AUDACITY OF PHAETON

In the story of Phaeton, *hýbris* takes the form of youthful daring, as seen in opposition to the experience and natural serenity of a god.[2]

Phaeton was the son of the god Helios, the sun, and went one day to ask for his father's help. His divine origins had been called into doubt, and he asked his father to promise to perform an action that would allow him to give clear proof of his lineage to everyone. Helios swore by the river Styx that he would satisfy the boy's request, and the promise was therefore irrevocable. It was only at that point that Phaeton asked to be allowed for the space of a day to drive the chariot with which Helios conducted the sun across the vault of the heavens. Helios begged his son to set aside his desires, but entirely in vain. He was likewise unsuccessful in his attempts to convince the boy that he would have to drive carefully, since controlling the powerful horses of the chariot of the sun was a far from easy task. Phaeton had decided to prove his ability to his sisters, and his mother gave him her encouragement. Having set out on his course across the sky, he soon lost control of the horses which his sisters themselves had harnessed. In Phaeton's mad trajectory across the heavens, the chariot flew at first too high, and then too low and too close to the earth. Trees burst into flame and rivers were dried up. Zeus finally put an end to the whole disaster by striking down Phaeton with a thunderbolt.

Here again, as with the myth of Daedalus and Icarus, the theme of imprudence and its consequences is developed through the pair of a father and a son. But what these two human poles represent is quite different, and they are connected to one another in terms of a different dynamic. The cause of the tragic end of Icarus is to be found in his father's inability to moderate his own ambitions, no less than in his inability to control the use that others might make of his creations. The premises of the destiny to be suffered by the son are already present in the personality of the father, and even while seeming to be unaware of it, it is Daedalus who truly commits the sin of refusing to show respect for his limits. Daedalus would seem to be nothing less than the incarnation of *hýbris*, and Icarus represents *némesis*. The father is a symbol of excessive pride, and the fate of the son is the punishment with which the gods reply to such a sin.

Helios and Phaeton are an entirely different pair. Whereas Daedalus and Icarus are both connected with creativity, the sun god and his child are linked to traditional attitudes of resignation and fatalism. Not even a god can save his sons from their destiny; and every new generation lacks qualities that the one before it possessed. The contrast here is between the ability of the adult and the daring of the boy; and there is also a contrast between the middle way that the chariot should follow and the *hýbris* of a flight that rises too high or sinks too low, the *hýbris* of a violence inflicted on nature by diverting a star from its natural course. The ruined harvest and the dried-up rivers are images of devastation that remind us of the uncontrollable terrors that our own technology can threaten to unleash. The error committed by Helios, on the other hand, is more indirect and insidious. He showed too little caution not in the use of objects, but in the use of words, which are even more powerful agents and therefore to be deployed within the strictest of limits. Not even a god can allow himself to make a promise before knowing precisely what he is promising to do.

And the loss of his son is the price to be paid for committing such an error. In symbolic terms, he loses his future; an irresponsible promise impedes the development of the heritage of which he should have been the source. Even if indirectly, irresponsibly spoken words already break the taboo of limits. Helios' excessive permissiveness implies an inability to establish prohibitions and moral limits. His exaggerated indulgence takes the form of a failure to play a paternal role, slipping instead into an attitude of maternal tolerance. In much the same way, the complicity of the mother and sisters encourage the boy's vanity and undermine the principle of virile austerity that lay at the base of the commandment of limits. Phaeton lacks the masculinity that the Greeks considered essential for a task such as driving the heavenly chariot of the sun. Phaeton was suspected of a certain feminine softness already at the time of Hesiod, who tells us that the boy while still quite young was kidnapped by Aphrodite and made to serve as the guardian of her temple.[3] For Zeus to intervene and put an end to the danger is also symbolic of a return to a principle of paternal order.

Punishment at the hands of Zeus is a common feature of the myth of Phaeton and the myth of Prometheus, to which we will shortly turn our attention. But the difference between the stories is greater than their similarity. There is an ever-present contrast between the Titan's desires for innovation and the conservative opposition of the gods, of whom Zeus is the general spokesman. But in the myth of Phaeton, on the other hand, the king of the gods makes no intervention until the very end of the tale, acting in the stead of the god Helios, who is incapable of acting sternly, and perhaps because of his natural heat. (But can a creature who satisfies the *hýbris* of his son still hold the rank of a god?) The two myths also differ with respect to the moral stature of their characters. Phaeton throws himself into his adventure out of pure audacity and vanity. Prometheus, whose purpose in stealing the fire of the gods is to better the human condition, is more generous and forward-looking than Zeus himself.

Unlike the myth of Prometheus, the myth of Phaeton announces no historical perspective of reform or evolution. It limits itself to insisting on the immobility of divine law, and on the inevitability of the punishment of human pride. In this respect its message is similar to the message of other myths. What makes it special is that it finds its vehicle of expiation in precisely those forces that the human being has so daringly appropriated: the chariot of the sun, which only the hand of a god can guide. This is a clear expression of a lack of trust in the use of tools which go too far in the manipulation of nature.

This story presents us with a warning about the paradoxical effects of techniques or technologies that are pressed into service by persons or forces of inadequate moral stature, and the myth of Phaeton thus adumbrates the scheme of Goethe's *Sorcerer's Apprentice*,[4] which is a modern tale that finds its theme in stories from ancient Greece.

PROMETHEUS

Every revolution is always against the gods, starting with Prometheus.
(Albert Camus, *Le Mythe de Sisyphe*)

(but, oh Zeus) you must allow me
my land and my hut,
which you have not constructed,
and my fire,
of which you envy the embers.
I know of no one under the sun
who is poorer than you,
oh gods!
(J. W. Goethe, *Prometheus*)

The modern age has learned to see Prometheus as the figure who opened the road to reason and to the principles of enlightened thinking. He is seen as a hero who fights for progress, and who directs his struggle against the immutability of fate and the conservatism of the gods. But since Greek tradition had no such thing as an idea of progress in any way similar to our own, the meaning of the story of Prometheus must have been a great deal more complex and it is far from easy to reconstruct it. Prometheus could hardly have been seen as a prototype of what we think of as free choice; but he can be thought to have offered an example of a particularly arduous personal destiny that could derive from a state of conflict with the gods, rather than from a condition of submission to them. Yet Greek tradition delved into this myth with unusual passion and insistence, and the frame of mind that Prometheus represents (Prometheus, more-over, means "he who thinks anticipatory thoughts") must surely have held a harbinger of the notion of progress, or of the need to declare an allegiance to human life, even at the cost of challenging the gods, and to stand on the side of change rather than of immobility.

The story of Prometheus is very widely known, and the primary reason for telling it again is to limit our discourse to its more important versions. We will consider the story as handed down to us by Hesiod's *Theogony*, Aeschylus' *Prometheus Bound* and Plato's *Protagoras*.

In Hesiod's version of the story,[5] Prometheus, who is one of the Titans, is entrusted not only with the task of furthering the evolution of mankind (among which his brother Epimetheus unwisely causes the appearance of womankind as well[6]) but also with the task of separating mankind from the gods. In Mecon, where that separation was to be solemnly celebrated, Prometheus cunningly portioned out the flesh of a great bull. He chose a great deal of meat and fat for himself and for humankind, but hid it all in the belly of the beast; the portion that he destined to Zeus consisted only of a heap of bones, but disguised beneath a layer of apparently attractive fat. "What an unjust division you have made!" Zeus exclaims, having seen

135

through the ruse. But Prometheus insists, and replies, "O lord of the gods, let you be the one to choose the part that you consider to be best." Zeus pretends to fall into the trap and selects the portion that is apparently rich with fat, but in reality much the poorer. However, his only purpose in doing so is to be able at a later point to show his anger and to allow himself the satisfaction of denying the use of fire to men. It was then – according to this version of the myth – that Prometheus purloined the fire of the gods in order to give it to mortals. And it was after this theft that Zeus excogitated a second punishment by creating woman. His perfidy – as Hesiod elsewhere adds[7] – lay in giving men the knowledge of an evil in which they incautiously would take delight.

Aeschylus' version of the myth can be only partially reconstructed, since only one of the plays of his Prometheus trilogy has been preserved.[8] Aeschylus relies on the tradition which tells us that Prometheus, who was more foresightful than the other Titans (once again maintaining the promise of his name), anticipated the victory of Zeus and was careful not to oppose him. Later, however, he took up the cause of men, whom Zeus had resolved to destroy. This decision was the beginning of Prometheus' sufferings. Hephaestus was ordered to chain him to Mount Caucasus, at the eastern border of the world, and even though Hephaestus felt pity for him, Kratos[9] insisted that the punishment was right and necessary. Prometheus here was destined to writhe beneath the beak of Zeus' eagle, who every day devoured his liver, which then grew back in the course of every night so that the torture could continue. Prometheus complained that the cause of all this suffering lay entirely in his benevolence to men. In addition to the use of fire, he had also given mankind its very first medicines for the cure of disease as well as the first rudiments for the understanding of dreams and the prediction of the future. But the final comments of the chorus remind us of a law that is far more important than generosity: "Wise are they who do homage to Necessity (*némesis*)."[10]

Plato offers the following version of the story.[11] "Once upon a time there were gods only, and no mortal creatures. But when the time had come that these also should be created, the gods fashioned them out of earth and fire and various mixtures of both elements in the interior of the earth; and when they were about to bring them into the light of day, they ordered Prometheus and Epimetheus to equip them, and to distribute to them severally their proper qualities." But Epimetheus (which means, significantly enough, "he who thinks afterwards") persuaded Prometheus to allow him to perform this operation alone ("Let me distribute and do you inspect") and then assigned "all the qualities which he had to give" to the animals, leaving mankind weak and without the ability to defend itself. To remedy this situation, Prometheus stole not only fire, but also the arts of Hephaestus and Athena – meaning the principal manual and intellectual abilities – and made a gift of them to men.

Prometheus is a highly fascinating mythic figure because he is everywhere shot through with a profound and paradoxical ambiguity. On the one hand, as is generally true of the characters who populate the scene of Greek mythology, his part has already been written by inscrutable fate and capricious gods, and he has nothing more to do than simply to recite it. On the other hand, he has the specific destiny of announcing a world in which everything will be turned upside down in favor of a faith in the freedom of men, in knowledge and in the search for improvement.

Such a hypothesis seems at first sight to diminish the novelty and grandiosity of the figure of Prometheus, but it allows us to preserve a consistent vision of the Greek way of thought, which anticipates the world of the west while none the less differing from it, because the destinies imposed by its tragic point of view are still a limit and every exercise of freedom shatters against it.

Much of the greatness of Prometheus seems indeed to lie in the fact that he does *not* assume the role, still unknown in ancient Greece, of the innovator and prophet; and all of his conquests, rather than rewarded, were a cause for punishment, suffering and the loss of freedom. If the sufferings of Prometheus derive from a preordained destiny, and not from an imperative to perform some brave new task, we understand why his myth was turned into tragic drama by the religious Aeschylus rather than the enlightened Euripides. Aeschylus, moreover, always preferred the superhuman to the human, and on this particular occasion he carried that preference to an extreme. *Prometheus Bound* is in fact a tragedy with no human beings in its cast of characters; all of its characters are either Titans or gods.[12] Prometheus' refusal, even after his enchainment, to collaborate with Zeus makes us wonder if his actions were truly moved, as he declares them to be, by motives of generosity towards men and by his love for the progress that will later see him as its herald. He can seem instead to be inspired by that supreme fidelity to one's own destiny (made manifest and reinforced by the expectations of the surrounding witnesses) that leads the Greek heroes – the Hector of Homer's *Iliad*,[13] the Eteocles of Aeschylus' *Seven against Thebes*,[14] the Polynices of Sophocles' *Oedipus at Colonus*[15] – in full awareness towards a death that, from our point of view, might still have been avoided.

The Greek hero, as revealed by these three prototypes, regulates his actions in accordance with what has been preannounced as his destiny, and with the opinions and expectations of his fellow citizens. The innovator, on the other hand, both in the Judeo-Christian form of the prophet and in the modern form of the revolutionary or scientist, has to accept a greater solitude, stepping out of line with respect to his society and his present, and acting on the basis of an intuition of the possible: his code of conduct descends from a hypothesis, and his values reside in the future.

A Greek hero or an innovator: to which of these two categories is

Prometheus to be assigned? Probably to neither. As an innovator and a humanist, he lacks a true image of the man of the future: his interlocutor is always Zeus,[16] and their conflict over the gift of fire to men remains a quarrel between superhumans. As a traditional Greek hero (we do well to remember that the myth of Prometheus has non-Hellenic origins) he lacks a clear submission to *dóxa*, the opinions of those around him. Prometheus' fidelity to his destiny primarily takes the form of an obedience to the specific quality of his own temperament, especially to his daring and his irrepressible cunning. In this respect he seems quite similar to Odysseus, Greek mythology's other great harbinger of the modern spirit.

What is the common feature of all the various versions of the story of Prometheus? He strikes our imagination as singular and unclassifiable, suspended as he is between heaven and earth, between Europe and that unknown world that lay to the east of it, at the limits of everything known, as we are reminded by his enchainment on Mount Caucasus. In a similar way, he seems to be suspended between a "theology" that had governed Greece and an "anthropology" that was then to supplant it. He is neither a god nor a man, even though capable of loving both. He cannot even be taken as an orthodox representative of his own race, the race of the Titans, who are usually described as extremely strong, but as arrogant and lacking in foresight: Atlas, as punishment for having participated in a revolt against Zeus, was condemned to hold up the sky at the western limit of the known world, at the edge of that ocean, the Atlantic, that bears his name. The arrogance and presumption that were typical of the Titans, and of many of the gods of Olympus as well, grow more refined in Prometheus. At first they appear in the guise of audacity and cunning, and later, once Prometheus has been enchained, they take the form of a patient recognition of his destiny. Myth, with the story of Prometheus, undergoes two transformations: it shifts from a superhuman to a human dimension; and rather than witness the archaic workings of power, it turns its attention to the manifestations of wisdom. (A similar development can also be seen in the Bible, where the patience of Job gives expression to a kind of wisdom with which the world of the divine was previously unacquainted.) Prometheus stands at the start of the ability to make tactical choices, and he likewise signals the beginning of the process of the progressive differentiation of the faculties of the intelligence; and these are the two central phenomena of the thinking of western civilization.

But in addition to anticipating the advent of a mode of enlightened humanistic thought that orphans itself of the gods, Prometheus also resembles, as mentioned above, the most modern of the archaic heroes, Odysseus. He does not, however, have the gift of Odysseus' piety and prudence, which is to speak of the fear of the gods and the perspicacious self-reliance that allow Homer's hero to extract himself from the most insidious situations. But on the other hand, he has something that

138

Odysseus lacks: a prophetic sense of his own task, which he places before anything and everything else, including prudence. Odysseus' goals are personal and relative: to defend himself, to succor his family and his loyal subjects, to nourish and reaffirm his alliance with the gods, whose benevolence was the food in which his intellect found its nourishment. Prometheus' mission is impersonal, abstract and absolute: to offer assistance to mankind, almost in the Christian sense of helping one's neighbor. But at a time of jealous gods who were wholly unacquainted with providence, such humanistic aims were premature, and therefore in conflict with the prevailing moral principles. Odysseus, even though modern and intelligent rather than strong and archaic, was first of all a hero. Prometheus was primarily a prophet. And that, precisely, is a considerable part of what makes the myth of Prometheus so disconcerting; we are accustomed to thinking that prophets belong to monotheism. Prometheus, finally, even in spite of his recourse to stratagems as a way of coming to the aid of man, gives proof of a loyalty that is not to be found in Odysseus. Odysseus was capable of deceiving the gods,[17] whereas Prometheus defied them.

The last play of Aeschylus' trilogy has unfortunately been lost, but we know it to have concluded with the re-establishment of the alliance between Zeus and Prometheus; and this was surely something more than a moralistic expedient for bringing the myth to a close. It was, quite to the contrary, the beginning of a theological compromise that was to lead the Greeks outside of their tradition and to prepare them for the assumption of an expansionistic frame of mind. Could it be said that archaic thought already felt the need of a pro-phet (he who speaks in anticipation) when it created the figure of Pro-metheus (he who thinks in anticipation)? Yes, from certain points of view, and the myth itself alludes to such a need. Even the most archaic civilizations knew that those who live to the east are the first to receive the light. Prometheus' imprisonment at the eastern confines of the world, where dawn appears, makes one think that the curse and the destiny in which he was entrapped were nothing less than the dawn of awareness; he had the destiny of being the first to see things clearly, the destiny of a state of pre-enlightenment.

Prometheus' principal gift to mankind was fire, and fire is the fundamental instrument for effecting transformations – for the cooking of food, for the forging of raw materials into objects and, symbolically, for the transmutation of instinct into culture and intelligence. But it is also something more than that: fire is also light. When man takes possession of fire, his eyes can begin to dispense with the sun. The possession of Promethean fire means that man's source of illumination no longer lies in the skies. This image contains the prophecy that men will find their future in the secular world, and in a world to be approached with infinite curiosity.

But still another allusion to progress can be found in the image of Promethean fire. Unlike material gifts, the various forms of knowledge, once acquired, never again become lost. So Prometheus' gift – since what it first of all represents is the illumination of the mind – was irrevocable. Zeus, even though omnipotent and full of ire, made no attempt to take it back. He would seem to have known that it had come to be mankind's inalienable property. But the culprit could be condemned to the dire and eternal punishment of having his liver eaten away every day. This image anticipates the most classical of the psychosomatic afflictions and suggests that the conquest of progress was destined to separate the body from the mind and to find its realization at the body's expense. We should remember that the schism of the body and the mind went virtually unnoticed in archaic civilizations, whereas it ranks today as a torment for millions of individuals: Zeus' punishment was truly eternal and while reaching down throughout history has grown always more severe.

So Prometheus does not repent. In Aeschylus' tragedy he pridefully continues to insist on the generosity of his theft, and he finally threatens Zeus. He has knowledge of a prophecy which announces that the king of the gods could be dethroned, but he adamantly refuses to reveal it. We have no idea of the terms on which Zeus and Prometheus made peace and reached a compromise in the lost conclusion of Aeschylus' trilogy, but it still remains certain that the stolen fire – the symbol of the overwhelming power of Zeus and of the nothingness of men for as long as it lay beyond their access and wholly enclosed in his thunderbolt – was never to be returned. The heavens were forced to bow down to the earth and forever to accept its possession of a spark of the divine.

This marks the birth of a new and different attitude that first came to life in Greece and that later grew robust in the other western civilizations. Man was to cease to throw himself prostrate before the gods and to feel himself in comparison to be a nothingness. A part of the power and fulgor of Zeus had become his own. Rather than project his emotions into the gods (Zeus–Jove, Hermes, Eros, etc.), man would begin to experience them as parts of himself, or as components of a life of the psyche (jovial, hermetic, erotic) that he himself could attempt to regulate.[18] The emotional gods descended from the skies and turned into emotions: into individual psychic experience rather than afflictions imposed by a superior authority.

People who formerly attributed their feelings to external agents and who then begin to succeed in seeing them as their own (a process to which we refer as the reabsorption of psychic projections) experience the benefit of an increase of consciousness; but they also suffer an impoverishment of the imagination. Very few people are truly capable of doing away with the gods and replacing them with reason; most people find it difficult to look for orientation in an imageless philosophy and to rediscover within themselves the psychic energies that they once projected into the heavens.

The story of Prometheus is more than simply another of the many tales of Greek mythology; it opened the road to the incorporation of the divine. It prepared the twilight of theology through a kind of gradual theophagy: the gods are swallowed. It follows that the sense of self-limitation was similarly destined to a gradual disappearance. If man had formerly been a nothingness – and a nothing that had to be careful not to become a something, so as not to excite the ire of powerful and jealous gods – this limit disappears for an even more basic reason than the demise of the gods themselves; this other reason for its disappearance is that men absorb it and make it a part of themselves.

The same omnipotence – and all its capriciousness – that had once belonged to the gods began little by little to stir within men; and it authorized them to envy their neighbors.

Through the re-appropriation of these psychic forces, man destroyed the mythic and heroic world that had previously had the function of containing them; and he thus destroyed a world that had given birth to one of the first and highest forms of human civilization.

10

THE CONTINUITY OF
THE MYTH OF LIMITS:
WESTERN STORIES

The golden mean

Two things have I required of thee; deny me them not before I die:
Remove far from me vanity and lies; give me neither poverty nor
riches; feed me with food convenient for me; Lest I be full, and deny
thee, and say Who is the Lord?

(Proverbs, 30, 7)

WHAT THE SERPENT KNEW

For God doth know that in the day ye eat thereof, then your eyes shall
be opened, and ye shall be as gods, knowing good and evil.

(Genesis, 3, 5)

If we are asked for a Biblical example of a limit that was never to be crossed,
our minds turn immediately to the story of the original sin. It constitutes
the prototype of the pride that the Bible sees as the root of all sin. In plot,
the story shows similarities with the tale of Prometheus; Nietzsche in fact
remarked that these two stories are brother and sister.[1]

The central theme of both of these stories is the breaking of a taboo that
reserved certain forms of knowledge – or the prototypes of all possible
knowledge – to the gods and thus denied them to mankind. But in the
Biblical story the relationship between the breaking of the taboo and the
guilt for having done so is clear, causal and unidirectional, and therefore
free of the ambiguities that allow infinite interpretations of the myth of
Prometheus. The Biblical story of the original sin (Genesis 2, 15–16; 3, 1–24)
is dramatic and full of suffering, but not tragic.

God placed Adam in the garden of Eden and gave him permission to
eat of the fruit of every tree, with the exception of the tree of the knowledge
of good and evil, "for in the day that thou eatest thereof thou shalt surely
die." God then created woman from one of Adam's ribs. Both Adam and
Eve were naked, and not at all ashamed of their nakedness. The cleverest
of the animals, the snake, tempted Eve by suggesting that God had lied.

He told her that eating of the fruit of the tree of knowledge would not bring about their death and instead would open their eyes, "and ye shall be as gods, knowing good and evil." Seeing that the fruit of the tree was "good for food" and "pleasant to the eyes," and thinking that knowledge was desirable, the woman therefore ate of it and gave it as well to her husband. This was the point at which they realized their nakedness and "they sewed fig leaves together, and made themselves aprons." On hearing the voice of God as He walked in the garden, they hid themselves. "And the Lord God called unto Adam, and said unto him, 'Where art thou?'" Adam replied, "I heard thy voice in the garden, and I was afraid, because I was naked; and I hid myself." God then said, "Who told thee that thou was naked? Hast thou eaten of the tree whereof I commanded thee that thou shouldest not eat?" Adam replied that he had been tempted by Eve, and Eve volunteered that the serpent had beguiled her. God then cursed the serpent and "put enmity" between the serpent and woman-kind, whom in turn he condemned to bring forth children in pain and sorrow, and to submission to man. Turning to Adam, He condemned him to labor in the fields; and in addition to drawing sustenance from the ground and eating his bread in the sweat of his brow, he was also to die and return to the ground, "for dust thou art, and unto dust thou shalt return."

The Biblical text then concludes with two highly interesting incidents that the modern reader often overlooks.

First of all,[2] God seems to become aware of the new human condition. Man is now "naked" and in need of shelter, both symbolically, since he is now exposed to evil and suffering, and materially, since he is subject to the inclemency of the elements and as well to a sense of shame. God therefore gave a "coat of skins" to the man and the woman. Rather than severity, God here seems more concerned with showing generosity.

God also knows that man's new condition has endowed him with something divine: the knowledge of good and evil.[3] He imagines as well that if man were to continue to live in the garden of Eden, he would also eat of the tree of life, and thus become immortal. To forestall such a possibility, God has to expel man from the garden and condemn him to work the earth from which he was made; He also finds it necessary to post His cherubim and a flaming sword at the entrance to the garden and thus to cut off access to the tree of life (and not, as is often imagined, to the joys of the earthly paradise).[4] God appears to be troubled by the thought that mankind might become too similar to Himself.[5]

This passage fits quite well with our thesis. God seems here to show an attitude that amounts to something more than the general irritability that He manifests at any number of points in the Old Testament: He seems to gives expression to a true and proper divine jealousy. His attitude seems to corroborate the words of the serpent and also to explain the reason for the taboo and the expulsion from paradise. The snake, paradoxically enough, seems to be more honest than God. Adam and Eve did not in fact die as a result of eating from the tree of knowledge, as God had forewarned (if not in terms of the death of natural innocence). And surely they took at least a step in the direction predicted by the serpent: they became similar to God in the understanding of good and evil. This is clear from the story's assertion that Adam and Eve grew aware of their nakedness and understood it to be shameful; and it is also clear from the words of God: "Behold, the man is become as one of us, to know good and evil." God is also distressed by the thought that humanity could acquire still more of the qualities of the divine by eating the fruit of the tree of life and thus becoming immortal. The serpent's honesty does nothing to mitigate the need for God's prohibitions, and in fact reinforces it. For humans to attain both knowledge and immortality would count as more than a simple infraction of the law: it would create a fundamental confusion in the order of the cosmos and totally upset its hierarchy.

But the serpent seems none the less to have been paradoxically honest with Eve, whereas God in part spoke a lie; and above all else there was something essential that God concealed. He seems to have made a secret of one of the most fundamental aspects of His taboo. There was no impersonal or pre-existent law that decreed that Adam and Eve should avoid the food that could make them similar to God. This was simply the will of God Himself, who was the source and principle of everything, inclusive of the law. God was unhappy with the thought that others might take on qualities similar to His own. Can we therefore conclude that the message of the Bible finds its foundations in a jealous God (even if animated by compassion and partly providential) who is prone to insist on exclusive ownership of His own particular prerogatives, and who would thus be similar to the gods of Aeschylus and Herodotus?

The answer to that question would belong to a study of theology. Here we can limit ourselves to observing that in the Hebrew myth once again, just as in the Greek myth, an act of excessive pride on the part of the man and the woman fills God with a fear of seeing Himself equaled by them. The Biblical story of creation and the myth of Prometheus both make it clear that mankind must be careful to keep its distance from *hýbris*. And in both of these cases humans go too far not by virtue of any simply quantitative acquisition of knowledge that might violate some abstract moral code, but by virtue of a new and qualitatively different achievement that brings them into direct conflict with the deity.

Neither the latent monotheism of Zeus nor the prototypical monotheism of Yahweh finds a resolution, in these episodes, of its ambiguous attitude towards humans. The gods' immediate reaction is to deal out punishment, but one also sees in both of these stories that mankind has set out on a path of untold potential. Having achieved a form of knowledge that releases them from their status as a passive appendage of God or the gods, humans will know a future of greater suffering, but also of greater responsibility.

Another important similarity between these two myths lies in the irreversibility of their new acquisitions; their sin becomes the viable embryo of possible enlightenment. Just as Zeus punishes Prometheus but makes no demand for the restitution of fire, the Hebrew God banishes Adam but does not rescind his knowledge of good and evil and decree that it once again must belong to Himself alone. The theft of knowledge can be punished but not reversed. This irrevocability of the acquisition of knowledge opened the road to the development and evolution of the west, where knowledge is a good tiding (literally, a "gospel") that has to be furthered and accumulated, and also to the way the west would distance itself from religious devotion, which has always found value in mysteries.

These parallels between the Greek and Hebrew myths suggest their observance of a common mythical model, but in the service of different divine principles. The Biblical God, in addition to creator, is also redeemer; Zeus, on the other hand, who could control the course of the life of humans but who had not created them, limits himself to punishment.

The Bible is concerned with absolutes; its emphasis is mainly theistic and it insists on the irreconcilable contrast between good and evil. In the tales of the Greeks, evil hovers about as a general menace; evil in the Bible, on the other hand, is denied all right to an anthropomorphic shape and finds itself expelled into the absolute otherness of the serpent.

The Greeks saw man as the center of all complexity, and man was a mixture of good and evil. It is of little importance that Prometheus was a Titan, since he chose to link his own destiny to the destiny of humanity and to enter with them into conflict with the gods. He is more tormented and complex than Adam. The myth leaves us uncertain as to whether he was moved by generosity towards mankind or by prideful competition with Zeus. Prometheus remains a torn and tragic figure. Rather than the power of goodness, what triumphs with Prometheus is the power of passion. The Bible, on the other hand, insists on the complexity of God, Who looks at Adam with jealous anger at much the same time that He feels the impulse to relieve him of the vulnerability of his sudden nakedness. And since the premises of the Bible demand the triumph of goodness, God acts accordingly.

An apocryphal book of Adam transposes this principle of divine compassion into the figure of an angel who brings comfort to the man, after his expulsion from Eden, by teaching him the arts of employing bulls for plowing, of using the blacksmith's hammer and of handling fire with tongs.[6] By giving Adam control of fire, this story makes him even more similar to Prometheus; yet it also sheds more light on the fundamental difference between the theism of the Hebrews and the incipient humanism of the Greeks: God Himself performs the act of generosity – an act of true and proper philanthropy – that the Greeks ascribed to the Titan. In Prometheus they found compensation for an attitude they knew their gods to lack.

The story of Adam gives the impression that in the Bible also a kind of *hýbris* constituted the gravest sin. But even if the Hebrew God can be suspected of harboring an ire similar to *némesis* and a jealousy akin to *phthónos*, He is different from the Greek gods by being substantially just. In turn, Adam's sin differs from *hýbris* by having transgressed against a limit established in defense of the nature of God and not against barriers that served to hobble the nature of mankind.

Genesis does not declare that desire for more is evil. Its only interdiction is that peolpe must not attempt to resemble God. The limits established by the Greeks were a part of a tragic universe where destiny was fixed and immutable, and their connotations were philosophical, whereas the taboo that ruled the life of Adam had more of the nature of an ethical norm of which the context was theological. The law in which the Hebrew perception of limits was grounded seems clearer and sharper than the Greek, but since it found its formulation as a prohibition (and not as an inwardly experienced emotion) it discourages the natural need to scrutinize the problem or to see it as a subject for more careful reflection. The Hebrew taboo is absolute and further includes the prohibition of delving into its meaning. The law is simply the law. Humans are permitted neither to break it nor to discuss it.

We can imagine that the ancient Jews, like the ancient Greeks, felt a need to set a limit to human greed. But their culture experienced that limit as a norm rather than as a mode of wisdom and thereby subjected it to a greater risk of losing its moorings; it more easily ceased to be accompanied by the ambivalent, complex and solitary feelings that completed the experience of limits in the tragic world of the Greeks. The limits established by Hebrew culture were exposed to the danger of being immediately compromised by the weakening of the system of dogma on which they rested, as we see today in the world that surrounds us – a secular world that knows no limits.

THE "MAD FLIGHT"

> And I bridle my thoughts more than is my wont
> So that they run no path unguided by virtue
>
> (Dante, *Inferno*)

In the *Divina commedia*, the eighth circle of hell hosts the *consiglieri di frode* or "evil counsellors."[7] Dante applied this term to individuals who made abusive use of intelligence by employing it for immoral goals, or simply for personal interest, and he was here concerned with a sin that can strike us as unusual, since it belongs to the framework of a severe code of ethics that has little to do with modern attitudes. In the fourteenth century, intelligence had to assume an attitude of humility with respect to faith, just as private interests had little legitimacy and had to bow to those of the church and the prince. In our own society, where the value of spirituality has waned as the value of rationality has increased, the use of intelligence for personal ends (which the Greeks would have described as "idiotic," since *ídios* meant "private," "personal," "separate" or "distinct") is far more highly tolerated, and frequently admired. So we now find it difficult to grasp the nature of the sin that Dante attributed to Ulysses.[8] The liberal, secular societies that followed the French Revolution no longer require the actions of the individual to place themselves in the service of the greater glory of God or the king, and personal aims cease to be legitimate only when explicitly prohibited.

At the time of Dante Alighieri, things stood quite differently. Every form of activity, no matter how mundane, took place within a vast theological context, and there was no such thing as an action that was exempt from religious responsibilities. Yet it has to be observed that Dante treats this class of sinners with a respect and almost a deference that he never extends to others. Intelligence remains the highest of the human faculties: from a theological point of view, the greatest of the gifts of God.

Each of the *consiglieri di frode* burned in an eternal flame, as though to imply that their lives transformed the experience of reason – ordinarily thought of as cold – into an ardent and uncontrollable passion. The soul Dante convinces to narrate its story is the soul of Ulysses. We know, however, that Dante's knowledge of the myths surrounding Ulysses was necessarily slight, since he surely had no acquaintance with the primary works in which we ourselves read the story of the adventures of the king of Ithaca. The *Iliad* and the *Odyssey* were unknown in the Middle Ages and Dante disposed of nothing more than a standard general theme – the legend of Ulysses as an inventor of ploys and ruses – on which to develop his creative imagination. With a passage from Ovid's *Metamorphoses*[9] as his starting point, he constructed one of his powerful images. He tells us that Ulysses – with his insatiable thirst for knowledge still intact after a year in the company of Circe the sorceress – dragged his companions into still another perilous adventure; and from this point onward, the legend that Dante recounts was most probably an invention of his own.

Neither the sweetness of his son, nor his respect for his father, nor his love for his wife Penelope could vie with Ulysses' desire for knowledge of the world and of human virtues and vices. With a single boat and only a few remaining companions, he sailed westward across the Mediterranean. Ulysses and his mates were already old when they reached the Pillars of Hercules, today's Gibraltar, where the hero delivered the following speech:

And now, my brothers, we have journeyed together to the ends of the earth and passed through numerous perils; and the span of life that remains to us is short. So this is surely no time to deny yourselves the experience of the other part of the world, unexplored and uninhabited. You are of human seed and not destined to animal existence, but to knowledge and valor.

Their souls burn with impatience and the ship throws itself into a "mad flight"[10] first to the west and then ever further southwards, until finally the stars in the sky of the "other pole" replace our own. After five months of navigation they reach a mountain of a height they had never seen before. Ulysses and his companions take joy in the sight, but only very briefly. A wave rushes down from the mountain and sucks their boat into a whirlpool; after spinning three times about itself, it disappears into the depths.

There seems to be no other source for this story than Dante's own creative imagination. His period's scant acquaintance with Greek mythology licensed him to develop his theme as he best saw fit, and the result was highly fortunate. Dante begins his story at the moment when Ulysses returns to the sea after his long sojourn with Circe on her island before that stretch of the Italian coast that is known still today as Monte Circeo. We find the background for this story in the way in which Circe was traditionally described. As the daughter of the sun, she was no less florid and sensual than the whole of the natural landscape in the Mediterranean, and we remember that peoples from farther to the north often suspect this climate of leading to attitudes of laxity and passivity. She had used her arts of seduction to enslave Ulysses and had turned his companions into pigs, which is an image of a life of mindless, crude and avid sensuality. But Ulysses was the model of consciousness itself and had proved to be capable of breaking away from such a condition of passivity and regression. We have already referred to some of the ways in which tradition saw Ulysses as similar to Prometheus, even if Prometheus showed a secular and humanist spirit that Ulysses lacked. Dante's Ulysses makes the similarity more conspicuous. Christianity for Dante was the only true religion, and the pagan piety of the king of Ithaca simply had no way of demanding his attention. Dante – who admired his hero to the point of virtually overlooking his sin – promoted Ulysses almost to the status of a hero of enlightened thought who speaks in defense of knowledge as a good in its very own right. Dante's Ulysses is even more noble than Prometheus; his most passionate desire was for knowledge itself, whereas the Titan was interested in the benefits that human beings might derive from it. Dante, moreover, presents us on the one hand with the passivity, animality and unconsciousness that fall to the lot of Circe's slaves, and with Ulysses' will to knowledge on the other, thereby creating an efficacious metaphor of the contrast between nature and culture, between biological life and the life of the mind. This is a typically European distinction; and like the whole of European civilization, Ulysses too was to move towards the west.

The story also perceives that the first of the tasks of this impulse to civilization is to produce stable forms of social organization, of which the family is the most primary; it calls our attention to Ulysses' son, Telemachus, his father, Laertes, and his wife, Penelope. But Ulysses' fidelity to his family is not as powerful as his commitment to his thirst for knowledge. The poet describes this need as an "ardor,"[11] thus alluding to the punishment of this class of sinners who burn in an eternal flame, and as well to the universal perception that the need for knowledge, though apparently in contrast with instinct, is in fact profoundly visceral. In the individuals who experience it most intensely, it can finally take the form of an agitated passion, or of an enantiodromia of conscious will.[12]

To persuade his companions to follow him, Ulysses delivers a brief but impassioned exhortation[13] that proves to be quite sufficient. This is reminiscent of the way in which consciousness can glorify itself and nourish a vicious circle that leads the individual to an overestimation of the power of will, and to an underestimation of the importance of obstacles. As previously observed, such attitudes are typical of the manic syndrome. The "mad flight" quickly pushes the boat into a different and unknown world where even the stars that signal its course are those of the "other" hemisphere. This image reminds us that the orientation of consciousness is archaically associated with geographical orientation – "orientation" is a question of knowing the direction in which the "orient" lies, and people who are confused can be said to have "lost their bearings" – but it also offers an image of the process of the gradual inversion of values (the shift in the stars) of those who push the need for knowledge to an extreme. Exploration ceases to be a means and turns into an end. And the goal, which is cultural enrichment, becomes a means: the already-achieved level of civilization and dominion over nature becomes the source of the instruments – the social cohesion of the group of explorers, the instrumentation of the voyage, the naval expertise, and so forth – required for new conquests.

This enantiodromia also includes a reversal of the feelings of those who set no limit to their frenzy for knowledge. The *némesis* that once turned the pride of *hýbris* into pain and humiliation, here "turns into tears"[14] the joy of the too audacious navigators. The newly discovered land – or their apparent achievement of their goal – is precisely the place from which their punishment comes. The story affirms its moral in the very same terms that bring its drama to a perfect culmination.

So Dante can virtually declare that there is nothing more to say. He simply informs us that the tale has taught him a personal lesson on the subject of self-moderation. Whenever he thinks back to it, he curbs his inventive intelligence somewhat more than he habitually does, in order that it should not press forward without being guided by virtue: *E più lo 'ngegno affreno ch'i non soglio perchè non corra che virtù nol guidi.*[15]

The verses that Dante dedicated to this ancient hero rank as some of his finest, and the terms he employs to reaffirm the law of the punishment of pride are hardly more than formally different from those of the Greeks. But there is also a much more general sense in which the whole of the grandiose construction of Dante's *Inferno* constitutes a re-elaboration, through an infinite range of tones, of the theme of *hýbris* and *némesis*. The punishment reserved for each and every sinner is based in fact on the concept, at the time quite widely diffused, of *contrapasso* or "retribution." This term was used in scholastic philosophy to indicate the conviction that divine judgment would strike the soul of every sinner with a punishment that corresponded to the evil committed in the course of his life. But this principle was largely quantitative, and Dante transformed it into something far more ample. As we have seen with the flame that torments the *consiglieri di frode*, the very quality of the punishment that sinners encounter in Dante's *Inferno* precisely corresponds to the nature of their sins. Divine justice is careful to assure that the specific transgression or act of *hýbris* contained in any particular sin (gluttony, sloth, licentiousness, etc.) unleashes its own specific *némesis*.

In Dante's story of Ulysses, the punishment of pride is far more precise than anything that might have been required by the general concept of retribution, and it can be seen instead to relate to the rules of the ancient Greeks. The rigid moral code of the Middle Ages did not regard the use of intelligence, or new explorations, or desire for knowledge as sins in their own right. The sin of Ulysses lay in the pride of his pursuits, which means that they were not unequivocally a part of a pursuit of the good. Shipwreck awaited Ulysses – as Dante saw it – because he entrusted himself to reason alone and not to divine grace, to which he had no possible access since he was not born a Christian. The inexorability of the punishment gives expression to an abstract and self-consistent theological tenet, which is also to say that here we stand at quite some distance from the anthropomorphic gods of the Greeks who meted out punishment for reasons of divine and passionate jealousy. Yet the depth of Dante's compassion for Ulysses makes it clear that humanism is not far away. Both the poet and his personage can be said to be its prophets. This Ulysses (a secular Ulysses since the only religion for medieval thought was Christianity) does not seem to present himself as a paradigm of the closed polytheistic world; he seems instead to be a prototype that harbingers the excesses of secular thought, which already had begun to develop at the time in which Dante lived. Dante had no other choice than to view it with the diffidence of a man who knew that humanity without the heavens could offer him no satisfaction; but he also admired the intelligence that was preparing to scale them. Dante paid a poetic tribute to intelligence even while always standing – loyal to his times and inspired by what today can assume the appearance of a detached foresightfulness – on the side of God. Ulysses, with all his new aspirations, is the man who has lost divine protection and learned the suffering of knowledge; and in this he resembles Prometheus with his dubious gift, and Adam with his useless apple.

FROM SUMMONING THE SPIRITS TO A PLEA FOR HELP

Master, I am in need of help! I am no longer able to free myself from the forces I have summoned.

(Goethe, *Der Zauberlehrling*)

Inventions, geographical explorations, secular philosophical thought and political revolutions were the characteristic features of the end of the eighteenth and the beginning of the nineteenth centuries in Europe and North America. The more the west turned its attention to things like these, the less it concerned itself with respect for limits. These years were the avant-garde of our present condition, in which the orientation to expansion has grown uninterrupted and spread to every other part of the world. The faith with which the elites entrusted themselves to technology and expansion was already substituting the faith that previous epochs had nurtured for providence and divine grace.

Johann Wolfgang von Goethe was one of the major witnesses of this transition, and here we would like to draw attention to one of his briefer works. *The Sorcerer's Apprentice* (*Der Zauberlehrling*) is full of concern and irony for the ingenuousness with which technology, a new figure of specialized intelligence, can transform means into ends and then propel ends into a state of autonomy. Goethe's poem will help us to proceed to the final part of this book.

The source of Goethe's poem is an episode of Lucian of Samsata's *Philopsuedés*,[16] which is a work that was written for the purpose of ridiculing tales of witchcraft and magic in which the common people of its time all too thoroughly believed. Like the other anecdotes of the *Philopsuedés*, this one too would derive from a collection of popular Hellenistic tales. Like the appearance of Odysseus in Dante's *Inferno*, Goethe's story and its background will help us establish a sense of a geographical and temporal continuity in the development of the notion of limits. Lucian's origins were barbarian, and he lived in the Roman era, but his language and environment were Greek.

The story finds its premise in the existence of a particularly powerful master of magical spells who in Lucian's version fittingly bore the name of Pancrates (he who is capable of everything).

Goethe's verses are a first-person narrative on the part of the apprentice, and their rhythms grow always more anxious and insistent and give way to frequent exclamations. The story begins with a temporary absence of the master, of which the apprentice takes advantage for the apparent purpose of pursuing material comfort; but his true concern is the satisfaction of his ingenuous vanity.

"Finally!" the silly apprentice exclaims, "Now the spirits who serve him will have to obey me as well. I have paid careful attention to his magic formulas."

"Come, oh waves, and let a flood of impetuous water fill my bath."

"And come, you too, old broom, and take up the rag. You are accustomed to serve, and now must listen to me. Rise up on two legs, and may a head grow out from your summit. Now take up the bucket and be quick about it."

"See how she runs to the bank of the river and down to the stream, and quick as a flash returns with water. And now for a second time. See how the water rises in the tub, how every bucket fills itself!"

"Enough, enough. We have already admired your work enough."

"Oh, God in heaven! I realize only now that I have forgotten the magic word!"

"Yes, the word to make the broom return to what it was before. My God, how it runs and carries buckets so easily! But can't you make up your mind to go back to being a broom? Here it is again, pouring out still more water, and a hundred streams overflow me. I can allow this to go no further. Now I shall grab it! But this is witchcraft. My God, I feel myself grow faint."

"You creature of the devil, do you intend to flood the house? Torrents of water now run everywhere. You cursed broom, you refuse to listen. You are nothing but a stick! So return to being what you are!"

"Won't you give it up? I'll grab you, throttle you, smash you in an instant with the axe."

"And now it's back again. Now I'll jump on top of it. You demon, this is your death! Crack! What a blow! I've struck through the very core of it! I have split it in two. And now I can breathe in peace again."

"Oh horror, oh horror! How quickly the pieces stand back up, two servants now ready to run! Oh you powers of the heavens, please come to my aid!"

"See them now as they run. Always more water in the room and pouring down the stairs! What a flood! O master, please hear me. Here he is! Now he is back. Oh master, such a tragedy! I can no longer free myself from the spirits I have summoned!"

The master: "Broom, return to your corner. This is enough. He, oh spirits, who has always been your master now calls you back into his service."

With Dante's Ulysses, we found it difficult to say if he was mostly a sinner or primarily a hero; here one cannot be certain as to whether *The Sorcerer's Apprentice* is mainly a replay of an ancient joke, or an intuition of a drama still to come. That's a very intriguing possibility, and especially if we stop to recall that Goethe was shortly to assume the status of the major poet of the German culture that soon would take up the reins, both for good and for evil, of modern European civilization.

We can read these lines in terms of both of these notions, sometimes thinking that they constitute a remnant of an ancient concept of *némesis*, at other times imagining that they contain a premonition of the excesses of the coming world of technology. The master could represent wisdom, anchored to the sure and steady values of a prudent tradition and a sense of responsibility. The apprentice's attitude, on the other hand, is new, superficial and prone to cede to temptation. As soon as the values of tradition relax their supervision, his *hýbris* takes over and guides events. What allows him to imagine that he can take his master's place is precisely the fact that he has learned his master's means – the magic words – while remaining unacquainted with his ends. His goals, as we immediately see, are banal and egotistic, and utterly out of line with so solemn an action as the summoning of magical forces. The silly boy wants only to take a bath. That may not at the time have been a simple operation, but surely it was not so arduous as to justify recourse to the supernatural.

Water is one of this story's most important symbols. The gap between the banality of a bath and the power of magical forces is precisely the space in which the apprentice's absurd behavior plays itself out, and his behavior anticipates the ways in which we ourselves are prone to act in the modern world. His haughty invocation of the spirits corresponds to our progressively greater appeal to the various technologies (and to a "progressive" conception of life) that magically multiply our capabilities. Yet his desire to do nothing more than to relax in a bathtub, while none the less refusing to conceive of this pleasure as a reward to be earned by the making of an effort, draws our attention to a level of profoundly regressive and impersonal needs to be freed from responsibility. (An ontogenetic and Freudian point of view would see it as a desire to return to the amniotic fluid, inside the belly of the mother; a philogenetic and Jungian point of view would speak of a return to the collective unconscious and to the waters where all of life first found its beginnings.) The conscious intent and the subconscious instinct that guide the action conflict with one another and configure a situation of dangerous self-deception. The former tends towards interventions that increase responsibilities; the goal of the latter is to refuse to assume them.

What about the broom? The apprentice appeals to this humble instrument that lives in daily contact with dirt, and he ennobles its stick by giving it a human form. The two legs added to the broom can be explained by the apprentice's intention to have it do his walking, but there is reason to remain perplexed by the addition of a head, which makes it totally anthropomorphic. Giving it a head would seem to imply a delegation of responsibilities to something that ought to be simply a tool. Does the apprentice not secretly imagine that the machine, after having worked for him, will also be capable of thinking for him? But one also notes that the tool created by the apprentice's magic is not at all sophisticated; it takes on the functions of one of the most archaic forms of human activity: transportation, an activity that establishes nearly no distinction between human beings and animals. The broom supplies an energy that replaces human effort, but it does so, as we see from the following inundation, in purely quantitative terms. It is incapable of any critical control or assessment of the final results of its actions. Gripped by panic, the utilitarian apprentice is incapable of returning to the roots of the magic, or to its original spirit. Without stopping to think that his actions will be irreversible, he then takes recourse to another and even cruder technical intervention. The aggressive banality of the axe has nothing to do with the magical connotations of the broom. This slippage can be interpreted as a regression to a simpler state of mind and serves only to make things worse. The broom is now an "automaton" and the danger implicit in its autonomous capacity for destructive action comes to be doubled when the thing is split in two. The apprentice is a picture of the psychological attitude of a person who daringly confronts a fire, but who does so without a method and therefore spreads the flames. Or it is rather like trying to eliminate a pollutant by throwing it up into the winds.

The master's return, from a psychological point of view, indicates the reappearance of a wisdom that still maintains its ties with tradition, and that still knows how to make use of a tool without allowing it to become autonomous. This wisdom restricts the tool to exclusively performative functions: its range of action is precisely limited, and it then returns to a state of rest. One notes, moreover, that the master does not direct his orders simply to the broom, but to those spirits that lie behind it; he knows that the problem does not lie in the machine – or in any given technology – but in the "spirit," or the depths of unconsciousness, that has called it into life.

Goethe's story was a concise, ironic and well-balanced way of dealing with the risks that are always inherent in unlimited desire; this theme was very dear to him, and he treated it much more extensively in *Faust*.

The apprentice's plea for help[17] can be a forebear of one of the most serious phenomena of the modern age: the cry of the technician who can no longer control the things that they have produced. But it also reminds us of the psychological event that lies at the origins of such a state of technological metastasis: the disappearance of limits and taboos that structured the ancient cultures that were not yet "forced" to pursue a course of growth and progress. The most conspicuous consequence of the lack of such limits is the pressing desire to take immediate possession of things; thoughts concerning the future no longer have the power to limit our actions in the present. We see this quite clearly in the apprentice, who unleashes uncontrollable powers because he is impatient to take a bath. Consumer society by now has accustomed us to the immediate enjoyment of our actions no less than of our purchases. (Some equate consumerism and hedonism, but they do so incorrectly, since unlimited consumption tends to the instantaneous elimination of anxiety, and not to *edoné*, or the experience of pleasure; consumerism finds its nourishment in negative reinforcements; hedonism aims towards something positive.) With the exception of money and a few investment commodities, the enjoyment of everything takes place within an ever more immediate present. When my grandfather wanted to capture an image of a landscape or a person who was dear to him, he engaged a painter. Time was required to complete the work, but the painting then changelessly lived in his home and was passed down to his heirs. My father owned a camera, which he always used with great respect. My own generation buys Japanese cameras, constantly replacing them with newer and more sophisticated models, and using them with little skill. My son is most comfortable with polaroid cameras that instantly develop and print an image; the image appears without leaving one time to dwell on what it was, or to imagine what it is going to look like; there is not even the inconvenience (or the tiny adventure) of having to return to the photo shop. And before being grown, he will probably feel at home with the new throw-away cameras; they go straight into the trash as soon as their film is used, in the name of our freedom from having to reload them. It grows ever more difficult to distinguish the consumption of the means that allows us to obtain an image from the consumption of the image itself. They tend to coalesce into an ever more general and single experience, which also takes place in ever briefer spans of time and with always greater ease. But we have to be aware that this shortening of temporal horizons satisfies regressive needs; and as we drug ourselves on technology, it becomes ever more typical of all of our attitudes.[18] The arts of seduction demand an immediate sexual pay-off; there is a tendency to abolish courtship, which is the richest and most distinctive element of human sexuality, even if it also exists among the animals. In much the same way, the learning of foreign languages has ceased to be a part of a gradual and complex process of cultural growth; there is an appointment this very afternoon for a deal with a group of foreign businessmen.

The lack of importance afforded to things that lie outside the immediate present appears at first glance to be simply frivolous, rather than destructive. But in fact it paves the road towards a head-on collision with the very nature of the world created by technological development. Our ability to assume responsibility tends to restrict itself to the immediate present; but our objective responsibilities are involved with a scale of ever vaster amounts of time. We are the first generation to be able to destroy its neighbors in an instant; and we can also cripple all future generations by profoundly altering the conditions in which they will have to live.

In spite of all its self-declared interest in peace, disarmament and the respect for nature, our civilization is a kind of global time-bomb – an essentially chemical time-bomb. Just how big a bomb is something we do not yet know, but something can surely be deduced from the millions of people who already die every year from cancers that primarily derive from alterations of the environment. The long-term destructiveness of our way of life is an absolute historical novelty that finds us unprepared. We are incapable of containing it, technologically or politically, or above all psychologically. And our ever-increasing influence on the lives that other human beings will have to live tomorrow is not the only cause for concern; this phenomenon, after all, goes perversely hand in hand with an ever-decreasing capacity even to concern ourselves with future events, since they lie outside the range of immediate anxiety or immediate enjoyment. Every notion of transcendence has been thoroughly undermined by our passion for immediate consumption. Our thought contains no space for faith, hope and charity, since they can only come to manifestation in the course of the passage of time, and we witness the crumbling not only of the postulates of Christianity, but also of Marxism's religious invitation to self-transcendence and sacrifice in the name of the generations of the future.

Part IV

NEMESIS RETURNS

Part IV

NEMESIS RETURNS

11

THE SITE OF THE CRISIS

THE PRESENT-DAY FORM OF THE MYTH OF LIMITS

New capacities for the self-regulation of human systems have to be developed since a number of automatic internal mechanisms have ceased to function.
(A. Peccei, President of the Club of Rome, *Cento pagine per l'avvenire*)

The Club of Rome had no intention of concerning itself with myths. It was founded in the 1960s by a group of experts from all the various branches of science and from all the corners of the earth, and their goal was to table a discussion on the state of the civilization of the world in the years to come. The Club subsequently commissioned the Massachusetts Institute of Technology to prepare a series of reports on the possible developments, in quantitative terms, that the planet Earth might undergo (population, raw materials, pollution, etc.). These reports were then to be synthesized into a series of reflections, in qualitative terms, that could capture the interest of the general public. This was the very first attempt to approach such problems on the basis of a systematic series of studies that considered the whole of the planet, and we can look at the collaborative efforts of MIT and the Club of Rome as an emblem of the ways in which present-day thinking has attempted to react to the global scale of the *hýbris* of the modern world.

The first volume of studies, *The Limits to Growth*, opened by declaring that the purposes of the Club of Rome

are to foster understanding of the varied but interdependent components – economic, political, natural, and social – that make up the global system in which we all live; to bring that new understanding to the attention of policy-makers and the public worldwide; and in this way to promote new policy initiatives and action.[1]

Various hypotheses were examined, and none of the forecasts was reassuring. The limits to be reached by humanity's various forms of

159

growth (technological, demographic, and so forth) appeared to be perilously close, as well as deeply intertwined the one with the other. (Growth of production goes hand in hand with a more rapid depletion of raw materials; growth of population brings greater pollution in its wake, etc.)

All the various data pointed to a single conclusion: uninterrupted expansion was shaping the terms of its own limits. Growth is destined to come to a halt: the *hýbris* of progress will encounter a *némesis* of deterioration.

The publications of the Club of Rome continued to appear, and they in fact excited discussion. It was observed, moreover, in more recent years[2] that the ecological system of the planet had in fact begun to approach a number of the breaking points that this group of publications hypothesized, and that virtually none of the general remedies suggested have been put into practice. But it also began to be clear that the planet had reacted with a level of flexibility that the model furnished by the Club of Rome had not foreseen. Even in the absence of a system of global organization, the planet had mobilized a series of compensatory reactions to its crisis, and we had not even been aware of the process or of having in any way determined it.

The model offered by MIT and the Club of Rome could never have predicted such a thing. It included no form of psychology. The very first report had attempted to circumvent the possible criticism of its lack of flexibility, and of the fact that it gave so little consideration to the human factor.[3] Since its premises were strictly "scientific," the model was to offer predictions and establish objective parameters, and the thorn of human afterthought was intentionally extracted from the huge and anguished body of civilization. Just as Socratic thought rejected mythology and appealed to the model of medicine, science sees its role in drawing conclusions from regular and universal causes that remain stable throughout time.

The human factor makes everything less predictable, since the human being is more than a biochemical sum of causes and effects. More than anything else, the human being is a continuous psychological process that constantly creates aspirations. The human factor includes a series of passions that modify all other factors by reimposing subjective order on the world of objectivity. Rather than in explanations, the soul finds its nourishment in narratives. The options with which it casts its lot are also new "myths" of history, or new formulations of its dominant themes. The soul's return into the ecological system of the planet marks a re-appearance of myth, dressed in the tatters of the technological opulence of the modern world.

If various sectors of the overall picture of the world have not collapsed at the predicted rate, this fact cannot be attributed to any general and rational human intervention. It results instead from a series of reciprocally reinforcing but individually unmeasurable initiatives that the renewal of a dormant narrative has prodded into life. This constructive turn of events has little to do with any response to the scientific validity of the reports of MIT and the Club of Rome; it counts instead as a diffuse reaction to their unconscious renarration of the myth of *némesis* – a *némesis* that now stands ready to punish the technological *hýbris* that daily parades before our eyes in the media of mass communication.

We began this book by suggesting that the literature on the limits of our planet has more than one aspect. Its most immediate level of content is technical and scientific, but its more hidden and lasting dimension is of a mythological nature. In the case of the reports of MIT and the Club of Rome, the scientific level has had little effect on those to whom it was directed; the sorts of remedies they suggested have largely been ignored. The second level of the message has had greater effect, even if it is difficult to measure it. The effects of messages vehicled though myth are always difficult to measure. But an emotion has none the less coursed through our souls, weighing them down with feelings of guilt for our involvement in a civilization of *hýbris*. The reports of the Club of Rome and all the technical language that ranks by now as the dominant form of communication can be seen to have opened a space for the appearance of a narrative of punishment: a negative western epic.

If our actions are shaped by a myth, we cannot be said to be influenced only by the conscious parts of it. So if the myth of growth is our universal secular faith, our actions are also influenced by the idea of punishment that functions as its complementary unconscious myth. This archaic threat mobilizes the soul as it faces the planetary crisis.

Moving in directions quite similar to those of the Club of Rome, other studies too have described the growth of industrial civilization as perverse or paradoxical or catastrophic, or as tending to implode into the opposite of all its established goals.

Ivan Illich has turned his attention to the expansion of schooling as a source of ignorance, to the burgeoning of our means of transportation as a cause for slower travel, to the advances of medicine as responsible for damaging our health.[4] Ranging out into anthropology, Illich also suggests that these deformations correspond to a model of *hýbris–némesis*. But his analysis is essentially sociological, and he makes use of this mythic model as a purely descriptive image that furthers an objective study of the degeneration of the planet; he does not treat myth as a movement on the part of the unconscious, or as a force that has the power to impose its will on the thinking of science and technology.

The scientific attitude gives precision to human knowledge, but it also has a way of imperceptibly cutting us off from what we know. Once disentangled from their roots in myth and purified of mythic thinking, astrology turned into astronomy, and alchemy into chemistry. This was all to the benefit of objective knowledge; but in addition to suppressing myth, such knowledge also did away with the psychological glue that holds the whole of human experience together. Astrology was a mixture of ingenuous astronomy and psychology, just as alchemy was a mixture of primitive chemistry and psychology. Having rid themselves of the real human being – the human being who is more than biochemical fact – the various sciences progressed at dizzying speeds. But they established themselves as purely scientific endeavor, and the final figure of the body of knowledge that derives from them can prove to be quite fragile. These sciences exist without the benefit of any principle that draws them together. They have lost the general code that makes them a part of human experience. Their explanations become ever less similar to narrative. In order to be convincing, or to draw us into its precincts, a story has to have some sort of mythic background that endows it with depth and sonority. Expositions of simple fact pour into our interior as though inertly, and they scatter in every direction like a jet of water that has no bed in which to flow, or like a sound that has no sounding box in which to resonate. To perceive the mythic background of a story is to feel that the narrative is something we already know, but have no idea as to when and how we learned it. The significant qualities of any such story seem to belong to the sphere of memory, which is why children will ask again and again to be told about things they already know, so as to recognize their emotions and consolidate their identity. Properly told stories become a part of the realm of inner truth. Rationally demonstrated "truths," on the other hand, remain exterior. Though fully absorbed at the conscious level and recognized as incontrovertible, they lack interior resonance and offer no orientation for feelings that are anchored in the personality. They are roads that the soul cannot travel when it wants to go back home, and they make no real contribution to the struggle against anxiety, or to the attempt to restore a sense of meaning to the fact that we exist. When we talk about the truths of science, we are talking quite frequently about things that make no difference to us, about things that cannot be shaped into aspects of a narrative. Truth as found in myth is something entirely different and restores us to dreams that we imagined ourselves to have lost. Rather than narrate, science only "in-forms." (We ourselves are what it forms, shapes and constructs, and without being allowed to participate in the process.) And science is alien to wisdom since it produces no real knowledge; its knowledge boils down to information.

Depth psychology does not practice the scientific method, but it is well aware of these short-comings.

Freud noted that "the gods of a superseded period of civilization turn into demons."[5] Jung remarked that "the gods have become diseases."[6] Hillman has added that "the repressed Gods return as the archetypal core of the symptom complexes."[7]

In the psychology of the maladies of the modern age, mythic forces no longer descend from the heavens, and instead rise up from the depths, which is the home of what we repress. Since myth is full of pain, it elects to reside in our new pathologies, where it once again recounts itself and returns to the story of its ancient pursuit of something that will heal it. It speaks of our current ills by appealing to truths to which we have lost all conscious access, and it thus repopulates the scene with gods, demons and heroes. The myth of Nemesis has discovered such a ploy and now re-appears in the narratives that study the global crisis; Nemesis assumes the form of the pathological limit of the growth of western civilization.

We face an apparent paradox. On the one hand, the disenchantment and secularization of the world, the dymythicization and denarration of scientific studies, have made a fundamental contribution to the enlargement of our body of knowledge.[8] Depth psychology, on the other hand – depth psychology is likewise an art for the pursuit of knowledge, and likewise one of the forms of modern culture that the world now fully accepts – studies psychopathology by looking back through the genealogy of myth and by entering into dialog with its personages. Depth psychology can never really share the methodology of the natural sciences, since to do so would shatter the link it has to have with the living subject who is always its protagonist. But it can point out the archetypes that condition the course of scientific research, and it can propose to read its findings in the light of the life of the human emotions: it can attempt to recognize the ways in which the findings of science correspond to the expectations of myth. Such a mode of investigation moves consciously back and forth through the distances that separate science from myth, and it thus presses myth into service as an instrument of knowledge.

From the psychological point of view, the "correctness" of the essays that study global limits lies in something more than their presentation of empirically verified fact; they can be thought to be most to the point when they find themselves in the grip of tremendous truths – technology's capacities for destruction, which are no less ferocious than the ancient gods – and find their way to the mythic structures that lie at the base of the crisis. To follow such a course is to mobilize the facts to which the psyche reacts; it reveals the symbols that the psyche recognizes, the symbols that the psyche pursues in all of its movements.

Elements of the myth of punished pride also appear in our circuit of mass communication. They can be found in popular literature, no less than in films. Unconsciously returning to the widespread self-flagellation of the end of the first millennium, the general public has recently consumed a vast production of "catastrophes" where technological *hýbris* is punished by a special *némesis* of its own creation.

The fact that this material is largely *Kitsch* makes no real difference; surely we are not to ignore its value as a signal of the general public's deep and morbid need for self-punishment. Psychology has little to do with aesthetic judgments since its task is to search out underlying evils: the horrid taste shown by pornography does not deny its pertinence to the problems of sexuality, and indeed reveals the disturbing depths in which such problems are rooted.

The crude and self-punitive superstitions of the recent genre of "catastrophes" give evidence of underlying drives that have hardly been able to rise beyond the threshold of purely physiological expression. The problem here, as with every instinct, is not so much to repress it as to allow it to grow less crude and to reach a more conscious and responsible level of expression.

There is an interesting parallel between these modern flarings of irrationality and the popular superstitions that surfaced in Greece after the upheavals of the fifth century: as the culture of the elites grows ever more rational, the culture of the masses can slip into a superstitious regression that takes a very dim view of progress. Greece experienced the strengthening of the cult of Nemesis; today we experience its unconscious counterpart in a self-punitive catastrophe-ism, and as well in a panacean naturalism that deifies the earth as a great primordial Mother; her mythic connections with the ancient goddess Nemesis by now are more than clear to us.

THE DIMENSIONS OF THE GLOBE

> Every form of life raises a claim to its right to life . . . The non-existent, on the other hand, raises no such claim, and therefore cannot even suffer a violation of its rights . . . But our search for an ethic has a great deal to do with precisely the sphere of the non-existent.
>
> (H. Jonas, *Das Prinzip Verantwortung*)

The body of essays that have undertaken the study of global limits is far from unsubstantiated, but it remains one-sided. Sooner or later, it will have to abandon its habitual point of view and look at things from a greater distance. Distancing,[9] even at the cost of a loss of detail, will increase its angle of observation and reveal a field that takes in the views of other specialists who have turned their attention to the same theme.

The global crisis requires an enlargement of both spatial and temporal perspectives. As previously suggested, a proper investigation of the problem of limits should turn less attention to the ideological superstructures presented by any particular narrative than to the substructures that call the narrative voice to life. Such substructures lie very deep and pay no attention to the spirit of the times; they are usually grasped only by following generations. We have to ask ourselves if the ancient notion of divine jealousy now has a meaning for us. We have to find another point of view from which to look at the process of infinite technological growth and the way it shatters the environment; we can dispense with the immediate vantage points of technicians or politicians and instead look out at ourselves through the distant eyes of Polycrates as he threw his ring into the sea. We have to retrace the genesis of a culture that recognizes (*re-cognoscere*: to know again) even today the very same taboos as Herodotus, but that speaks a different language (the language of science), makes use of different means (the means of technology) and rejects the reproduction of the immobility of myth, desiring instead to fathom the transformations of the past and to imagine those of the future.

The territory that concerns us extends in all of these directions; in addition to studies of the past, such as those that till now we have attempted to present, it also requires a reflection on tomorrow: precisely the kind of reflection from which the sorcerer's apprentices flee.

Spatial barriers, which are fairly easy to overcome, have been chipped away by technology: first by our means of transportation, which have made travel very fast, and then by our means of communication, which have made travel almost superfluous, now that our voices, images and written words can instantly flash from continent to continent. We live in fact in what has been described as a "global village."

But we are less aware of the ways – after having shattered the barriers of geography – in which we begin as well to pass through the barriers of future history, which is to speak of the barriers of time. We have already begun to colonize the future. Perhaps this rapid unification of time is something we refuse to notice, since it is even more menacing than our victory over space.

Up until the day before yesterday, our responsibilities remained with our neighborhoods: our moral tasks were close at hand, easy to understand and still quite largely described by the Gospels. But now, quite suddenly, our responsibilities have become infinitely more complex; and in order to understand them we have to entrust ourselves, essentially, to precisely those technologies that we see as having invaded the globe and plunged it into crisis.

Dumping one's trash into another epoch is not a peculiar trait of our times. Until only a few decades ago, such behavior was in some ways justified. Civilizations made their options, but all of their options remained reversible. Nature could be subjected to violent human interventions, but human beings still had the chance to give things a second thought, since the homeostatic forces of nature were in any case sure to restore the world to a state quite similar to what it had been before. Entire countries of Europe have been deforested; but in the past such forests might have been allowed to regrow in only a handful of years. Our parents were capable of wounding or murdering their neighbors, but they did not threaten to compromise the health and the lives of their still unborn descendants or to contaminate their future habitat. In the course of the last century, nature's principles of homeostatic self-regulation succumbed to technology. Technology ushered us into an era of options that have direct repercussions on generations yet to come. We constantly talk about democracy and the extension of various entitlements, but these men, women and children of the future will never have had the chance to contribute to basic decisions of which they none the less will bear the weight. We discover the limits of democracy when we enter the dimension of time. Democracy possesses no time machine that allows it today to query the inhabitants of the future that our present technologies already exploit.

Thinking that looks beyond technology and turns its attention to the future of the various forms of life regards the suppression of a human culture or of an animal or vegetable species as a crime against the integrity of the planet.[10] And any such crime is felt to be qualitatively different – much more than a question of numbers – from the murder of an individual. No matter how painful, the loss of an individual mends and recedes in a different way and is somehow limited in time. The destruction of a species or of a human culture seems to be a graver crime than the sum of the individual crimes of which it consists, since what dies is a whole living system, and the ways in which it interacted with everything around it can never again be reconstructed. Such orders of responsibility transform the entirety of our planetary environment into a global village, seeing it also as having a temporal dimension in which what we do today is immediately operative in the future as well. The global village is held together by an order of responsibility that we cannot keep whole without seeing that it also cuts through time. The unity of the global village is established more by ethics than by communication.

Some of the ways in which moral problems stretch the edges of time were already known to the Greeks. The tragedies pressed back the confines of the epochs they traversed. The events of the drama were set into motion by *hýbris*, and *némesis* sealed their outcome. The inevitable was clearly foreseen, charged with meaning, and simultaneously absurd: a relief, as the manifestation of justice; a pit of desperation, as the ritualized proof of its iniquity.

The morality of the tragedies was ambiguous, but convincing and inescapable. An unchosen evil was followed by a greater evil, which again allowed no subsequent choices. The passion of an instant was a source of nearly infinite malediction that droned through the generations. Eternity hung balanced against a moment, and the whole life of an unknowing child made up for an incautious action on the part of a distant parent.

We look today at the snares in which our growth is so entangled. Why, we ask, is technology so poisonous? What have we done to resuscitate the absurd?

166

In the Greek tragedies, questions on the cause of pain were answered by the chorus. Rather than heal the wounded, these voices washed their sores, making their bodies once again fragile and beautiful. Today there is no reply. There are many choral voices; but while making us listen to everything else, they speak no wisdom. The bodies of the wounded lie out of reach, hidden beneath the trappings of technology.

Links of blood relationship once chained the passionate crime of Atreus to Orestes' back. That chain was a suffering, but also a source of certainty; a weight, but still an identity; an identity made out of memory, and out of respect for a man whose suffering is the name he bears. Today we hammer nails into a nameless future. As years go by, some child will feel them rust in their body, but why and by whom they was wounded are things they will never know.

For thousands of years we have shaped our identity on the basis of a cult of our ancestors, giving meaning to our very existence by rooting it in a sequence of figures that we experience as having been necessary. These are the figures that created us. We ourselves are future ancestors; but for the first time in history we run the risk of possibly being remembered as negative and destructive figures: not as individuals, but as a whole generation. The material devastation that we leave behind us is likely to be accompanied by an unforeseeable but none the less tremendous level of psychological damage. Having proclaimed the dogma of endless growth and taken it as authorization to aspire to immortality, it is as though we want to impose our presence on our descendants, forcing them to remember us. But it seems that we can manage to elude their forgetfulness only by turning into monsters, since the disappearance of myth has also extinguished the race of heroes, as well as all transcendent forms of the cult of founding fathers.

MYTH AND TIME

And here we now find the result of that Socraticism that undertook the destruction of myth.
(Nietzsche, *Die Geburt der Tragödie*)

The global crisis has inserted itself by now into private spaces that western societies had long since deeded to the individual. Sexuality finds itself linked to overpopulation; acquiring, using and disposing of goods raises questions of pollution and respect for resources. Democracy in the life of the common people seems also to include a sharing of the power of destruction. Unlike the people of the past, they can exercise a direct influence on the ruin of the planet. The modern age thought of the redistribution of power as a positive contribution to the life of society, but the process now comes to completion in negative terms that work to our harm. And at the very same time that private life comes to be saddled with such a wholly new level of responsibility, the politicians of the modern secular world are discovering their inability to impede the dissipation of that freer mode of life that modernization had seemed with such great pains and effort to have set on its course.

Let's look at a simple example. The campaigns against overpopulation are technically fairly simple, and they often produce rapid results – rapid but limited. The birth rate sinks and then grows stable at a somewhat lower level, but still not as low as desired. It is as though the techniques for birth control rapidly reach those persons who already wanted to limit the size of their families, but who had lacked the necessary information; the problem would seem to lie in the existence of another group of people whose traditional belief in the benefits of a large family remains unchanged and unshaken. We see once again that technical innovations are relatively simple, whereas cultural and psychological changes are immensely more difficult to enact. On the one hand we find the precept "Be ye fruitful, and multiply"; its opposite suggests that "the rational choice is to have at most two children." But these two opposing notions do not stand on an equal footing, which means that the choices they represent are not truly alternative to one another. The voice that discourages conception, offering techniques to avoid it and explaining its undesirability, gives nothing more than rational, specialized information. Rather than tell us what we ought to do, it only tells us what we ought to avoid. The exhortation to "be fruitful and multiply" is something quite different. It offers no information and is simply a commandment. It issues an order and creates a meaning for the living of a life; it cannot be separated from the overall world view in which it inscribes itself. It finds its source in myth, and it speaks with the voice of prophecy.

Politicians who attempt to address the problems of the global crisis quickly discover a defect in all their available tools. Their tools have nothing to do with any dimension of the sacred, and their interventions are accordingly limited. They cannot rely on faith and thereby command obedience; and the articles of faith that counter their efforts cannot be deflected simply by contradicting them. The faithful can only be converted. These politicians are likewise unable to step beyond time and currently given circumstance. That again is something that faith can do and that reason cannot. Religion can show proof of its generosity by accepting history; but it can likewise do without it, since it is not a product of history nor strictly dependent on historical events. A religious view of the world embraces the whole of time, preserving the past as a part of the present since it elevates the past to liturgy and myth; and its future commitments are likewise clear in the present, since the truths transmitted by prophecy require no verification.

Any public personality who attempts to deal with the problems of global ecology becomes involved in transmitting a message that talks about the ultimate meaning of our actions, and the nature of any such message is potentially religious, even if the spokesperson has nothing to do with any religious institution. But secular knowledge remains unconcerned with the soul. And it likewise knows no involvement with a dimension of time that unifies the past, the present and the future. The timeless images and absolute emotions of myth are replaced by the constantly changing facts and figures of the world of information. Conversely, prophecy stimulates an openness to the future but finds no ear among those whose lives are totally lived in the present. The wane of Christianity and the collapse of revolutionary promises have shortened the range of the gaze that once looked out towards the future as a place of redemption. The forms of security offered by the state attenuate our worries about our future and our children. Objects grow ever more functional and their life-span grows ever more brief, so it ceases to be possible to think of them as media of our inorganic survival, much as our children can represent our biological survival. The achievement of a level of relative material well-being has gone hand in hand with a decline in our ability to draw up projects that project us into the future. And the ability to project ourselves into the future is not only a spiritual faculty; it also works in the service of the creation of stable improvements in our material lives, and it ranks in any case as one of the fundamental qualities that distinguish humans from animals. Animals enjoy the present and can also learn from the past, but they lack the faculties of abstraction that allow us to shape an image of what we will be in the future. Our world seems to have inherited the very worst forms of the Greeks' lack of foresight. Few follow in the footsteps of the wise inhabitants of the island of Melos. Most of us offer a new lease on life to the arrogance of the Athenians who denigrated the people of Melos by remarking "you are the only men who regard future events as more certain than what lies before your eyes."[11]

POLITICAL PSYCHOLOGY

It is no longer our common goal to flee from *phthónos*.
(Euripides, *Iphigenia in Aulis*)

In the field of psychodynamics, every investigation, just like every therapy, can generate a counter-transfer. The author can become emotion-ally involved with theit theme and psychologically identify with it. While writing this text, I have often experienced a feeling of impotence that I cannot entirely attribute to the complexity of the problems of the outside world. I have also rediscovered an internal limit of my own. The obstacle was something more than any general attack of writer's block and presented itself as an interior and still quite diffuse expression of precisely

169

the tabu to which I hoped to give a written formulation. I have begun to think that my encounter with such a difficulty may even have something to do with the reasons for depth psychology's lack of participation in the studies of the limits of our planet. All of us find it clear that revising the notion of unlimited growth and replacing it with a concept of limits is of at least as much concern to psychologists as to any other group of specialists. But the psychologist who confronts this theme is required, here once again, to deploy a more personal level of involvement. So, the psychologist is more vulnerable and exposed, and subject to a higher level of disorientation and discouragement. If we consider the viscosity and elusiveness of the dynamics of the personal psyche, it can hardly be surprising for psychologists to refuse from the very start to confront the psychic dynamics of a collective of such vast dimensions.

A similar point of view has been indirectly expressed by the author of one of the very few psychological studies of the problem of limits that do in fact exist:

> We analysts discovered a frightening level of ingenuity in the suggestions these scientists have offered for the purpose of effecting the transformation not of individuals – which we already know to be a highly difficult affair – but indeed of the whole of humanity. Their suggestions have ranged, on the one hand, from the control of the sphere of social life by means of rationally chosen objectives and insistent appeals to reason, and, on the other, to the reproposal of religious visions of the world and to appeals to the churches.[12]

Almost all innovational visions have encountered such difficulties and learned some sort of lesson from them. The rational explanation of the need for a change arouses very little enthusiasm, and even among those who most stand to benefit from it. But what makes it so difficult to sensitize the public to the planetary crisis is more than a question of the chronic conservatism of the collective psyche. Much of the problem resides in the difficulty of pointing out an adversary, and the indication of an adversary is always essential to spurring the passions of minds that think in exclusively secular terms. How can people be mobilized for a struggle against an unspecifiable enemy?

An habitual laziness therefore induces our politicians to avoid a global or synergetic view of the problems of the planet. They overlook the ways in which these problems interlink and thus shatter them into fragments that they then necessarily approach as expressions of all the old-style conflicts between interests, nations and classes.

In this way, the expulsion of the negative dynamics of the psyche and their consequent attribution to an adversary – what Jung describes as the projection of the "shadow"[13] from out of the interior of the individual subject and onto an external object – can coexist with the production and

170

accumulation of military and economic arms and with all the other manifestations of a faith in unlimited growth, or at least until we pass a certain threshold where our very own actions begin to produce an immediately perceptible "negative residue." Such an obviously evil side effect, the unmistakable mistake, can no longer be outflanked, concealed or projected off in the direction of our neighbors or the future. It can no longer be attributed to others, and it ceases to be something that will only later be visible through *a posteriori* historical analysis; it comes to be perceived as deriving directly from our own behavior. When the devastation of nature is already far advanced, every new industry can be seen to produce a quantity of pollution that the environment can neither hide nor absorb; it stands out immediately as a harmful residue. We can foresee that a nuclear war that totally destroyed the enemy would result in a level of radioactive poisoning that would also ravage the homes of the victors. And so forth. We reach a point where we find ourselves forced to understand that we are threatened by our own behavior, and not only by the behavior of others.

To lead ordinary citizens to an act of self-criticism once required the use of difficult and highly specialized tools of analysis, but such times belong now to the past. Traditional expansionist politics today throws off a negative residue that constitutes an immediate manifestation of the shadow of the whole of our society, and this residue offers access to a psychological attitude that no longer sees the the enemy as an adversary that stands before us, but as a presence inside us. Politics here runs aground if it attempts to continue to think in exclusively political terms.

It becomes ever more difficult to point out social groups or nations of which the interests are incontrovertibly opposed to one another. It likewise seems impossible to attribute specific bodies with specific responsibilities for the cause of specific damages. So our task has less to do with viewing the system of our civilization as a patient to be cured – a point of view that would give us the job of continuing *ad infinitum* to perfect it – than with seeing humanity itself as a crazed cultural machine that has begun to run amok: we now promote the metastasis of a culture that has long since lost all equilibrium with the minimum quantity of nature in which it has to be housed.

"Nature" and "culture" are now perhaps the only terms that can inherit the confrontations that once saw nations or social classes in conflict with one another. The treatment of the ills contained in this contraposition most certainly involves political measures, but it calls above all for a re-habilitation of the psychic life of the individual. The imbalance of nature and culture comes unmistakably to manifestation not only in an infantile dependency on the products of technology and in an overestimation of their worth, but also, more subtly, in the arrogance of an overextended intellect and in the individual's exile from a forgotten body.

The crisis in which we are currently entrapped is a question of excessive growth and development (culture) on the one hand, and of the depletion of resources (nature) on the other, and its reflection in the life of the individual is to be found first of all in the way we give overweening precedence to cultural as opposed to physiological needs. The basic or in-born drives are constantly in conflict with the drives that result from education. It is only secondarily, and with much greater difficulty, through numerous abstractions and a variety of oversimplifications, that we can identify the poles of nature and culture with particular political systems. All of them, in fact, promote forms of exterior violence against the environment as well as an interior perversion of the natural person.

It is clear that all of the principle confrontations created by human beings can be seen as conflicts *between* individuals, and also as conflicts *within* individuals. Even conflicts between classes and nations can be seen to correspond to interior clashes of various elements of the psyche. The conflict between the bourgeoisie and the proletariat might find a parallel, with a bit of simplification, in the contrast between the need for order and the impulse to vitalism, or between our aspirations for quality and quantity. But questions such as these are quite difficult to see in terms of psychological introjections; the arguments seem fairly abstract and only make sense to people with a specialized use for such language. The contrast between nature and culture, on the other hand, can be much more easily grasped as existing both in organized society and in the interior of the individual.

Having been banished from the circumambient environment, nature takes ever greater refuge in the interior of the individual, where it assumes the form of a new and higher evaluation of the body. Culture has come to dominate the body, but has not finally and eternally denatured it. The body is felt to contain a series of interior "nature reserves," and without them we would have no access to or useful enjoyment of the external wilderness parks that nature has created but which culture has decreed and fenced off. The theories of the psychological disciplines – which were born from the need to treat the psyche that organicistic medicine ignored – in fact now lend renewed attention to corporeal experience, and physical interventions have been introduced into the praxis of psychotherapy. The primarily western distinction between the mind and the body[14] translates into a way of life that finds its expression not only in the integral, definite and finite form of the human being, but also in the infinite, abstract and potentially alienating form of the world of concepts.

Such general dualisms always go through phases of both inter- and intrapersonal historical development. Their terms coexist with one another, and the decision to turn more to the one than to the other comes to be dictated by the particular circumstances in which history places us.

Until the time when the opposition grows irreversible on a planetary scale – as for example with a total derangement of the balance between humanity and nature – an underestimation of the importance of psychological and intrapersonal terms is quite likely to remain the case, since the pertinence of the interpersonal terms of sociological thinking is much more immediate and visible.

Psychology and politics have grown ever more specialized and now present themselves as two radically separate disciplines; but we live under circumstances that have made that separation untenable. So the time may have come for the development of a discipline of political psychology; and that is surely a difficult thing to create, if only for the reason that the respectively introverted and extroverted minds that work in psychology and politics are of radically different kinds, in terms of initial temperament no less than of subsequent education. But such a coupling is none the less necessary, since traditional politics – which ignores introspection and thus avoids all thought of the kinds of guilt it bears – is blasted by a mode of unilateral thinking that is rife with notions of persecution. It seems hardly less irrational and obsolete than a modern-day return to the practice of ostracism. The traditional division of the planet into opposing camps was based in fact on attitudes of aggression and paranoid interpretation (which describes a neo-ostracism). And to move beyond the stage in which the limits of the globe have called a halt to expansionistic politics will first of all require a psychological transformation, inclusive of moments of discouragement and depression. These in fact are the visible signs of a confrontation with a guilt that individuals come to recognize as their own. But precisely the appearance of this attitude of introversion (not only of rational self-criticism) should enable us to transfigure the gravity of external circumstances into a psychological resource that prompts the spontaneous rejection of expansion.[15]

The political options of the global *pólis* also demand, now perhaps for the very first time, the payment of a clear psychological price that belongs to the sphere of interior economics and cannot be charged to others. The problem of the limits of growth assumes its truest guise and presents itself as a limitation of human expectations, which means that it poses an essentially psychological question. This *cul-de-sac*, though apparently created by the age of modern technology, gives the Greeks a new pertinence. The Greeks were more tempted than any other people by the notion of infinity, and that was precisely why they afforded limits the status of a faith and inscribed it onto the single table of their law.

12

ROUTES TOWARDS RECONSTRUCTION

IDEATIVE COURAGE

This ambitious passion was what the Greeks called *hýbris*, and it was from Greece that Europe inherited it (in spite of Christianity, which in a certain sense made it even made more potent). This inheritance has the quality of a vice that contrasts with all of Europe's virtues, and she has always been severely punished for it.

(B. Snell, *Die Entdeckung des Geistes*)

Till now we have regarded the disappearance of limits as the source of a psychic void. But there are other possible points of view. It can also be seen as the appearance of something new. To convince ourselves that the disregard of limits can only be an act of arrogance is to court or accept an enantiodromia of modern attitudes, and this is a trap we should be careful to avoid. To think of the disappearance of limits as the inauguration of something new does not turn *hýbris* from an evil into a good, but it opens the road to an understanding of its cumulative contribution to the history of the west. While growing ever less concerned with traditional castigations, the west has experienced *hýbris* as a largely constructive impulse.

Expansive thinking often seems to lie at the roots of the problems of the modern world, but it is also the source of our ability to see it in constantly changing lights. Our constant recourse to the ideative optimism of expansive thinking is what gives us the power to revise our attitudes, values and actions. Pre-Socratic melancholy, of which Nietzsche so profoundly lamented the loss, could offer us no such agility; its structure was determined by the modes of aesthetic contemplation and not by premises required for action. Rather than unfold the potential of thought, it submitted it to rigid taboos.

Ideative courage as we know it in the western world made its first appearance in fifth-century Greece and then followed an unbroken course of development that issues into the modern age. Its extremes have been known to collapse into massive epidemics of greed, but the conceptual

174

ability that enables the west to project itself into infinite forms and extensions of itself is none the less its greatest strength.

The ability to deal with abstract concepts – which, unlike notions that relate to specific images or emotions, can be linked by reasoning into ever more ample configurations – has extremely concrete consequences. The general idea of the hunting implement, as something detached from the hunter's particular need to procure his own food and disconnected from his own particular memories, is the necessary premise that enables such a hunter to dedicate a part of his time to producing arms that can be usefully exchanged. No such thing as the artisan's workshop could have been conceived without such premises, even aside from the question of mass production. In tandem with the invention of the monetary unit, which again is abstract and conventional, the notion of the economic enterprise as an independent entity with autonomous possibilities of development opened the road to the accumulation of a new kind of wealth. Wealth needed no longer to express itself in terms of necessarily finite quantities of land, herds and bars of gold, and entrepreneurs could turn their ambitions to its endless multiplication. Similar functions were served by the abstract notions of dominion for the military captain, of lands discovered and explored for the navigator, or of redeemed souls for the missionary who followed them. Intentions could be quantified without making reference to their visible results, and greed could expand accordingly.

Such activities found a definition as autonomous entities that stand apart from the persons who create them. Even without their founders, they can and must continue to thrive. The concepts of education, as distinct from the image of the person to be instructed, and of knowledge, as separate from any particular matter to be taught, had to be developed before science, philosophy and studies of any and all other kinds could take on the status of treasures in their own right, worthy of a life of their own and not necessarily incarnated in single individuals. Culture and civilization would otherwise amount to precarious and unstable islands, entirely circumscribed by the lives of those who possess them; they could be neither cumulative nor structurally continuous since they would die with the persons with whom they were consubstantial.

Only the Greeks, spurred by *hýbris*, conceived of knowledge as an indirect form of immortality. No such conclusion had ever been reached before. It is clear that a certain expansion of knowledge also took place among the peoples whom the Greeks called barbarians, but it seems to have found its basis in the intuitions of certain individuals, rather than in any coherent program. Since it did not have the character of transmissible abstract knowledge of which the parts could be combined and interrelated, it tended to disappear with the deaths of those who gave it formulation. It was salvaged from forgetfulness only by being rethought and newly formulated by other individuals.

Though repeated, collective and even perhaps choral, the Persians' military conquests likewise give no impression of having been conceived of as integral and necessary parts of a culture intent on its own expansion; they seem instead to have owed their existence to the personal caprice, no matter how powerful, of individual kings. On reading the dialog between Xerxes and his uncle Artabanus,[1] we come away with the feeling that what was then the world's most powerful dynasty had not yet seen its endeavors in the light of a unifying idea. The meaning of that immense expedition, already underway, might seem to have been the subject of no previous discussion, and even this talk between Xerxes and Artabanus seems virtually to have arisen by accident. Xerxes is conducting a massive expansion that his father Darius had already attempted a decade earlier, and he seems to be aware of attempting to emulate this precedent, and others as well;[2] but still he seems less interested in continuing his father's program of conquest than in pursuing an action of his own, indirectly inspired but never foreseen by Darius. Xerxes' goal is to take revenge for the great humiliation that the Athenians had inflicted on his father. He is fighting a personal war, like a duel or a gigantic feud. His motives lie more in instinct than in any political ideal, and the actual waging of the war has the character of a series of reactions that follow no pre-established strategic plan. The enterprise is guided by an impulse rather than a concept. The king of Persia, as seen through the eyes of Herodotus, also seems to have been accustomed to the adulation or endless admiration of courtiers;[3] the Greeks, on the other hand, are known to have regarded verbal exchanges as acts of real criticism where something was truly at stake, or even as a challenge that spurred a process of learning. Barbarian dialog was static, whereas Greek dialog explored new territory. Herodotus makes us presume that the barbarians were unacquainted with anything equivalent to the notion of *paideía*, or to the duty to pursue and systematically develop one's natural talents. The conquests of knowledge remained confined to isolated places, even within the life of the individual.

It is clear, of course, that the expansionist attitudes that course through European history unfolded in ways that were not entirely linear or discontinuous, and they frequently encountered obstacles. Doubts were raised from time to time, and mainly on the part of the church, but rather than question the legitimacy of the constant expansion of human knowledge, achievements and expectations, they focused ever more on perplexities aroused by a few of its details. Europe's less than central position on the earth and the earth's less than central position in the universe were impugned by the Roman Catholic church at a time when they were already subject to scientific measurement. We have branded the church's negation of the facts as an act of arrogance, which in fact it was as an abuse of doctrine; but it was actually guided by a need for prudence: by the need to prevent the endless dilation of the limits of the world that God in

Genesis had consigned to man. The payment of interest as a reward for the investment of money was also obstructed for quite some time. Non-invested capital strikes the modern world as more wasteful and immoral than speculation, but the church's prohibitions were prior to the formation of an ethics based on economic thinking, and they aimed to prevent capital from assuming a life of its own. The church was afraid that the growing ductility of the economic system might nourish a kind of *hýbris*.

But as these checks became ever less frequent and proved to be ever more impotent, science, technology and the hunger for conquest aimed ever more resolutely at the infinite. In growing antithesis to the non-European civilizations, the west gradually ceased to find its orientation in a God who kept ever less jealous custody of His exclusive right to the figure of the infinite. Since everything infinite belonged to God, and since civilizations are extensions of humanity, the constant growth of their earthly acquisitions could be taken as proof that the concomitant emptying of the heavens was an absolute necessity, rather than any mere co-incidence, since God by now was forever to find His domicile in the human mind and the human hand.

Having been created by humanity for the satisfaction of human needs, science and technology apparently presented themselves as wholly secular values, in no way transcendental; but their pursuit of the infinite was essentially equivalent to an act of competition with God. The growth of wealth and power found its only limits in the growth of the wealth and power of others. Colonial conquests were limited only by the similar aims of other European nations, and so forth.

The rest of the world was to have no other choice than gradually – and then frenetically – to adapt itself. Every area of knowledge and geography was rapidly occupied by the west's rush forward, and the world's other peoples were to live in lands that were governed by western colonists and swamped by western languages. The way in which European civilization inundated the globe knows no precedent, and it explains the bitter resentment of all those peoples who surely never wished to compete with the west, but who wanted to preserve their own ways of life. Today, suddenly, there are no more sanctuaries. Without necessarily having wanted to do so, we have also trameled the limits of all the other cultures of the world.

From the great innovations of fifth-century Greece and down to the present day – the exception of the Middle Ages is more apparent than real – the defining characteristic of the western mind has always lain in its ability to dispense with all thought of pre-established limits while theorizing its principles of development and pursuing its material conquests; and in the ability to do so without incurring conscious feelings of guilt.

The constant quality of western thought is an ideative audacity that can thrust itself out into the limitless. Its premises were already active in the secular courage of Socrates, Thucydides and Euripides; and today it forms the basis of a doubly universal culture. It has gradually assumed control of every corner of the earth. And it deploys a single approach, omnidirectional and free of all limits, towards all the forms of knowledge and human achievement. Historical criticism, which allows us to look at progress as a relative value and to reconstruct an image of simpler and more serene societies, is itself the fruit of a widened ability to think in terms of comparisons, and no such faculty could ever have taken shape outside of the context of a radical dilation of the dynamics of ideation. The disappearance of the taboo of limits is the matrix of our every subsequent course of evolution; as divine authorization to proceed to the construction of history, and to refuse to remain the slaves of destiny, it counts as the driving force of twenty-four centuries of events.

ETHICS

In the course of the last generation, humanity has consumed more energy resources than in all of its previous history. That is a frightening realization. But it is even more frightening to realize that the expansionistic presuppositions responsible for such a level of consumption were certainly more suited to the Athenian culture in which it was forged – now dead for twenty-four centuries, or a hundred generations – than to our own, which has had to take cognizance of global limits.

Expansive thinking guided the history of the west up until the end of the first half of our century. The years we are currently living through perhaps belong to a new phase of thinking of which we glimpse the necessity, while still not grasping its essence.

A few of the thoughts of Jaspers and Jung could prove to be of some help to us.

Jaspers divides history into three periods.[4] He sees the primeval human cultures as a long period of latency; very little can be known about any such original condition, but we can presume it to have seen the growth and demise of any number of civilizations that left no traces behind them, and none of which prevailed in any definitive way. Next came a sudden reawakening in various parts of the world, some few hundred years before the birth of Christ, and men began to put forward radical questions (Confucius and Lao-Tse in China, Buddha in India, Socrates in Greece, the prophets in Palestine, Zarathustra in Persia). This is what Jaspers refers to as the "axial" period, since it was to prove to be the axis of history. Humans ceased to think mythically, with their minds turned backwards to the origin of things, and began to think rationally and prophetically, with their minds turned towards the future. And the west, as the heir of the Greeks, has ever since crafted an uninterrupted course of development that tends to unify the world. Jaspers then proposes a third period, which he sees as having recently begun: the period that consolidates the cultural unity of the globe under the aegis of science and western technology, which constrain humanity to adopt new ways of thinking. The poverty of this new departure, as compared to the great leap forward of the axial period, lies in its finding its origins in the overwhelming power of external circumstance and not in the novel reflections of great new thinkers; rather than a product of human will, it is a product of the will of technology.

Jaspers came to these conclusions before the appearance of the notion of global limits, and he anticipated its major premises. Today, the limits of development in fact contribute to the unification of the globe, in terms of ethics no less than technology.

We can follow Jaspers' scheme by saying that in some first and imprecise phase of human life, humanity did not feel incited to the pursuit of cumulative conquests; it had no notion of any such thing, or was totally indifferent to it, or even, like the Greeks, considered it sinful. After those primordial times, a canon of limitless action, both mental and material, became the axial ethic of the west: it was forged in the so-called axial period, and it served as the axis of the actions of the west, and was thus its *de facto* moral code.

Today the conditions for the appearance of a third ethic seem to present themselves; but, unlike the second, it lies outside of the sphere of human control; it simply imposes itself upon human life as one of the results of the globe's having reached its point of saturation with respect to growth. The third of the historical phases that Jaspers postulates is governed by technology's repercussions on the forms and contents that live in the human psyche, and on all of our profoundest modes of being. So it leads to a fundamental question: what new ethical themes have been generated by this universe that in all its technological obesity has been drawn together and unified by western culture?

In Jungian terms, the ethics of unlimited action might be called the ethics of the *hýbris* of consciousness. Jung employs the ancient Greek notion of *hýbris* to describe the arrogance of rational consciousness – its denigration of the unconscious and irrational dynamics of the psyche – which is typical of the modern western world, and he could therefore be said to turn his attention to *hýbris* as an intrapsychic phenomenon.[5] Though of course unacquainted with psychoanalysis, traditional cultures felt widespread respect for what we now refer to as the unconscious. The uncontrollable components of the psyche found expression in other dimensions of daily experience, and mainly in the dimension of religious experience. They were freely allowed to communicate messages in ways that were not to be classed as pathological: the imposing dream was a divine portent, the attack of hysteria revealed possession by a spirit, and so forth.

Jung sees these traditions of respect for the psyche's irrational contents to have gradually disappeared from our civilization as a result of their incompatibility with the emphasis that the dominant western values place on the realm of the concrete. Academics seem often to believe that the life of the psyche comes completely to flower in the measured and rational thought of the conscious mind.[6]

We have already discussed the way in which the intellect's ambitions for expansion proceed simultaneously in two directions: towards the outside material world, and towards the interior psychic world. This second direction of expansion is the mode of what Jung refers to as the *hýbris* or inflation of consciousness. But the constant intertwining of humanity's two conquests – over the external world and the internal world – may also prove to be salubrious. Our constant confrontation with the ever more critical conundrums of technological expansion exerts considerable pressure on the dynamics of the psyche and could gradually attenuate the presupposition that consciousness is destined to take possession of ever greater areas of the unconscious.

The history of depth psychology testifies to and anticipates this development. The first phase was opened by Freud and is summed up in his exhortation: "Where id was, there ego shall be."[7] He saw consciousness as asserting control of the territories of the unconscious in much the same way that society appropriates sites that still belong to nature: "It is a work of culture – not unlike the draining of the Zuider Zee."[8] The second phase, inaugurated by Jung, concerns itself with the relativization of consciousness. Here the consciousness is criticized for its one-sidedness, and the equilibrium of the psyche is shifted from the Ego to the Self, or into an intermediate position between consciousness and unconsciousness, rather than in conflict with unconsciousness. Jung writes:

> Looked at from the outside, the psyche appears to be essentially a reflection of external happenings – to be not only occasioned by them, but to have its origin in them. And it also seems to us, at first, that the unconscious can be explained only from the outside and from the side of consciousness. It is well known that Freud attempted to do this – an undertaking which could succeed only if the unconscious were actually something that came into being with the existence and consciousness of the individual. But the truth is that the unconscious is always there beforehand as a system of inherited psychic functions handed down from primeval times. Consciousness is a late-born descendant of the unconscious psyche. It would certainly show perversity if we tried to explain the lives of our ancestors in terms of their late descendants, and it is just as wrong, in my opinion, to regard the unconscious as a derivative of consciousness.[9]

The stages of western ethics might therefore be summed up as in the following subsections.

Mythic ethics

To speak of mythic ethics is to appeal quite intentionally to the ambivalence of the word "myth." We are referring on the one hand to the ethics of civilizations that find their guide in myth; and we are also calling up the image of the ethics of epochs that are now too distant and fuzzy to be known through anything other than reports in which fact and fiction lie enclosed as a single flesh within the shell of non-history and can never be separated from one another. We are thinking of the contexts in which human action is limited by the fixity of myth, and by the *phthónos*, in the Greek world, that reserved all achievements to the gods, forbidding man to conceive of them as his own. This is an aristocratic ethic; it endorses the supremacy of the nobility, and it shows disinterest for every quantitative form of progress, of which it has not yet intuited the rationality. Culture and civilization circulate among only a few, which radically restricts the possibility of military, commercial or other kinds of conquest that require collective participation.

Rather than with a true and organically structured system of ethics, we are dealing here with a spontaneous phenomenon of societal self-regulation that articulates itself through canons of aesthetics, in sets of predominantly contemplative attitudes, and in feelings of guilt more governed by taboos than by commandments.

Axial ethics and the *hýbris* of consciousness

Human action is guided by a need for expansion that helps to dislodge taboos. For action to be circumscribed by limits is ever less felt to be a virtue and gradually reverses into a vice.

This is a democratic ethics, as a natural ramification of its greater rationality and also of its propensity to the use of quantitative terms. In moments of commercial or military expansion, such attributes show unequivocal advantages and therefore tend to dominate.

At the political level, this form of ethics achieved its definitive hegemony with the French Revolution. But that was no more than the final phase of a process of rationalization that revolved around the axis of Greek civilization. Transformations of such great depth inevitably require the passage of enormous periods of time.

The ethics of the reappearance of limits

The world in which we live no longer permits us to follow God's behest: "And you, be ye fruitful and multiply; bring forth abundantly in the earth, and multiply therein."[10] This Biblical command was followed for centuries and gave no cause for alarm, but it functions now as the fuse of a mammoth explosion that annihilates all demographic and environmental equilibrium. Humankind's absolute dominion over the whole of the environment, inclusive of every form of animal and vegetable life, may once and for a great deal of time have found its authorization in the words of God, but this distinction now seems pernicious and impious.[11] Our civilization is in stable conditions when it grows, and not when it is stable. But the earth that hosts this growing civilization is of fixed and given dimensions and cannot grow. No heavenly voice has supplied a new commandment, but the old injunction that spurs expansion has led us to the edge of the terror of *global phthónos*; that central metaphor of Greek morality that seems ready to reassert itself on a planetary scale. Rather than no longer personal or national, it is global in every way: its finds its mark in every living human being, and it breeds in every sphere of human activity.

But material and technological expansion run parallel to the expansion of the Ego, and its crisis can therefore contribute to curbing the excesses of interior colonization.

The mastery of rational consciousness over the totality of the psyche is a basic but far from absolute conquest. The mind continues to be made as well of dreams, emotions and zones that lie beyond control. Rationality's claim to a right of unlimited expansion, to the damage of alternative but not consequently eliminable functions, sooner or later perverts itself into rationalization: the dogmatic justification of a masked unconscious impulse. Rationalization prepares the way for fanatical or one-sided attitudes.

By displacing our deepest emotions – the pools of ambivalence that constitute the very substance of the soul – reason has produced the one-directional clarity of scientific objectivity, and also of the decisional processes required for the exploitation of its findings. But the expulsion of doubt and the accumulation of knowledge and material goods are consigning us to a diseased civilization that threatens to grow perilously irrational.

We can "study" – and yet not "feel" – this peril for as long as our analyses rely on no more than the one-directional reason of which the metastasis counts as the root of the disease. We can *comprehend* the disease only by reviving the ambivalent emotions that once resulted in introversion or paralysis, but also in a vision that was much more balanced and complete since it addressed both sides of reality.

Calling a halt to rationality – embarking on a route that again leads to doubt, to ambivalent feeling, to the wound that the soul inflicts on whatever the intellect constructs but refuses to interrogate – puts a stop to a course of action that is associated with guilt. Guilt is a feeling of responsibility for the world of "existence," and also the perception of an imprecise debt that remains to be paid. (Heidegger reminds us that the German word *Schuld* means both "guilt" and "debt.") And the feeling of guilt is no simply sporadic presence in the life of the psyche; it is quite a stable part of the dynamics of the workings of civilizaton. Mankind is an animal whose actions are determined by a highly special relationship to guilt. Something similar is not necessarily unknown to the rest of the animal world, but "guilt" in other animals determines no more than the inhibition of an action or, at most, an immediate action of reparation; in humans, on the other hand, it sets up a gradual and complex reordering of activity in ways that can flow into cultural creations. Or if the individual is unsuccessful in integrating the feeling of guilt and indebtedness, it flows instead into a negation of guilt and an equally complex but delirious reconstellation that projects it onto others (paranoia, or the conviction of suffering persecution).[12] Feelings of guilt can be redirected, but not canceled out.

Technology itself spins endlessly on, always further spawning itself like a chain of numbers, but the human citizens of the world of technology preserve within themselves a memory of the limits that regulated the rhythms of archaic civilization and that held control of instinct in their animal pre-history.

Since historical humanity is moral (*mores* are societal customs) the sense of limits, which the expansion of technology removed from consciousness, comes primarily to manifestation as an unconscious sense of ill-being, and is therefore considered neurotic. The word, moreover, rather than "illness," is indeed "ill-being," since the experience lies in the re-emergence of the ancient principle of self-regulation that brings nausea in the wake of satiety. After the explosion of the nuclear plant in Chernobyl, various analysts reported an unusual number of apocalyptic dreams among their patients; these nightmares' common denominator was a superhuman *némesis* in the act of scourging a technology that represents human *hýbris*. None of these patients, obviously enough, bore any personal guilt for that explosion, but all of them experienced it as a source of collective guilt and felt themselves involved in it, even though living at distances that precluded all direct endangerment. Analysts have also noted that one of the most frequent forms of agoraphobia involves housewives whose activities are wholly anonymous and who are thus deprived of affects. These patients are taken by panic among the endless shelves of supermarkets; the glare of an infinity of objects that seemingly beg to be purchased fills them with shame and nausea.

The unconscious continues to experience the *hýbris* of technology as ridden with guilt, and it still experiences the infinite as surrounded by taboos and states of panic which consciousness has canceled out; and it brings them back into consciousness in the form of a twisted sense of disorder and ill-being.

The God who purified sin personified a provident and pre-existent infinity. Now that this God has abandoned us, we encounter an infinity of possibilities. They seem to lie at our fingertips, as though we had only to reach out and grasp them; but they are unexplored and alien. The perception of this state of abandonment combines with the offers of the new encounter, and the persons in whom this event takes place discover themselves to be swamped with anxiety. To be open to too many broad expanses and attracted by too many possibilities gives rise to the para-doxical sensation of embracing the void.

We here lean out to beyond the edge of the possible, and we discover a place that is full of vertigo; it is also the place where we can call our discourse to a halt. When all sense of limits has been left behind, we intuit the existence of a zone of terror not at all dissimilar to the feeling encountered by the people of antiquity when they stood in the face of their pitiless, powerful and tremendous gods. But we now discover no powers that block our way, and no merits that offer absolution. The person who appeared to have abandoned metaphysics now finds himself in the grips of the metaphysical terror of the infinite number of their possible actions. This, perhaps, is precisely the place – this place no longer regulated by external or dogmatic limits – where they encounter an existential *Angst* that re-echoes the ancestral experience of standing exposed to *phthónos*. The difference lies in the fact that by now we have swallowed the gods, and it is therefore humans, tragically, who envy and punish themselves. It would be arbitrary and superfluous to attempt to relate this new condition of the soul by taking recourse to new psychologies or philosophies. The narrative has already found its form in the language of Kafka and Joyce.

We face a new version of the ancient clash between the individual who yearns for happiness, and the gods who out of jealousy deny it. Here again we find a conflict between actions in pursuit of satisfactions, and counter-actions – complex social reactions no less than states of psychic ill-being – that impugn them. The gods of antiquity have re-appeared on the scene of our modern evils quite truly as a jealous aggregate. The denial of our cravings, and our encounter with a jealous limit are clearer today than ever before because the different planes on which they lie are now in substantial agreement: the external response that nullifies our demands is social and environmental, and it concords with a more obscure but no less violent "no" that resounds from a dark corner of our psyche. Existential philo-sophy sees it as the *Angst* of existence: *ex-sistere*, the painful awareness of relativity, separateness and limitation with respect to the universality of being. I am almost nothing; how can I desire to have everything? The feeling of guilt that falls to the lot of arrogant and lonely human beings has nothing to do with specific sins, but is consubstantial with the fact of existing as infinite possibility and irreversible separation. This duplex rediscovery of the experience of limits could lead us towards an attitude of moderation that unassisted rationality is unable to create.

13

DEATH, DEPRESSION
AND GUILT

The meaninglessness of any process of purely worldly self-perfection
... was something that religious thought could already see in the
obvious meaninglessness of death, which seemed in turn to furnish
final proof of the meaninglessness of life as "cultural" fact. The peasant
could die "an old man, and full," like Abraham. . . . But not the
"cultivated" individual who aspired to self-perfection through the
appropriation of "culture." Such a person might grow "tired of life"
but could never be "sated by life. . . . " The very premise of his
perfectibility lay, at least in principle, in its possibly infinite prolongation, like the possibly infinite quantity of cultural goods themselves.
(M. Weber, *Gesammelte Aufsätze zur Religionssoziologie*)

Death, as physiological fact, is postponed by medicine. Death as cultural
fact risks total effacement.

Technology discovers its ever greater progress at the cost of the regress
of social customs. In the course of the last few decades, as human existence
has distanced ever more radically from natural life, the most fundamental
event, on a par with birth, that lies along our paths has been demoted from
a cultural to a physical phenomenon. It turns into an object that belongs
to medicine. Death is no longer a power with a voice of its own, a
protagonist of mythology, of religious and philosophical experience; it is
no longer the font of those thoughts on the sense of life that are only
imposed by radical events.

People once died in their homes, surrounded by others, both family and
strangers, who were prepared for the sight of death to teach them
something. Death imparted a lesson on the relativity of earthly things and
was the source of a supramundane wisdom. Today, the very word is
avoided, and everything that might call it to mind is rejected or repressed.
So mourning and the cult of the dead – which were the customs that
allowed the dead to continue to live in the soul of the individual and the
rites of the group – have disappeared. Medical treatment of terminal illness
is still referred to as "therapy," almost as though its aim might lie in
helping people to live rather than to die.[1]

Life in the pre-modern cultures, characterized by active processes of symbolic exchange between the members of the group, was not defined as a single dimension of itself; life included the constant presence of death, and people continually confronted it. Like consciousness and unconsciousness, life and death were not so much contraposed as reciprocally intertwined. Given the ease with which persons of any and all ages might die, it would have been arrogant and in any case unthinkable to expunge the image of death from the realm of daily life. Preparing oneself for its arrival was a constant and necessary activity. In turn, death always had something to teach, as a great public rite, and the dying always had a truth to pass on to us; death and the dying delivered a message on the vanity of things, on the uselessness of the accumulation of goods, honors or simply a few more years. Death, in its quality as the absolute limit, pointed out the end of everyone and everything, and it inculcated the awareness of the uselessness and foolishness of every unlimited aspiration.

Civilizations too made no claim to eternal life. The early Greeks devoutly sang of the fall of Troy and made it a part of their myths, since by narrating the ruination of their enemies they were preparing themselves for the future collapse of the walls of every city.

Death in the era of science is entirely negative – a loss. Life on the other hand is only and entirely positive, having forgotten its contrary pole and interred all awareness of its own limits. Deprived of that frame of reference, life loses its qualitative meaning and transforms itself into a process of quantitative accumulation. The death that people would choose to die is as fast and silent as possible. The person in the midst of dying, once the priest of their own final rite of passage, no longer has anything to say. No longer an active subject, that person turns into the passive object of medical procedures, performed by physicians who are priests of technology.

This turnabout may limit the sufferings of the body (when medicine in fact succeeds in reducing rather than prolonging them) but it torments the soul: the dying, who in the past were subject to pain but who also experienced the respect of their families and neighbors, thus becoming a link with the great beyond and therefore the voice of a metaphysical wisdom, are now requested to exit on the tips of their toes.

The binding reciprocities and compensatory exchanges that typified archaic societies have been replaced in our civilization by systems of oppositions that reveal themselves in a culture of adversary relationships and in a psychology of the projection of the shadow; such systems of oppositions generate conflict with the Other, which degenerates in turn into rejection. Primitives too will of course be remembered to have fought and killed their enemies; but the warrior would stop beside his adversary's fallen body to celebrate rituals to propitiate it. If at times he ate of it, that was surely no expression of scorn and had little to do with hunger; cannibalism – like ritual exchanges of gifts, or like the Greek who donned the battle dress of the fallen Trojan – was an active way of reinforcing the symbolic link between victor and victim.

Modern westerners, on the other hand, atomize their enemies, wiping them off the face of the earth and erasing them from history as well, rewriting history into entirely the story of the victorious. The novelty of the political conflicts of the twentieth century cannot truly be seen to lie in the thorough extermination of non-Aryans in central Europe, of class enemies in eastern Europe or of forces of political opposition in Latin America. Every epoch has given proof of its ability to slaughter its adversaries; but the Greeks, for example, had a Homer who kept the Trojans alive in memory. Songs were sung about the enemy in order to preserve a state of psychic mobilization that would continue to be available in epic, with epic then to be elevated into myth. One spared the enemy's women and took them home, often to bear the victors' children (the partial continuity of the vanquished by way of reproduction, just as cannibalism gave them partial continuity by way of absorption). Today's novelty is not the extermination of peoples, but of rites and memories: the slaughtered cease to survive even as symbolic presences, and the slaughterers exculpate themselves not by declaring that the massacre was just, but by denying that it ever took place. Another final solution is to declare that there are simply no records – not even a birth certificate – for persons who are claimed to be missing, thus denying not only their death but their very existence. Analogously, western civilization replaces the complexity of the unconscious psyche and its "interior adversaries" with the clarities of consciousness; the ambivalence of symbols with the one-sidedness of rationality. Its processes are linear rather than circular, of accumulation rather than exchange, of signification rather than symbolization. Where life and death are turned into irreconcilable opposites, the value of life no longer derives from a meaningful dialog between them, but from a quantitative accumulation of life that relegates death to invisibility. Scientific zeal and lofty intentions have allowed human *hýbris* to fill out the whole of its figure, appropriating the role of God in determining the forms and the terms of life. "Daring and desire for novelty" may have allowed the Athenians and their descendants to produce vast realms of knowledge, but they also produced a forgetfulness of myth. There is a myth in which Aesculapius, the founder of medicine, is stricken down with a thunderbolt for having attempted to use his art to cheat death of its rightful sway.[2]

The repression of death, confined to the lucubrations of philosophy and theology, is thus the final product of the repression of limits. God is the limit of man, but in our oblivion of all transcendence He does not reveal Himself or show His power on His own. If God disappears, people simply take His place; their identification with God is in fact the very source of the notion that everything is possible and unlimited.[3] Death, on the other hand, continues to exist for believers and non-believers alike, and it proposes an eschatology (a reflection on the last things, *éskata*) for both. But when something that cannot be abolished becomes incompatible with the values of the culture that surrounds it, it can simply be forgotten: death is an event that continues to assert itself, but our times have expelled it from their value systems. Death is repressed, since it is the prototype of the limits with which nature has circumscribed life.

The vitiation of death is the final term of a process of which the beginnings fade back into the era of the passage from myth to history. A civilization that for centuries had pursued the nullification of limits was destined sooner or later to tread a road that also does away with death. Conquest that disregards all confines turns into addiction; the existence that pays no regard to death becomes a life-directed neurosis. In the course of the past several decades – the period in which the process has taken shape – the expulsion of death from consciousness has hastened in turn the destruction of every other taboo of limits, since the repression of death is itself the force that nourishes the unconscious figure of unlimited life: the fantasy of immortality. Freud had a clear understanding of the process when he affirmed that man was transforming himself into an ersatz god.[4]

The western drive to expansion is primarily visible in terms of geography and space, but here we catch a glimpse of its temporal dimension.

The circular exchanges of traditional societies promoted the symbolic integration of differences, and their psychological effects included the inhibition of enantiodromias. By rejecting such modes of exchange and replacing them with habits of linear and potentially infinite accumulation, today's civilization simplifies the originally polyvalent and sees nothing as more than one-sided, thus shattering natural equilibriums which are based on alternations. Consumption obeys no other finality than its own self-incrementation through the creation of new needs and therefore of new consumer goods, thereby mimicking an infinite prolongation of the nutritive function and the life that it supports. The retention of wealth, undirected to any foreseeable utilization in life, already implies an unconscious fantasy of immortality.

The simpler societies of the past had a clear understanding of the need to avoid such *hýbris*. Things were social facts that did not concern their proprietors alone, and the circulation of goods was imposed and steered by the culture's dominant system of symbols. Objects were subject to ritual donation, to ceremonial destruction (the "potlatch" in which a chieftain displayed his power but relinquished accumulation and protected himself from envy), and to sacrificial destruction (to "make them sacred") in the course of the life or at the moment of the death of their owner. All of this lived still in the minds of the Greeks when Aeschylus made his chorus chant: "if with well-measured cast, caution heave overboard a portion of the gathered wealth, the whole house, with woe overladen, doth not founder nor doth it engulf the hull."[5]

Those who are ready to recognize, accept and at certain times to provoke a loss are not ill. The experience of mourning and of the potential for depression that each of us harbors within us (but which only a radical loss or an encounter with death reawakens) is essential to the formation of the sense of responsibility, the moral sense and the sense of limits of the mature human being. An "availability to depression" or at least to slow, thoughtful, silent and introverted reflection is a necessary part of any mature civilization that fosters self-responsibilization and self-limitation. But it is always more alien to our own civilization. It is only indirectly that our "negative epic" betrays the malaise of living in a state of dissatisfied satiety. The single individual has little awareness of bearing the weight of the unilaterality of history and the return of the repressed.

The common frame of mind that ignores the notion that economic development has limits and that available resources have an end likewise rejects the experience of depression and guilt. Proud of its defeat of enormous material obstacles, it fears their possible rebirth in the form of psychological limits.

A culture marked by an "availability to depression" has not yet managed to assert itself since depression is experienced as an illness rather than as the restoration of an equilibrium. The recognition of the complementarity of activity and thoughtfulness, of mania and depression, of extroversion and introversion is no less necessary to the life of the individual than it is to the whole of a culture, but it finds itself blocked by those acquisitive attitudes for which normalcy is only to be found in ever more rapid, superficial and extroverted rhythms of activity.[6]

This is why normalcy, which was once an intermediate state between mania and depression, seems gradually to shift towards the former; so those who have simply maintained a position of equilibrium are more and more branded as depressed. A frenetic race to nowhere disguises its perversity as normalcy, simply by virtue of statistical frequency.

History knows no precedents, but that could hardly be said of the psyche. History has a linear development, the psyche lives out a cycle, from birth to death. If history also records events that are repetitions of others, that results from the constant intertwining of collective and personal events, where the former, which are always new, can never be separated from the always ancient passions of the latter. True and proper history, much as Herodotus intended it to be, remains the story of the activities of human beings, as seen in terms of a "research" that attempts to comprehend them.

Since history knows no precedents, our civilization is the first that *believes* itself to be immortal; but perhaps, in reality, it is simply the first civilization to lack a conscious feeling of limitation. As an alternative, however, one could also suggest a more pessimistic hypothesis. Our society has returned to a radical competition for growth and means of sustenance, and also, in the present-day world, pursues the elimination of minor cultures and most of the residues of nature; as such it might well constitute a direct continuation of the world of animals.

When human beings abandoned the conditions of animal life and entered the era of history and civilization, our forms of life ceased to evolve according to the principles of natural selection: the survival of the fittest and the death of the weaker. Human evolution came instead to be directed by the principles and ever more rapid rhythms of cultural development and technological growth. And yet its rejection of all respect for limits, for God and for death can almost make it seem that our civilization has followed an inverse path of regression. Its history begins with the highly civilized chapter of a culture that rooted itself in self-limitation – perhaps in some way inherited from mechanisms of the self-inhibition of instinct – but then rapidly ceded to the most primordial rules of competitive expansion, issuing finally into a kind of Darwinism that controls the lives of the very forms of culture. In the face of the omnipotent charge of technological society, all other cultures are disappearing.

Our civilization presents itself as something new, but the psyche – the principal organ of the individuals who make up civilization – remains what it has always been, and it cannot ignore the fact that death and the intuition of the divine set up limits both to life and in life. Unlike the Orient and the Third World, which in order to participate in modern life have not transformed their traditional systems of belief – in the course of the last few rapid generations they have simply learned to flank those systems of belief, perhaps somewhat discolored, with our rational rules for life in the secular world – western civilization is the only civilization to have directly, profoundly and relentlessly incorporated into itself all of the forms and infinite qualities of God. In the course of the centuries, the Greeks transformed themselves into modern men; and while doing so they swallowed up all of their adversaries: first the Persians and then the gods. They left no meaningful qualities on sites that lay outside of themselves, and this explains the near impossibility of telling whether a Greek statue represents a god or a human being; far beyond the realm of all mono-theistic prohibitions of graven images of God, the forms of Greek statuary speak already of the divine satiety of secular life.

This is the path that westerners have continued to follow, shifting their contraries and limits into their own interior. Secularization has implied a great deal more than adapting to new rules that control the outside world. It also includes an interior metamorphosis: a transmutation of the soul into a place so complex as to prove ever less amenable to description. If God has been removed from the heavens and re-incarnated into human aspirations that are no less infinite, death too, removed from sight, has likewise been displaced and not eliminated. It makes its re-appearance in the interior of the individual, assuming the guise of states of depression

190

that escape all rational explanation. At the core of such an absence of *élan vital* lies a sense of absolute guilt which again, in rational terms, seems wholly unmotivated; it accompanies the perception of living a life that knows of no sufficient justification for continuing to exist. Guilt, as an interior feeling of which the causes remain imprecise, is a survival of the death we deny and the soul we devalue; so it makes unconscious allusion to the traditional figure of the death of the soul. The feeling of bearing a guilt of which the origins remain inexplicable finds no referent in specific responsibilities; it refers to the ancestral terror of spiritual demise.

Tolstoy tells a tale about a man who struggled against a limit. The title asks: "How much land does a man need?"[7] The reply appears at its end. A man was purchasing land in a highly unusual way. For an already determined sum of money, he was to become the proprietor of all the ground he could circle on foot in the course of a single day. He is to begin to walk at sunrise, and he has to return to his starting point by sunset. His legs are good, and he expects to acquire a vast estate. Only a dream has told him that he is dealing with the devil. He walks all day long and never allows himself to rest; there is nothing that he is willing to forgo. He constantly redoubles his efforts and his breath grows short, but still he manages to make the circuit of his walk include that patch of woodland. The sun seems very low, but he cannot really tell, since his vision is growing ever more hazy. He still wants that field, that valley. As he re-approaches his point of departure he fears that he has taken too long. But no, the sun still hangs on the horizon, and he is surrounded by people who are offering congratulations. Why then should it be so terribly dark? His servant begins to dig a hole, and this is the point at which we understand how much land a man needs. If he knows no limits, a few square feet will suffice: he needs nothing any larger than a burial plot.

NOTES

1 THE MYTH OF GROWTH, THE MYTH OF LIMITS

1 Ortega y Gasset, 1930, Chapter 1.
2 This book makes use of the most open possible definition of myth. Many works have been written on the subject, but few unanimously accepted conclusions have been reached. One of the most exhaustive treatments of the theme is to be found in Kirk, 1971. Kirk considers the meanings of the word "myth" to be virtually numberless, and in any case irreducible to a common denominator. See also the more highly focused discussion by the same author, 1975.
3 The use of these terms inevitably gives rise to a certain degree of ambiguity. I have attempted to observe the distinctions formulated in the now classic work by Kluckhohn and Kroeber (1952).
4 See Jaeger, 1943–4, "Introduction."
5 The mystery cults dedicated to Dionysus are particularly pertinent to our subject. In their most widespread form, which included drunkenness, ecstasy, possession and dismemberment, they constitute an image of the abandonment of stasis and the surpassing of limits (even if here it may be a question of a state of omnipotence on the part of the unconscious, which is quite different from the arrogance of consciousness that interests us). But even if a great deal has been written on the subject, it cannot be said, unfortunately, that a similar volume of sound conclusions has been reached. Such cults were experienced in highly individual ways. And the ways in which they have been reconstructed – even aside from the limits imposed by the scanty sources – have been equally individual. As personal religions they were quite different from the collective religions. (See Burkert, 1987, Chapter 1.) Their very center was based on the inexpressibility of subjective experience. Dionysus' variability and unpredictability were also underlined by his lack of a specific residence (and thus by his lack of territorial limits). Dionysus was always everywhere. He was by character a foreign god, and not necessarily by virtue of his geographical origins. Detienne (1986), for example, informs us that Dionysus in Thebes was the god of invasion, and yet was much more discreet in nearby Attica; he remained a god of wine, but he also taught that wine should be tempered with water; he presided simultaneously over excitement and moderation. From a psychological point of view, the profusion of Dionysian mysteries in ancient Greece gives the general impression of an unconscious compensation for the morality imposed by the doctrine of self-limitation. It functioned perhaps as a safety valve that gave that compensation the tolerable form of a religion.
6 Rohde's grandiose study (1890–4, see Rohde 1903) of the multiform Greek

beliefs concerning the soul dates from the very same period that was prone to insist too highly on the unity of Hellenic culture. For a discussion of the reception of the various Greek cults, see also Guthrie, 1951.

7 The Greeks considered poets to be the greatest of the artists, since poets were the most generous. The works of sculptors, architects and painters (who primarily decorated vases) entered the outside world and offered enjoyment to a limited number of people. With time, they could bring the temptation of material wealth. The word, on the other hand, was eternal and belonged to everyone; it lived in the interior of the individual and always in personal ways, much the same as emotions. No one was too poor or illiterate to possess the verses of Homer. Everyone could recite them and give them to others without in turn being deprived of them. Their riches were inexhaustible and everyone could own them.

8 The thought that the purpose of such models is to offer a guide is also expressed in recent studies. The following words, for example, are found in the introduction to Pohlenz's *The Hellenic Man* (1947):

> Beyond all variations, there was a single Hellenic man, and our goal is to capture his essence. This is more than a simply historical task. In fact, it is only by succeeding in truly understanding the Hellenic man that we will be able to answer the question as to whether or not Hellenism still has a value for the culture of our own epoch.

9 An investigation that concerns itself less with precise dates and developments than with conjectures on the evolution of a *Weltanschauung* cannot be referred to as history in the traditional sense. Genealogy, from Nietzsche to Foucault, has established itself as an autonomous genre.

> History attempts to discover the real beginning of an idea, and the historical conditions that generated it; genealogy, on the other hand, is on the lookout for the *availability to meaning* that a certain idea inaugurates and expresses, which is to speak of the sense of meaning that makes itself visible in the ideas that it generates. (Galimberti, 1987, p. 264)

Such a procedure requires a constant even though implicit reference to current meanings of growth and limits.

10 See, for example, Vernant, 1967, part 7, Chapter I: "Ionian 'physics'.... transposes the system of representation elaborated by religion into a secular form and places it on the plane of a more abstract mode of thought. The cosmologies of the philosophers return to and prolong the cosmogonic myths. . ."

11 Plato, *Phaedo*, LXII, 14d (Jowett 114).

12 Freud, 1907, p. 151.

13 Though it ranges through the fields of anthropology and history and attempts to avoid being specialistic, my investigation conserves the emphases of Jungian psychology, which is always attentive to the conscious and unconscious contents of the psyche, both personal and collective. The dominant values of a culture constitute its collective consciousness. Their cultural transformation and their separation from official mythology does not mean that they cease to exist. Myths can continue to exist below consciousness and return to light in altered form, or in somewhat different dress. Several of Jung's essays move in this direction, and attention might be called to his analysis of the re-appearance of the Germanic god Wotan in Nazism. See Jung, 1936.

14 *Hóros*, in the sense of "law" or the source of order, has also been identified with Christ. For this use of the term see, for example, Jung, 1951, par. 85.

15 Diehl, *Anthologia*, 24–5.

16 Horace, *Carmina*, II, 10, 5.

17 Freud, 1926, pp. 87ff.

18 A musical composition does not develop an endless number of variations since it follows the expectations of the listener's ear, and they demand that the theme return towards its origins. See Mumelter's (forthcoming) discussion of the difficulties that Schönberg encountered in his attempt to escape from this obligation.

2 TOWARDS A PSYCHOLOGICAL TERRITORY

1 "Psychodynamics" and "depth psychology" are general terms that refer to all of the schools of analysis. "Psychoanalysis" and "analytical psychology" are the disciplines that were created, respectively, by Sigmund Freud and Carl Gustav Jung.

2 See also Calasso, 1988, p. 114, in reference to Greek mythology: "No subsequent psychology has taken a step beyond it, if not in the invention of different names for the powers that control us – names that are longer, more numerous, clumsier, and less efficacious."

3 "Modern humanity is proud, above all else, of its sense of responsibility, but it thus presumes to speak with a voice that it could not truly prove itself to possess. Homer's heroes knew of no such cumbersome word – the word 'responsibility' – and they would have given no credence to any such thing. They seem to have thought of every crime as being committed in a state of mental infirmity" (*ibid*).

4 Culture here is not to be understood in the larger and more general anthropological sense that allows us, for example, to speak of "primitive" cultures or of simple tools as part of a "material" culture. The relationship of *paideía* to European notions of culture has been explored in the classic text by Werner Jaeger (1943).

5 *Pythian II*, 72. For the translation see Pohlenz, 1947, pp. 598 and 609.

6 For a general reflection on the affirmation of these values in Greece, see *ibid*, chapters III, VIII, XI.

7 *History of the Peloponnesian War*, II, 41.

8 See the last part of our Chapter 5, "Divine jealousy and Athenian politics." The religious aspect of the Greek relationship between the individual and the state in ancient Greece is particularly clear in Toynbee, 1956, part I, chapter III.

9 In Pericles' Athens, theater was never entertainment; it was a public rite in honor of Dionysus. Architects did not dedicate themselves to building private homes, even in spite of the abundance of wealthy citizens who might have been prospective clients. The wealthy were allowed the honor of financing public works and ceremonies, or of building ships for the state.

10 Discussion of the instincts (for example, the instincts of self-preservation or reproduction) is sometimes imagined to be grounded in physiology, but here again we in fact are expressing ourselves by way of conventional metaphors. What we discuss is nothing that we actually observe, since flight or the excitement of the genital organs is a consequence of an instinct and not an instinct itself. We therefore make hypothetical reference to something we have not seen (instinct) but of which we perceive the effects (self-preservation or reproduction).

11 In psychology the psyche has to study itself, whereas the other scientific disciplines make use of active or transitive modes of thought in which a thinking subject studies an external object.

12 The most noted is Karl Popper, who insists that the theories of psychodynamics are false not by virtue of proofs that demonstrate their falsehood, but rather, quite to the contrary, because the objects studied by depth psychology are inherently subject to no confutation. Their nature is such that they cannot be falsified. Popper's criterion for the scientific status of a theory lies in fact in its falsifiability, which is something excluded by the apodictic character of psychodynamic interpretations. See Popper, 1992, part I, Chapter I, and as well 1934, part I, Chapters I and VI.

13 We do well to remember that the original term from which this concept derives is Cicero's *cultura animi*, the cultivation of the soul. See Kluckhohn and Kroeber, 1952, *passim*.

14 This is no question of any peculiar optimism on the part of psychologists. The search for the earliest forms of modern thinking finds philology to be a source of highly useful reflections.

> At least as far as the Greeks are concerned, there is no need to be . . . too skeptical. Greece is a question, after all, of our own spiritual past, and . . . things that at first may seem entirely alien to us can prove to be very natural, or at least a great deal simpler than our highly complicated modern concepts. . . . And our participation in the Hellenic past can be a question of more than memory; the possibilities it offered are preserved within us, and we can rediscover them to hold the strands of the various forms of our own modes of thought.
>
> (Snell, 1946, "Introduction," p. 14)

3 THE LIMITS OF ENDEAVOR IN NON-WESTERN CULTURES

* This chapter is not directly concerned with our principal thesis and in fact attempts to restrict our field of inquiry by stressing that the problem at hand is alien to non-western cultures. It might be considered an appendix (for future reference) to the first part of the book, and the reader may prefer to proceed directly to Chapter 4.

1 See, for example, Eliade, 1978, Chapter XVIII.

2 *Ibid.*, Chapter XVI.

3 Van der Leeuw makes use of phenomenological classifications and considers Confucianism to constitute the first example of "a religion of distancing and flight." He sees the second such religion in the deism of eighteenth-century Europe, which found its inspiration in Confucianism. See Van der Leeuw, 1956, part V, para. 90.

4 See Toynbee, 1956, Chapter 1.

5 The Sanskrit *daivam* (a later substantivized adjective that indicates a nameless divine quality) is India's expression of an idea that in many ways corresponds to the Greek notion of fate. (See Zimmer, 1951 pp. 100ff.) One also notes that *daivam* and *deves* (god) derive from the same root, implying the divinity of the former, and the unswervingness of the latter.

6 Genesis, 1, 26–9.

7 See Perrin, 1979.

8 In the seventh century BC. See Archilocus, fragment 3, in Diehl, *Anthologia*. One

of the reasons for the superiority of the barbarians at the beginning of the Persian Wars lay again in their corps of archers. The Greeks had no such troops, and their code of honor demanded that a free man equip himself with heavy armor and enter into hand-to-hand combat with the enemy.

9 See also Cipolla, 1965.

10 See Morris, 1975.

11 See Weber, 1904, "Introduction." See also the more recent Rosenberg and Birdzell, 1986, especially Chapter IV.

12 Needham, 1954, volume I, para. 239, remarks that there was a constant flow of Chinese technological inventions into Europe in the course of the first thirteen centuries of the Christian era, just as later the current of technology began to flow in the other direction. Cipolla, 1983, p. 410, insists that Europe was the third, if not indeed the fourth world with respect to the culturally more refined and economically and technologically more advanced worlds of the Byzantium of the Macedonian dynasties, the Islam of the Omayadis and the Abassidis, and the China of the Tang dynasty.

13 We know that China, while certainly in no way indifferent to problems of equity, has never developed a tradition of abstract jurisprudence. The Chinese have always preferred to evaluate right and wrong by looking case by case at concrete situations. This deeply ingrained attitude was also responsible for their having ignored the study of abstract geometry, which flowered so notably in Greece. The Chinese approaches to these two fields of knowledge show great similarity and express the same attitude. The Chinese looked at purely abstract things with a mixture of indifference and suspicion. See Needham, 1954, volume II, section 18 and volume III, section 19.

14 This development was in a certain sense announced, quite early, by Heracleitus. See Diels and Kranz, 50, *Die Fragmente*, "When you have listened not to me, but to the Law [*Lógos*], it is wise to agree."

15 See Needham, 1954, volumes IV and V. We also know that the ancient Mexicans were acquainted with the wheel and yet only put it to use in their toys.

16 See Cipolla, 1967.

17 *Ibid.*, p 103.

18 The success of such attempts to establish a relationship of optimum compatibility between human life and the natural environment is not, of course, absolute; their efficacy has to be understood from the socio-religious point of view. Reliance on backward techniques can also cause damage to nature. One remembers, for example, that bees were killed in order to harvest their honey in the era before the invention of the artificial hive with removable honeycombs.

19 Such gratuitous or arbitrary interventions of the gods, or their irrational use of their powers, remind us of the more ancient phases of Greek civilization. See Dodds, 1951, Chapter I, and Snell, 1946, Chapters II and III.

20 Lévy-Bruhl, 1922, Chapter VII.

21 Eliade, 1949, Chapter IV.

22 Towards the end of the nineteenth century, the Ghost Dance Religion was one of the politico-religious resistance movements with which the Native North Americans opposed the advance of the white settlers. It was widely spread in the north-west part of the American continent and it was charged with a profound awareness of the relationship between technical innovations and the survival of autonomous cultures. Its adepts were forbidden to make use of a whole series of implements introduced by the white settlers. See Linding and Dauer, 1964, pp. 56–8.

23 See also Toynbee, 1956, chapter XV, pp. 210ff.; and Cipolla, 1965, chapter II.

24 Lévy-Bruhl, 1963, is here quite noteworthy. We are told (p. 13) that for the

primitive, "It isn't a good thing to be too durably happy" (*trop constamment heureux*). A native of Célebes thus made the following remark (p. 14.) on a hunting expedition that was too successful, thanks to a dog that did too good a job: clearly the animal had intuited that its master was about to die and therefore made great efforts to procure the food that would be needed for the visitors who would come to pay homage at his funeral. In eastern Africa, excessively beautiful ears of maize in the harvest could be a source of worry. A farmer who found his harvest to include the "chief of the field" (apparently the description of the plant that was taller and finer that all the others) would be quite disturbed, since such a plant contained too much power for a poor and simple man. Before eating it, he would ask others to taste it, without telling them what it was. He was afraid of being poisoned (pp. 14–15). Lévy-Bruhl's account, moreover, never gives reason to think that the unhappy warnings seen in such signs are in any way connected with feelings of excessive satisfaction, pride or arrogance. It is not a question of a punishment that balances out a sin, since there has been no question of human responsibility. The primitive simply perceives that the natural order of things has been disturbed. That fact on its own is significant and magical and can only foreshadow the work of great and dangerous forces.

25 It is widely recognized that reactions of collective panic on the part of some of the pre-Columbian cultures of Central and South America – peoples whom it would be incorrect to speak of as primitives – were encouraged by previous prophecies on the arrival of divine beings. See, for example, León-Portilla, 1964.

26 Black Hawk, Sauk Chief, as reported in Hamilton, 1950, p. 165.

27 Smohalla, Wanapum Chief, as reported in Eliade, 1959, p. 138, quoting from Mooney, 1896, pp. 721, 724. In spite of its lack of supporting ethnographical evidence, Jean-Jacques Rousseau's reconstruction of the way in which the notion of property split man off from nature is in perfect harmony with the typical feelings of primitives:

> The first man, who having fenced in a plot of ground, said "this belongs to me" and found a group of people stupid enough to believe him, was the true founder of civilized society. How many crimes, how many wars, how many murders, how much misery and error the human race might have been spared if someone had ripped up the stakes or sprung across the ditch while crying out to his fellows, "Be careful to give no heed to this impostor! If you forget that the fruits of the earth belong to everyone and that the earth belongs to no one, you are lost!"
>
> (Rousseau, 1750)

Religious respect for material goods and the sacred limits of their commerciability are found with particular clarity among the Native Peoples of North America, thanks to the relative simplicity of their societies and to the tenacity of the resistance they showed to the penetration of European culture. Such phenomena are more difficult to perceive in Africa, where European influence dates much farther back. A greater willingness to compromise on the part of African peoples led as well to the creation of numerous intermediate situations. Mühlmann observes that "the 'territorial complex' of the Kikuyu," in eastern Africa,

> was one of the major definable causes for the Mau-Mau revolt. The Kikuyus hold that there is no such thing as land that belongs to no one, that the right to possession of a territory can never be lost, and therefore

that no foreign land can ever be "conquered" or "annexed" without offending the will of the supreme being (Ngai).

(Mühlmann, 1964, pp. 110–11)

Even this relatively recent conflict between English settlers and the native people of eastern Africa, in a period just preceding decolonization, is therefore seen to have derived not so much from economic than rather from religious considerations. In reference to the Kikuyu migration of the sixteenth century, Mühlmann remarks,

> The land that the Kikuyu wanted was woodland: one of the hunting grounds of the Ndorobo. If the Kikuyu were to acquire it, they and the Ndorobo had to enter into an act of solemn ritual communication – a "reciprocal adoption" – through which the spirits of the ancestors of the Ndorobo were transformed into Kikuyus. The juridical act that sanctioned the territorial agreement would thus take place "within the group," which was the only condition under which it was possible.

(ibid., p. 111)

4 THE EGOISM OF THE ARCHAIC GODS

1 We can imagine such a person to have felt himself different from people whose lives were just and proper. But he cannot be imagined to have felt "guilty" in the modern sense of the term. Guilt in the world of Archaic Greece was a form of damnation or contamination that had little to do with an individual's good or evil intentions. There was an objective cause (aitía) for the evils that afflicted the individual, even perhaps in spite of himself. It might, for example, have been áte (the blinding of reason), which in turn was personified as one of the daughters of Zeus. (The Iliad, IX, 504–5 and XIX, passim.)

2 This text will continue to make use of this conventional name for the person or persons who composed the Iliad and the Odyssey during the course, approximately, of the eighth century.

3 See Dodds, 1951, Chapter I; Snell, 1946, Chapter I; Pohlenz, 1947, Chapter I. It could even be said that twentieth-century psychology has been mainly a rediscovery of this ancient conviction.

4 The Iliad, XXII, 38–130. In our discussion of theater, we will also see that the crime of Euripides' Medea comes from her thymós rather than her will, which struggles against it.

5 The Odyssey, XX, 1–30.

6 See Snell, 1946; and as well Pohlenz, 1947, Chapter I.

7 One generally prefers to speak only of Greek religion, and not of a Greek theology. Greek religion was lacking in a revealed and well-organized doctrine, which is the meaning of theology, strictly defined. The place of theology was originally held by myth. See, for example, Burckhardt, 1929, volume I, part 3a. This text will respect this convention, though not perhaps rigidly. "Theology" is a better term than "religion" for dealing with the divine as self-sufficient and indifferent to the human being, such as we find it, in fact, in the realm of the Greek gods.

8 As said at the start, I refer to the gods of Olympus not because they were the only divinities of ancient Greece but because they are the best-known images of such deities, and, above all, because they are already a part of our world of metaphor. Their prevalence is doubtless also a product of the recent European culture that has studied them.

9 An example we will later discuss is the *áte* thrown by Zeus into Agamemnon.

10 On the other hand, interaction with subjective entities such as *thymós* or the *daímon* was much more autonomous. In the course of such confrontations, the Greeks practiced a kind of interior dialog, which was able to survive the decline of polytheism in the form of philosophy or proto-psychology. A renowned example is Socrates' attention to the *daímon* who spoke to him in a dream. Plato, *Phaedo*, IV, 60c–61b.

11 The ancients must to some extent have been conscious of this mechanism of psychological defense through expulsion. Lucretius was to say that the gods were born from the dreams of men. See *De rerum natura*, V, 1169–82

12 The *Iliad*, XXI, 538–611.

13 *Ibid.*, V, 792.

14 The *Odyssey*, I, 178–323.

15 The *Iliad*, XIX, 86ff.

16 *Ibid.*, 270ff.

17 The *Odyssey*, XI, 559ff.

18 The *Iliad*, III, 64–7.

19 The reconstruction of the two centuries, the seventh and sixth, that lie between Homer and Pericles in fact has to entrust itself almost entirely to the virtually psychological descriptions furnished by these personal voices. When documents that speak of the whole of society reappeared, the society had already changed. See Bowra, 1961.

20 See Snell, 1946, Chapter IV; and as well Di Lorenzo, 1988.

21 Fragment 1, Diehl, *Anthologia*.

22 Herodotus, VII, 10–18.

23 *Ibid.*, VII, 15.

24 *Ibid.*

25 The transformations of the religious ethics of the Greeks are treated in various ways in Dodds, 1951, Chapter II; Snell, 1946, Chapter X; Latte, 1920–2, pp. 254–98.

26 The Greek cosmogony is to be found in Hesiod's *Theogony*. It should be noted that Hesiod dedicates the whole of this work to the gods, without reference to men. No such thing is to be found in any of the monotheistic religions. According to Herodotus (II, 53), we owe the classification of the ancient gods according to attributes and categories to Homer and Hesiod.

27 See Burckhardt, 1929, volume I, part 3, and volume II, part 5.

28 Even though with reference to the immortal horses of Achilles. They pity man, "For in sooth there is naught . . . more miserable than man among all things that breathe and move upon earth." The *Iliad*, XVII, 443–47.

29 As Priamus reminds Achilles, the *Iliad*, XIV, 527ff.

30 As, for example in Minnermus (fragment 2, Diehl, *Anthologia*):

> But we, like the leaves that come in the flowery Springtime when they wax so quickly beneath the sunbeams, like them we enjoy the blossoms of youth for a season but an ell long, the Gods giving us knowledge neither of evil nor of good; for there beside us stand the black Death-Spirits, the one with the end that is grievous Eld, the other that which is Death.

> Or Simonides (fragment 9, Diehl): "Men's strength is slight, their plans impossible; within their brief lifetime toil upon toil; and death hangs inescapable over all alike: of death an equal portion is allotted to good men and to bad."

31 A few examples: Aeschylus, *Prometheus Bound*, 753ff., "Ah, hardly would'st

thou bear my agonies to whom it is not foredoomed to die; for death had freed me from my sufferings." Sophocles, in *Electra*, 1169–70, has his heroine cry "I fain would die to share with thee thy tomb; / For with the dead there is no mourning, none." The chorus of *Oedipus Rex*, 1186ff., exclaims, "Races of mortal man / Whose life is but a span, / I count ye but the shadow of a shade! / For he who most doth know / Of bliss, hath but the show; / A moment, and the visions pale and fade." The chorus in *Oedipus at Colonus*, 1224, likewise pronounces, "Not to be born at all / Is best, far best that can befall." In *Antigone*, 582ff., we find the words, "Thrice blessed are they who never tasted pain." Euripides' Medea, in *Medea*, 1228, remarks, "For among mortals, happy man is none." In *Hippolytus*, 189, "O'er all man's life woes gather thick"; and at line 367 of the same drama, "O troubles that cradle the children of men." The wisdom that Herodotus attributed to the gods lay in revealing to us that death is preferable to life, *History*, I, 31; VII, 46.

32 The Greeks' capacity for reacting to pessimism can be seen as the interior equivalent to their ability to react to the geographical difficulties presented by their outside world, a capacity which has been frequently underlined. (See note 2, our Chapter 7.)
33 See Latte, 1920–2; Snell, 1946, Chapters I, II, and X.
34 *Homeri Hymnus in Venerem*, 45–190.
35 The *Iliad*, XX, 375ff.; 443ff.
36 *Cheíron*, "inferior," *ibid.*, XX, 434 and 436.
37 *Ibid.*, XXII, 226ff.
38 *Ibid.*, XXII, 99ff.
39 See Snell, 1946, Chapter X.
40 See Latte, 1920–2, pp. 261–5.
41 The *Iliad*, XIV, 159–353.
42 The *Iliad*, XIII, 631–5.
43 The *Odyssey*, I, 32–4.
44 Fragments B 11 and 12, Diels and Kranz, *Die Fragmente*.
45 *Ibid.*, B 18. For the relationship with the notion of progress, see Childe, 1942.
46 See Dodds, 1951, Chapter II. The world *philótheos*, lover of god, was not to make its first appearance until Aristotle.
47 See Benedict, 1946, Chapter X.
48 See Dodds, 1951, Chapter II.
49 See Bowra, 1961.
50 As Freud was to note when he observed the survival of superstitious acts and unmotivated fears among civilized men. See Freud, 1912–13.
51 Perhaps from *phten-*, which in turn derives from a Zend or Avestic root that would signify "to diminish." See Chantraine, 1968, p. 1202. It is ordinarily rendered both as the "envy" and the "jealousy" of the gods, even if these terms are not truly synonymous. From the etymological point of view, envy, from the Latin *invidia*, implies simply the hostile glance (*in-video*, "look at from a slant") directed at those whom one considers to be more fortunate. "Jealousy," from the Greek *zélos* and the Latin *zelus* (which correspond as well to the German *Eifer-sucht*) is the glance that sees the fortune of the other as merited, and thus implies admiration or emulation (see our own Chapter 5) rather than jealously in the modern sense. Both translations seem inadequate: they imply a point of view that belongs to later epochs, when it was thought that mortals can have qualities that the gods lack. In its modern meaning, jealousy is primarily an obsessive defense of what one has, and envy is the desire for what belongs to others. In accord with modern usage, we should translate *phthónos* with "jealousy" when dealing with authors who accepted the traditional

religion, and with "envy" when dealing with authors who assumed a more critical stance.

52 Homer was less concerned with revealing any general law of "envy" than with narrating the desires for revenge that were felt by specific gods. Instead of the word *phthónos*, he employs the word *ágamai* (to admire, to envy).

5 THE GREEK SENSE OF LIMITS

1 We have already noted that Zeus' indifference to injustice, even at times his exploitation of injustice, had made his right to his divine scepter seem somewhat questionable. See the *Iliad*, XIX, 87; XIII, 633; and elsewhere.

2 *Anánke*. From our own point of view, it is of little importance that *anánke* is also at times personified as a deity. *Anánke* is of less significance as a mythic figure in its own right than as a law that gives cohesive meaning to the whole of Greek mythology.

3 Thucydides, *History*, I, 6.

4 *Ibid.*, II, 40. This is the celebrated funeral oration for the Athenians fallen in battle.

5 Herodotus, *History*, III, 39–43.

6 *Ibid.*, III, 43.

7 *Ibid.*, III, 125.

8 For the concept of *phthónos* as a divine distributive, or redistributive, principle as opposed to an expression of egoism, see also *ibid.*, I, 32; III, 40; VII, 10; VII, 46.

9 One cannot of course exclude the possibility that the fear of the envy of the gods was also a way of exorcizing the fear of the envy of one's neighbors. Such fears may perhaps have been sublimated and projected into the heavens. As we will see with the pity the Greeks could feel for their historical enemies, virtually to the point of identifying with the Trojans and the Persians, one of the typical instincts inherent in the Greek sensibility was to place oneself in the position of others. But there is little real reason to insist too heavily on the role of human envy, which in fact is found everywhere. The Greeks, on the other hand, are the only people ever to have seen the envy of the gods as a central consideration; it even gave them the crucial explanations for all historical events.

10 See for example Herodotus, I, 34.

11 Our principle sources of information are: Tournier, 1863; Roscher, 1884–1937; Posnansky, 1890; Volkmann, 1920–1 pp. 294–321; Murray, 1907; Del Grande, 1947; Kerényi, 1939.

12 The *Iliad*, I, 202 and 214. We have previously met this word in Menelaus' invective against the Trojans.

13 The *Odyssey*, XVII, 485–7. The first adjective is *hýbrin*, the second is *eunomíen*, which indicates a person who respects the law. The words have been aptly chosen and contrasted since *eunomíen* contains the same root (and thus the same idea) as the word *némesis*.

14 *Ibid.*, XXII, 40: "Ye dogs, ye thought that I should never more come home from the land of the Trojans, seeing that ye wasted my house, and lay with the maidservants by force, and while yet I lived covertly wooed my wife, having no fear of the gods, who hold broad heaven, nor of the indignation of men."

15 *Works and Days*, 134, 137, 145–6, etc.

16 Evil spirit: *Persians*, 354.

17 Demon or spirit; *ibid.*, 345, 354, 472, 724, 725, 845.

18 *Ibid.*, 808 and 821.

19 *Ibid.*, 362.

20 See Burckhardt, 1929, volume I, part 2, Chapter XX, section 4; Glotz, 1986, Chapter XVIII; Flaceliere, 1959, Chapters III and IV.

21 The *Iliad*, VI, 442 and XXII, 105.

22 Such an invocation is spoken, for example, by Poseidon, when he incites the Greeks to resistance against the Trojans, who seem about to overwhelm them. The *Iliad*, XIII, 122.

23 *Works and Days*, 197.

24 We have noted that Ulysses, before striking down the suitors of Penelope, reproved them for having forgotten all respect for *némesis anthrópon*, which in addition to being an irate reaction was also revenge, and distributive justice as administered by mortal men. The *Odyssey*, XXII, 40.

25 See also Roscher, 1884–1937, volume III.1, 118.

26 Murray, 1907, p. 89.

27 *Nichomachean Ethics*, 1108a30–b5.

28 Murray, 1907, pp. 91ff.

29 A century after Homer, the poet Archilocus dared to boast of having saved his life by throwing away his shield, a gesture that traditionally would have covered him with shame. See Archilocus, fragment 6, Diehl, *Anthologia*; and also Anacreon, fragment 51, Diehl.

30 Kerényi, 1939, p. 50.

31 Posnansky, 1890, p. 1ff.

32 *Theogony*, 223, 224.

33 Roscher, 1884–1937, volume III.1, pp. 130–2.

34 I here make use of the information furnished by Kerényi, 1939, pp . 35–8, and by Roscher, 1884–1937, volume III.1, pp. 118–20.

35 Kerényi, *ibid.*, p. 51.

36 Kerényi, *ibid.*

37 Kerényi, *ibid.*, pp. 55–6

38 See, for example, Posnansky, 1890, pp. 6–23.

39 The *Iliad*, III, 156–8.

40 A change was already perceptible in the classical age. In *Agamemnon* (verse 11) the chorus attempts to attribute responsibility to both Helen and Clytemnestra, and clearly considers the latter to be guilty of *hýbris*. But one also notes that Clytemnestra's guilt derives from her possession of "a masculine heart."

41 The intertwining of the various components of the reform is underscored by Jaeger, 1943, book I. Aristotle's *Constitution of Athens* already speaks of those changes as an evolution in customs that was of wider scope than mere judiciary reform. For an overview of the institutional reforms, see Chapter IV of *The Fifth Century BC*, the fifth volume of *The Cambridge Ancient History* (Lewis *et al.* 1992).

42 See also Pohlenz, 1947, Chapter XII.

43 Fragment 1, Diehl, *Anthologia*, 71–3.

44 Fragment 5, *ibid.*

45 Fragment 1, *ibid.*, 16–28.

46 Fragment 25, *ibid.*, 25.

47 Plutarch, *The Life of Themistocles*, 22, 5, was already to remark, "ostracism was not a penalty, but a way of pacifying and alleviating that jealousy which delights to humble the eminent, breathing out its malice into this disenfranchisement."

48 Even Aristotle accepted the legitimacy of slavery. See *Politics*, 1252 a.

49 Plato too respected this tradition. The number of the fully enfranchised citizens should have been fixed at 5,040 (*Laws*, V, 737–40); and the dimensions of the

city were to neither increase nor decrease (Plato, *The Republic*, V, 460; Aristotle *Politics*, 1326a-b.) See also Mumford, 1961, by now a classic, Chapters VI and VII. Concern with limiting the sizes of cities was unknown both in the ancient cities of the Near East and in Rome, and it disappeared with Hellenism. It is significant that a taboo that limited citizenship to 5,000 to 6,000 people appeared in periods of hardship. After the defeat of Sicily, the Athenians chose to submit to an oligarchy, entrusting the state to the 5,000 people who were considered to be its best. As we will see further on, the number of citizens who directly participated in the governing of fifth-century Athens were at most 6,000.

50 *Politics*, 1326a–b.
51 As Finley seems to do, even while insisting on the limited size and ideally total independence of every community as the dominant political taboos. See Finley, 1964, Chapter III.
52 Finley, *ibid.*, insists that the tenacity of the small independent community can be explained only as an attitude that found its resolution in a deep and irrepressible conviction on the way in which mutual coexistence had to be organized. Toynbee in various works expresses the conviction that the *pólis* deified itself and became the true object of religion for the Greeks. This point of view seems to fit quite well with the fact that the gods of Greek tradition were entirely inadequate as objects of veneration. It is difficult to imagine a society that has no positive points of reference in its religion. See Toynbee, 1934–61, volume IV, Chapter XVI; and 1959, Chapter IV. See also Pohlenz, 1947, Chapter V.

6 HISTORY BEGINS TO MOVE

1 *Poetics*, 1451b.
2 See also Snell, 1946, Chapter IX; and Toynbee, 1956, Chapters I and III.
3 See Farrington, 1947, and Mondolfo, 1982.
4 See also Bury, 1932. Similar ideas are also found in the essay "The Ancient concept of progress," in Dodds, 1985. Since the terms we employ include both "growth" and "progress," we have to be clear about the distinction between them. "Growth" is a general term that makes no reference to the source of the growth involved. "Progress," on the other hand, is intentional growth and implies improvement. As we use the word today, it derives most of all from the period of the Enlightenment. But a critical assessment of the term can be based on a glance at a more distant past. We can discover it to contain the notion of a guiding force (the Latin *pro-gressus*, a step forward, is precisely the same as the German *Fort-schritt*). This is a notion that has not always existed, and that in many ways has come to replace the Christian notion of a guiding Providence (*pro-vedere*, or looking forward), which in turn supplanted the Greco-Roman notion of fate. But as we look into the future, we find it difficult to imagine the relativity of the notion of progress and to see that it might again be subject to decline and come to find itself replaced by still other notions of a guiding force. (See also Bury, 1932, pp. 241ff.) Each of these ideas has incorporated the notion that preceded it, throwing it into historical perspective. But the new notion evaluates the old notion without evaluating itself. The distortion of our point of view lies in our inability to imagine a value successive and superior to the idea of progress, thus presuming that the notion of progress is absolute and definitive, just as the Middle Ages would have maintained with respect to Providence, or as the Greeks and Romans might have held for the

notion of fate. Every epoch that enjoys relative stability has the unconscious tendency to see itself as the final stage of civilization. For the Greek concept of fate, see also Dodds, 1985; the first pages of that essay contain a brief summary of the Greek ideas that correspond to the Latin *progressio, epídosis* and *prokopé*. In the quotation in Chapter IV, *Die Fragmente* (fragment B18, Diels and Kranz), Xenophanes makes use of *ameíonon*, the comparative of *agathós*, which means "good."

5 *Works and Days*, part I.

6 The compensatory dynamics of the psyche that are connected to its bipolarities are constantly present in the thought of Jung, who takes the concept of enantiodromia from Heracleitus.

> I use the term enantiodromia for the emergence of the unconscious opposite in the course of time. The characteristic phenomenon practically always occurs when an extreme, one-sided tendency dominates conscious life; in time an equally powerful counterposition is built up, which first inhibits the conscious performance and subsequently breaks through the conscious control.
>
> (Jung, 1921, par. 709)

7 Herodotus, VII, 60. The Scythians were known once to have counted their troops by making a pile of their arrow heads (*ibid.*, IV, 81). In order to capture the Greeks on the islands, the Persians held each other's hands and advanced as a human chain from which none of the island's inhabitants could escape (*Ibid.*, VI, 321).

8 Burckhardt, 1929, II, IV, 2. Just as the Greeks were responsible for the word *barbarian*, they also supply us with most of the descriptions of these peoples. A barbarian, as far as the Greeks were concerned, was anyone who did not speak their language. But in fact they knew quite well that all of "the other peoples" were not the same. The peoples in the north, for example, were thought of as fairly uncivilized, whereas the Asiatic peoples were even the object of a certain measure of admiration: they were powerful and rich, and the Greeks were also aware of the complexity of their culture and systems of organization.

9 Herodotus, VI, 48.

10 *Ibid.*, VII, 133. Herodotus' story of the Persian ambassadors who came with demands for submission has been held to be unreliable. (See, for example, Bengston, 1986, section III, part I, 2.) But if the story is seen as a later mythological embellishment that accentuates the victory of the just, its symbolic character is indeed quite telling. Herodotus does not seem to see the Greeks themselves as responsible for their treatment of the Persian ambassadors. Quite to the contrary. The reply of the Greeks is presented as a emblematic and metaphorical form of justice that strikes down an act of *hýbris*.

11 Given the logistic difficulties of moving from one place to another, and above all owing to the circumscribed notion of the nation to which a citizen belonged: the *pólis*. The distance from Athens to Marathon was in fact 40 kilometers – the very same distance as the marathon race.

12 The two armies were separated by more than 8 *stádia*, a unit of measurement that corresponds to 185 meters. So the total distance was about 1½ kilometers.

13 See Herodotus, *History*, VI, 112. For the Athenians to have run the whole distance dressed in heavy armor is highly unlikely. Herodotus also exaggerates in attributing the entirety of the initiative for the encounter to the Athenians. My general reconstruction of the events is based on Bengston, 1986, and especially Glotz, 1986.

14 *Ibid.*, VI, 117.

15 The main source is Pausanias, I, 33, 2 and 3.

16 Other sources indicate that the sculptor was Agoracritos. The statue is no longer in existence, except for a few important fragments in the British Museum. See Posnansky, 1890, pp. 100ff., and Roscher, 1884–1937, III.1, p. 148ff.

17 Posnansky, 1890, pp. 40 ff.; Roscher, 1884–1937 III.1, pp. 127 and 131. The attribution of the victory to this deity probably dates from later times, and the story of the block of marble can be imagined to date from the epoch in which the veneration of Nemesis reached its peak. Otherwise there would be no explanation for the fact that the highly religious Aeschylus attributed the Greeks' second victory over the Persians not to Nemesis, but to a simple *daímon*. This is the view of Posnansky, who however draws no distinction between the campaigns of Darius and Xerxes, of which the latter was the inspiration for Aeschylus' drama. In any case, Aeschylus' omission of any mention of the goddess Nemesis is proof that the affirmation of the cult of Nemesis came somewhat later than that of the cults of most of the other gods.

18 Writing at a time not much later than the end of the Persian Wars, Herodotus, posterity's principal source, certainly accepted exaggerated reports from witnesses. See also Burckhardt, 1929, part VIII, Chapter VI, and part IX, Chapter III. Herodotus rarely makes direct comments, but in addition to offering descriptions he makes cunning use of exclamations or conversations he has heard as a way of underlining what strikes him as essential.

19 Herodotus, VII, 8.

20 *Ibid.*, VII, 10

21 *Ibid.*, VII, 34.

22 *Ibid.*, VII, 35.

23 *Ibid.*, VII, 56.

24 *Ibid.*, VII, 40.

25 *Ibid.*, VII, 56.

26 Herodotus himself was aware of this problem, but gives it a mythic dimension, as confirmed by other unusual events: "I am not at all surprised that the courses of several rivers were depleted," referring to the army's consumption of water, "but I ask myself in amazement how sufficient food was found." (*ibid.*, VII, 187).

27 Boardman *et al.*, 1986, Chapter I.

28 Glotz, 1986, Chapter II.

29 The way these figures related to the contemporary world are revealed by considering that the entire population of fifth-century Attica (including a majority of half-breeds and slaves) amounted to a figure between 200,000 (De Sanctis, 1975) and 500,000 (Flacelière, 1959, Chapter II, p. 78). An intermediate figure is also given by Glotz, 1986, Chapter VII. In Athens, which was then the most populous city of the known world, the citizens entitled to vote numbered no more than 30–40,000.

30 Herodotus, VII, 56.

31 See Burckhardt, 1929, part VIII, Chapter VI.

32 Herodotus, VII, 188–90.

33 According to Glotz, 1986, volume II, Chapter 2, who also sees little likelihood in Herodotus' report that the allied troops were dismissed and sent home.

34 Herodotus, VII, 226.

35 *Ibid.*, 225

36 *Ibid.*, 238.

37 Herodotus, VIII, 75.

38 *Ibid.*, 84–96; see also Aeschylus,*The Persians.*

39 Herodotus, VI, 17.

40 See, for example, *ibid.*, VI, 105 and 107; VII, 57, 141 and 189.

41 See Chantraine, 1968, p. 400. (See also our preceding distinction between envy and jealousy.)

42 Aristotle, *Constitution of Athens*, XXII, 3.

43 See also Burckhardt, 1929, part IX, Chapter III.

44 One might consider a few Jungian interpretations, and in particular with reference to Stalin: "When you fight a thing you have to get very close to it, and it is likely to infect you. . . . Stalin fought so much against the Czar's bloody oppression that he is now doing exactly the same as the Czar" (Jung, 1938, p. 130).

45 Herodotus, *History,* VI, 112.

46 Even though our narrative does not include a discussion of the figurative arts, it is worth remembering that at the end of the sixth century the principal statues representing the human figure (*koúroi*) were still quite static and endowed with an almost inscrutable expression. All of that was to change quite radically in the fifth century, when everything was set into motion, in the plastic arts as well.

47 Herodotus, VII, 139. "It was they . . ., naturally after the gods, who repulsed the king Xerxes." But even in the mouth of Herodotus, that homage to the gods sounds formal and irrelevant, inserted, as it is, into an entire chapter that sings a hymn of praise to the merits of the Athenians.

48 Thucydides, V, 89. See as well VI, 83.

49 See also Burckhardt, 1929, part V, on "The ability to listen to adversaries."

7 NEW HORIZONS

1 See Chapter 6, note 29.

2 The birth of autonomous civilizations is often explained in terms of such a model, of which the most well known is Toynbee's hypothesis of "challenge and response." After employing this theory as the fulcrum of an explanation of the origins of autonomous civilizations in general (1934–61, volume II, Chapter VII, and again in volumes III, IV and V, *passim*) he applied it in detail to Greece in a later work (1959, Chapter II). The notion is particularly pertinent to Athens, where the challenge was especially intense and came quite early. Virtually no other country has arable lands that are both so good and also so scattered, scarce and difficult to irrigate. But Greece also boasts a variety of landscapes, ports and maritime routes that stimulates travel. Snell's observations (1946, Chapter XVII) are quite similar. One notes that Toynbee's most eloquent critic, Ortega, is here in substantial agreement with his theory. (See Ortega y Gasset, 1966, lecture X.) This is not in fact a modern idea and its antecedents can be found among the ancient Greeks themselves. Their scientific curiosity led them to explain cultural differences as the fruit of different environmental circumstances. A passage (16) from *Airs, Waters and Places* in the Hippocratic Collection affirms:

> With regard to the lack of spirit and of courage . . . the chief reason why Asiatics are less warlike and more gentle in character than Europeans is the uniformity of the seasons, which show no violent changes either towards heat or towards cold, but are equable. For there occur no mental shocks nor violent physical change, which are more likely to steel the temper and impart to it a fierce passion than is a monotonous sameness.

One notes that this explanation indirectly confirms the Greeks' ability to identify with their adversaries. It insists on contingent rather than structural differences between peoples, avoiding all racist distinctions. Hippocrates was also aware of how greatly individual temperaments can vary: "You will find that Asiatics also differ from one another, some being superior, others inferior" (*ibid.*).

3 See Glotz, 1986, volume II, Chapter XIV; for the relationship between the economic system and the supremacy of the aristocracy, see also our Chapter 5.

4 See Glotz, 1986, volume II, Chapter I. For the particularly anticonformist way in which Athens encouraged the development of new techniques, see also Vidal-Naquet and Austin, 1977, Chapter V.

5 For the general expansion of the Greek city-state, see Smith, 1967, part I, Chapter II.

6 Thucydides, II, 38.

7 *Ibid.*, I, 102.

8 *Ibid.*, II, 65.

9 See Glotz, 1986, volume II, Chapter XIV.

10 See Colli, 1975, Chapter I.

11 Fragment B107, Diels and Kranz, *Die Fragmente.*

12 *ouk emoú, allà toû lógou akóusantas* (Fragment B50, *ibid.*).

13 Fragment B45, *ibid.*

14 But was it truly Socrates who brought about these changes? And who was Socrates? Like Christ, he was a man who was written about by others, and who wrote nothing of his own; a symbol, to whom we attribute essential innovations. But perhaps the things to which we refer as the innovations of Socrates were developments to which he no more than opened the road by unsettling traditional certainties. Perhaps it was only in later years that they slowly came into existence. Socrates as the inventor of concepts is a figure whom we know from Plato. And the Socrates who laid the bases of modern thought by ripping the soul from its origins is a figure that appears in the brilliant though slanted thinking of Nietzsche. But this is in any case the tradition from which we derive, and we will continue to respect it. We discuss the innovations of Socrates, without truly knowing the extent to which they were truly his own, and we do so because the subject of our discussion in not a man, but a culture and a symbol. And such a culture and such a symbol are unquestionably a part of the cultural memory of European civilization, even if perhaps they partly date from somewhat more recent times. It is in much the same way that we continue to talk about Homeric attitudes, since this is the epic heritage that has reached us, even if someone may some day prove that Homer never existed.

15 Plato, *Apology,* 21b–23b.

16 These were the consequences of the invention of philosophy, but not at all the intentions of its founders. The philosophers were mistrustful of these new activities, since that knew them to lead to change and greed, which were feared by the philosophers' typically conservative social views. See Plato, *Laws*, IV, 704aff.

17 Jaeger, 1943, volume II, pp. 48–50, and volume II, pp. 3–76, pays particular attention to the ways in which Socratic thought constructed its new ethical vision on the basis of precedents found in the first medical treatises.

18 See, for example, Aristotle, *Nicomachean Ethics*, 188b 7–10 and the following citations.

19 Plato, *Laches*, 198d.

20 See Plato, *Politics*, 299c; *Laches*, 198d; Aristotle, *Nicomachean Ethics*, 1104a 9; 1112b 5.

21 Aristotle, *Metaphysics*, 982b 10–22.
22 Plato, *Laws*, III, 698a; IV, 705b; V, 742a–e.
23 Aristotle, *Politics*, 1362b.
24 Plato, *Gorgias*, 467b–468a.
25 Plato, *Lysis*, 218a; *Laws*, IX, 963c-d.
26 According to Plato, for example, the gods keep watch over men, and are good and free from jealousy. See *Timaeus*, 29e, and *The Republic* II, 379a–d.
27 Aristotle even refers to the circumstances under which the gods took on anthropomorphic qualities, thus relativizing the forms if not the substance of faith. See *Metaphysics*, 1074b.
28 "Is not this the conclusion? – that the soul is in the very likeness of the divine, and immortal?" (Plato, *Phaedo*, 80b).
29 "For nothing that belongs to happiness can be incomplete. Such a life as this however will be higher than the human level: not in virtue of his humanity will a man achieve it, but in virtue of something within him that is divine. . . . If then the intellect is something divine in comparison with man, so is the life of the intellect divine in comparison with human life. Nor ought we to obey those who enjoin that a man should have men's thoughts and a mortal the thoughts of mortality, but we ought so far as possible to achieve immortality, and do all that man may to live in accordance with the highest thing in him; for though this be small in bulk, in power and value it far surpasses all the rest" (Aristotle, *Nicomachean Ethics*, 1177b 25–1178a 5). See also *Metaphysics*, the entire second chapter of book I.
30 Plato, *Timaeus*, 29c–e.
31 Aristotle, *Metaphysics*, 982b–983a.
32 Aristotle, *Rhetoric*, 1386b.
33 Colli, 1975, p. 13.
34 Herodotus, I, 1.
35 The epic poems opened with a ritual invocation to the Muse. Her voice had to sing the stories of its heroes. We have already drawn attention to the first line of the *Odyssey*: "Tell me, O Muse, of the man . . . ."
36 See Chapter 6.
37 Herodotus, II, 53.
38 Snell, 1946, p. 215, remarks that for the Greeks of the Archaic period, a mythical event could be the "cause," practically speaking, of some present-day fact, but that what happened in the past was otherwise something apart and without relationship to the present.
39 *phthonerón te kai tarachódes* (I, 32). It is hardly an accident that Herodotus puts these words in the mouth of Solon, the father of Athenian law.
40 Herodotus' profound belief in a divine morality, paradoxically enough, is the only thing that renders comprehensible the sufferings to which the heavens subject men who are substantially good but gifted with an excess of fortune that the gods will not tolerate. This is the substance of the story of king Croesus (I, 26–61) and also of the already cited story of Polycrates.
41 IX, 109.
42 *Macbeth*, V, V, 26–8.
43 "We Europeans have recounted the history of the world, starting with the Peloponnesian Wars and the historical writings of Thucydides. . . . *This war is the beginning of history*" (Sini, 1989, p. 106).
44 Thucydides, II, 41. Thucydides attributes this statement to Pericles, who clearly voices the historian's own opinion.
45 See also Jaeger, 1943, book II, Chapter VI.
46 Thucydides, V, 84–113.

47 "since you have immediately set up the debate on the theme of what is useful, ignoring the theme of justice . . ." (*ibid.*, V, 90).

48 *Ibid.*, V, 98.

49 *Ibid.*, V, 95.

50 *Ibid.*, V, 116.

51 *Ibid.*, V, 113.

52 *Ibid.*, book VII, which recounts the defeat of the Athenians in Sicily.

53 *Ibid.*, V, 105

54 *Ibid.*, I, 22.

55 The dates of the birth of Aeschylus and Euripides can be calculated to have been separated by no more than forty-five years.

56 In the play *Persians*.

57 For Aeschylus, as for every responsible citizen of the time, this was not only a poetic feeling, but also a political and civic conviction. Though aware of the importance of the victory at Marathon, where he himself fought, he did not hesitate to condemn the anxious desire for continued victory that inspired the policies of Pericles. That was no punishment of *hýbris*, but a form of it.

58 It is surprising to note how modern categories of interpretation can impoverish this complex vision. Farrington insists that Aeschylus throughout the whole of his career was concerned with a political problem, or with the attempt to secure the bases of Athenian democracy, and that in *Persians* he had sung a hymn of victory for the triumph of democracy over its barbarian enemies. But this is to forget that for Aeschylus the laws of the city of Athens belonged to a realm of religious more than political or juridical order and descended directly from Solon. One finds, moreover, not a single passage of *Persians* that asserts a Greek supremacy. The barbarians (a word that assumed negative connotations only in later times) were subject to such an order just like the more advanced Greeks themselves. What the drama recounts is not a political victory, but the victory of *némesis* over *hýbris*. See Farrington, 1946, Chapter VI.

59 *Agamemnon*, 918ff.

60 *á-phthonos*, *ibid.*, 471.

61 *Ibid.*, 11.

62 *Ibid.*, 1501.

63 *Ibid.*, 1485.

64 *Ibid.*, 1505ff.

65 For a view of the relationship between Socrates and the Greek tragedies (a view less pessimistic than the views of Nietzsche, to which we have previously referred), see Jaeger, 1943, book III, Chapter II.

66 The nurse in *Hippolytus* repeats the phrase "Nothing too much" (265). But it is hardly an accident that she is the play's most ambiguous figure, and the person who is involuntarily responsible for unleashing the evils it recounts.

67 See *Medea*, 255ff.; Phaedra at line 474 in *Hippolytus*; *Electra*, 246–67 passim.

68 *The Madness of Hercules*, 1341–6. See also the Euripidean fragment, "a god who behaves badly is no god." (fragment 292, 7 Nauck). Or again, "Ever men's folly is their Aphrodite" (*Trojan Women*, 989).

69 "All of the instincts that are not discharged towards the exterior, *turn instead towards the interior*. This is what I refer to as the *interiorization* of man. This alone accounts for the development in man of what will later be called his 'soul.'" (Nietzsche, 1887, Chapter XVI). And later, "The man who in the lack of external enemies and resistances, closed up in an oppressive narrowness and normalcy of custom, impatiently tore himself into tatters, persecuted himself, ate away at himself . . . became the inventor of 'bad consciousness.'" (*ibid.*). One notes

Nietzsche's anticipation of the Freudian notion of the super-ego and of the sadistic force that it unleashes against the individual.

70 Euripides, *Iphigenia at Aulis*, 1400ff. We are by now at quite a distance from Aeschylus' respect for the enemy, and from the Homeric tradition that never referred to the Trojans as barbarians.

71 We do well to remember that Euripides was condemned to slight success, that Thucydides lived in exile for twenty years, from 424 to 404, and that Socrates was made to drink the hemlock in 399.

72 *Medea*, 1078–80.

73 See De Sanctis, 1975, book III, p. 411.

74 Nietzsche's nostalgia for Greek "pessimism" is undoubtedly linked with his personality. But in addition to having been a part of a fundamental rediscovery of the Greeks (his *Birth of Tragedy* is subtitled *The Greek Spirit and Pessimism*) he also affected the intellectual climate in a way that we still, after more than a century, find it difficult to understand. Burckhardt is another of the great protagonists of this shift of attitudes. Nietzsche was a few years younger, and he was deeply impressed by the lectures of the older man, who was then in the course of writing his most powerful pages on the subject of Greek pessimism. These writings exercised a powerful influence on the German culture of later generations, imbuing it with specific qualities of which the other countries of Europe were to feel the brunt in the course of the two world wars. (See Burckhardt, 1929, part V.)

75 See Hillman, 1971, and Samuels, 1989. Samuels makes use of a different approach that addresses the multiplicity of conscious contents and cultural structures.

76 See Nietzsche, 1886, chapter IX, "What is aristocratic?" See also Burckhardt, 1929, part II, Chapter II.

77 *Weisheit* rather than *Wissenschaft* (science) in German.

> Its principal characteristic consists of its finding its highest goal not in science, but in wisdom, which without allowing itself to be deceived by the seductive deviations of science, turns its immobile gaze towards the total image of the world, attempting to grasp within it, with empathetic feelings of love, one's own eternal suffering.
>
> (Nietzsche, 1872, p. chapter 18)

78 *volumen* (or "scroll") from *volvo*, or "roll up."

79 See, for example, Lanza and Vegetti, 1975, Chapter V.

80 See Pohlenz, 1947, Chapter VXI.

81 See Jaeger, 1943, volume I, Chapter III.

82 See the chapter "Il monoteismo della ragione," in Galimberti, 1984.

83 Burckhardt considers the fifth century to have been a period of decline and he associates the spread of democracy with the spread of greed. He contrasts this period of democracy with the precedent aristocratic age (1929, part IX, Chapter III).

84　Socrates: And as for the Muse of Tragedy, that solemn and august personage – what are her aspirations? Is all her aim and desire only to give pleasure to the spectators, or does she fight against them and refuse to speak of their pleasant vices, and willingly proclaim in word and song truths welcome and unwelcome? – which in your judgment is her character?

Callicles: There can be no doubt, Socrates, that Tragedy has her face turned towards pleasure and the gratification of the audience.

Socrates: And is not that the sort of thing, Callicles, which we were just now describing as flattery? Then now we have discovered a sort of rhetoric which is addressed to a crowd of men, women, and children, freemen and slaves. And this is not much to our taste, for we have described it as having the nature of flattery.

(Plato, *Gorgias*, 502b–d)

85 Tournier, 1863, part II, Chapter X.
86 Kerényi, 1960, Chapter VI.
87 "But when they had formed a barrier of ships between the beach sacred to Artemis of the golden bow and the beach of Cynosura, after having in a madness of hope destroyed the flourishing city of Athens, Dike was to cancel out their arrogance, daughter of hybris, who in the greatness of her fury imagines herself to swallow up everything" (Herodotus VIII, 77).
88 Posnansky, 1890, pp. 57–9; Roscher, 1884–1937 III.1, p. 135 and *passim*.
89 See above, in the pages dedicated to Thucydides.
90 See Sinclair, 1988, part 5, Chapter II.
91 Snell, 1946, Chapter II.
92 See Roscher, 1884–1937, III.7, pp. 130, 136, 141; Posnansky, 1890, pp. 52ff.; Volkmann, 1920, p. 321; Tournier, 1863, p. 225; Dodds, 1951, Chapter IX.
93 Roscher, 1884–1937, III.1, pp. 141ff.

8 CONTINUITY AND TRANSFORMATION

1 In the course of his study of history, Toynbee formulates a list of twenty-eight original civilizations. Eighteen of them are seen as totally extinct, and nine of the remaining ten have in some way or another collapsed. Toynbee speaks of western civilization as the only one that currently survives and flourishes. See Toynbee, 1934–61, volume IV, Chapter 13.
2 See Quinzio, 1984, Chapter II.
3 According to the myth, the Greeks who went to do battle at Troy left Philoctetes on an island. He suffered from an incurable wound. But he possessed the bow and arrows of Heracles, without which the enemy city could not be destroyed. Odysseus therefore returned to Philoctetes, who preferred to continue to suffer in solitude rather than to collaborate with those who had abandoned him. Odysseus was full of self-awareness and challenged such archaic stubborness, remarking that he was only what circumstances required of him (Sophocles, *Philoctetes*, 1049). And he was ready to make use of a ruse to extract the bow from Philoctetes. The root word *odys-* indicates scorn and hatred. Homer tells us that Odysseus means "he who feels scorn and hatred" (he received the name from his maternal grandfather: *Odyssey*, XIX 407ff.) whereas Sophocles interprets the name to mean "he who excites the scorn and hatred of others" (fragment 964, Nauck).
4 In the distribution of the arms of Achilles. The only occasions on which Pindar mentions Odysseus pass this accusation along, and without attenuation. *Nemean* VII, 20ff.
5 Euripides, *Trojan Women*, 721 and 723.
6 See our remarks above, in Chapter 1, on the notion of *cultura animi*.
7 St John, 1, 1. The new cohabitation of God with man was also visible in architecture: the church is conceived for both, differently from pagan temples, which were dedicated to the gods alone.
8 *Ibid.*, 1, 14.

9 First Epistle to the Corinthians, 1, 23. Toynbee remarks, in reference to this passage:

> For the Jews, this revolutionary Christan doctrine of God's incarnation was a blasphemous importation into Judaism of a myth that was one of the most damnable of all the errors in Hellenic paganism. This was a betrayal of everything that Judaism had achieved in a long and arduous struggle to purify and elevate man's vision of God's nature.

In this sense, Christianity is a radical grafting of the Greek mentality onto the matrix of monotheism (Toynbee, 1959, Chapter I, p. 16).

10 Nietzsche, 1883–5.

11 *Ibid.* The meaning of *über* as "out" leads us back to the relationship between *hýbris* and *outrage* (raging or ranging "outwards"). *Hýbris* can also be rendered in German with *Übermut*.

12 The psychological dynamics of Nietzsche's profound identification with God were analyzed by Jung in a long series of seminars, of which the stenographic notes have recently been published; see Jung, 1988.

13 See Quinzio, 1984, Chapter II.

14 Matthew, 5, 37

15 See Nietzsche, 1872, Chapter XVff. (The title, *The Birth of Tragedy, or the Greek Spirit and Pessimism* was added by the author in the edition of 1886.)

16 See Eliade, 1949, Chapter III.

17 See again Eliade, 1949, especially Chapters I and IV. "Men of the archaic cultures found it difficult to accept 'history' and periodically attempted to abolish it."

18 This variety of images is often praised by Jung as being more psychological than anything to be found in Protestantism, which is constructed almost exclusively around the image of God the Father, and where the overall attitude is more abstract and philosophical. See above all the publication of 1952. In particular he sees the presence of chthonic forces and numerous female figures as corresponding more to the range and multiplicity of psychic needs. The intensely practised cult of the Virgin Mary can also be seen to recuperate a variety of aspects of the archaic religion of the Great Mother, who herself is a personification of nature.

19 One remembers that ideological considerations kept the painting of religious icons immobile for thousands of years, with its figures detached from any and all context, as opposed to the art of western Europe where movements and background scenes reveal the complex inter-relationship between its images and the cultural developments in the surrounding world in which they existed. See the essay by Florenskij (1922).

20 See Ariès, 1986, Chapter IV: "History ... at its origins, to the extent that it separates itself from myths that are independent of time, embodies the concerns of the princes and scribes at the moment in which states were coming into existence and taking control of rural communities that had previously been regulated by customs."

21 Toynbee too was deeply influenced by Spengler; see 1934–61, volume IV, Chapter XIX and 1948, Chapter II.

22 See, for example, Mauss, 1926.

23 Their previous conviction of their own impending destruction finds documentation in any number of sources. Though itself influenced by the teachings on the coming of the Millennium of Gioachino da Fiore, a fine example can be found in de Sahagun, 1840, especially Chapter I.

9 THE CONTINUITY OF THE MYTH OF LIMITS: GREEK STORIES

1 I refer to various different versions of the story, as reported by Roscher, 1884–1937; Graves, 1955; Kerényi, 1960; *New Larousse Encyclopedia of Mythology.*

2 See the previous note for bibliographical references. Most of the sources of the story of Phaeton are Roman.

3 *Theogony,* 987ff.

4 See pp. 265ff.

5 *Theogony,* 507ff.

6 *Ibid.,* 513–14.

7 *Works and Days,* 53.

8 We now have only *Prometheus Bound; Prometheus the Bringer of Fire* and *Prometheus Unbound* have been lost.

9 *Krátos* means force or power. Here he punishes the Titan who helped humanity to go beyond the miserly limits that the gods desired to impose. The Greek concept of *krátos* is often associated with the problem of the limits of action. We can note that the name of the tyrant of Samos, who obtained even what he did not desire, was Polycrates (he who can do much – see Chapter 5, p. 46); we will later see (p. 149) that the personage who inspired Goethe's story of the sorcerer's apprentice was named Pancrates (he who can do everything).

10 Aeschylus, *Prometheus Bound,* 936.

11 *Protagoras,* 320c.

12 This would likewise appear to be true of the trilogy's two lost tragedies.

13 Hector's wife Andromacha implores, "Stay here with me on the tower, and concentrate the army near the wild fig tree where the walls are more vulnerable." But Hector, as we have seen already, replies, "Such things are important to me as well. But I am shamed before the feelings of the Trojans. And I have learned to know glory fighting in the front lines. Thus there will come a day in which the city will succumb, and you shall be dragged away as a slave to some Greek. But I will not see that day. I already will be dead" (*Iliad,* VI, 429–65, in paraphrase).

14 The chorus begs Eteocles not to enter battle against his brother Polynices, but Eteocles replies, "If indeed man should suffer ill, let it be clear of dishonour; for that counts as the sole gain when men are dead. But of ill coupled with dishonour thou canst not say aught that's good" (*The Seven against Thebes,* 683–5).

15 After listening to the curse of Oedipus that predicts his death at the hands of his brother Eteocles, Polynices exclaims, "I dare not whisper it to my allies / Or turn them back, but mute must meet my doom. . . ." Antigone: "One boon, O Polynices, let me crave." Polynices, "What wouldst thou, sweet Antigone? Say on." Antigone: "Turn back thy host to Argos with all speed, / And ruin not thyself and Thebes as well." Polynices: "That cannot be. How could I lead again / An army that had seen their leader quail? / . . . .' Tis shame to live in exile." (*Oedipus at Colonus,* 1402–21, *passim*). We have to note that these last two texts are from the fifth century, and thus – in partial contradiction of the theory of a civilization of guilt – that still in this epoch shame was the most crucial feeling. See our notes 35–40, Chapter 4.

16 The conflict between Prometheus and Zeus almost takes on the character of a personal conflict. See also Burckhardt, 1929, volume I, p. 53, where he insists that the legend of Prometheus is not concerned with the gods in general, but with Zeus.

17 "Odysseus the sailor cheated the natural divinities just as civilized voyagers once took advantage of the savages to whom, in exchange for ivory, they offered beads of colored glass" (Horkheimer and Adorno, 1947, p. 56).

18 See Jung, 1929–57, volume 13, par. 54. "We are still as much possessed by autonomous psychic contents as if they were Olympians. Today we call them phobias, obsessions and so forth; in a word, neurotic symptoms. The gods have become diseases; Zeus no longer rules Olympus but rather the solar plexus."

10 THE CONTINUITY OF THE MYTH OF LIMITS: WESTERN STORIES

1 Nietzsche, 1872, Chapter IX.

2 Genesis, 3, 21.

3 *Ibid.*, 22.

4 Ibid., 23–4.

5 This is the way in which the episode is read by several commentators. See Graves and Patai, 1964, Chapter XII.

6 Preuschen, *Die apokryphischen gnostischen Adamschriften*, pp. 24 and 33.

7 *Inferno*, cantos XXV and XXVI.

8 Here we will respect Dante's use of the name "Ulisse." It is obviously a question of the same personage to whom we elsewhere refer as Odysseus.

9 The tale of Macareus, Ulysses' companion (VXI, *passim*).

10 *Inferno*, XXVI, 125.

11 *Ibid.*, XXVI, 97.

12 Nietzsche, 1886, Chapter I.

13 *Inferno*, XXVI, 122.

14 *Ibid.*, XXVI, 136: *Noi ci allegrammo, e tosto tornò in pianto*, "We brightened with delight which soon turned to tears."

15 *Ibid.*, XXVI, 21–2.

16 *The Lover of Lies* (from about 177 AD).

17 *Die ich rief, die Geister, Werd'ich nun nicht los*, "I can no longer free myself from the spirits I have summoned." This phrase has become a German proverb that alludes to the worst forms of imprudence.

18 Immediate and futureless use also empties the means of communication, as according to the axiom "the medium is the message." See McLuhan, 1950, Chapter I.

11 THE SITE OF THE CRISIS

1 Meadows, *et al.*, 1972, p. 9.

2 See also Meadows, *et al.*, 1992.

3 Meadows, *et al.*, 1972, p. 150.

4 See Illich, 1971, 1974, 1976.

5 1930, p. 99, note 1.

6 1929–57, volume 13, par. 54.

7 1972, p. xvi.

8 Two concepts here encounter one another, and their dialectic is of utmost importance for a large part of the field of psychology. Proceeding by analogy with the models of the natural sciences, Freud, who considered myth to be a kind of collective dream, seems primarily interested in explanations that grasp its structure, and thus its underlying causes. In Freud we see the

restraint of the scientist who would not take recourse to myth if he could not filter it through rationality. Jung, who was much more highly influenced by romantic culture and by anthropology, raises a different problem and exhibits a different kind of restraint. He was less concerned with the scientific analysis of myth than with grasping its interior meaning; and he frequently refuses to dissect a myth since he is much more interested in preserving its wholeness and grasping its purposes (an act of comprehension). Jung feels that symbol dies when its meaning is revealed. Parallels to these two conceptions are also found in theology: Bultmann and Jaspers entertained highly different relationships to myth and made them a subject of public debate in the 1950s (now collected in Jaspers and Bultmann, 1953, 1981). Bultmann had undertaken a rereading of the holy scriptures by separating mythic language, which he thought of as historicized and by now inaccessible to the modern mind, from the essence of the Christian message (*Kérygma*) which was to be recomposed in a demythologized language. For Jaspers, on the other hand, myth is, yes,

> a bearer of meaning, but the meaning it bears can only be expressed in the language that it itself offers. Symbols speak in the forms of myths, and their nature lies in not being translatable into any other language. . . . Their interpretation is not possible in rational terms, but can rather take place through new myths.
>
> (Jaspers and Bultmann, 1953/1981, p. 42)

9 This operation was typical of the analyses of Foucault, and it was also proposed by Claude Lévi-Strauss as the specific research attitude of ethnology – so much so as to lead him to use it as the title of one of his last books: *Le Regard éloigné*.
10 For example Lévi-Strauss, 1984, Chapter I and especially Chapter XXII..
11 Thucydides, V 113.
12 Dieckmann, 1982, p 94.
13 "By shadow I mean the 'negative' side of the personality, the sum of all those unpleasant qualities we like to hide, together with the insufficiently developed functions and the contents of the personal unconscious" (Jung, 1917–43, volume 7, note to par. 103). Such undesired qualities are the first to be attributed to a rival.
14 On the basis, most fundamentally, of the thinking of Plato and Descartes. See Galimberti, 1983, Chapter I.
15 A few years back, before the shift in global politics had become as clear as it is today, I attempted to hypothesize its evolution with the parallel use of the Kleinian and Jungian models of psychodynamics: as a collective passage from a schizoparanoid position to a depressive position, and from the archetype of the *puer* to that of the *senex*. See Zoja, 1986.

12 ROUTES TOWARDS RECONSTRUCTION

1 Herodotus, book VII, and partially quoted in our Chapter 6.
2 *Ibid.*, VII, 8.
3 In order to give Xerxes a critical view of the great expedition, Artabanus himself, no less than the brother of Darius, felt obliged to begin by remarking that conflicting opinions are useful since they permit the making of choices; but still it is only his family relationship with Xerxes that keeps him from being punished (*ibid.*, VII, 10–11). There are also later moments in which he counsels prudence, but he has to resort to the paradoxical and adulatory tactic of simultaneously underlining the grandiosity of the undertaking (*ibid.*, VII, 49).

4 Jaspers, 1959.

5 See Jung, 1937–40, pars 141ff.

6 "In the absurd supposition that the intellect, which is but a part and a function of the psyche, is sufficient to comprehend the much greater whole" *ibid.*, par. 141.

7 Freud, 1932, lecture 31, p. 80.

8 *Ibid*. And what is the purpose of civilization? "The principal task of civilization, its actual *raison d'être*, is to defend against nature" (Freud, 1927, p. 15). Things today stand suddenly reversed. We now have to defend nature against civilization.

9 Jung, 1931–4, par. 676.

10 Genesis, 9, 7.

11 The relationship between Christian ideology and the expansionistic attitudes that lead to the global crisis is one of the themes most dear to the thinking of modern German ecologists.

12 Such a dynamic can take possession not only of individuals, but of whole civilizations. Guilt and expiation are central themes of classical mythology – for example, with Prometheus and Sisyphus – and also of Christianity, where they find majestic representation in Dante's *Divine Comedy*. But their importance is also more than clear in events that belong to our own time. We know, for example, that the Allies' attempted to see the First World War not as a question of Germany's "defeat" (military) but rather of its "guilt" (moral). The "debts" that Germany was asked to meet were *Schulden*. This was a wholly new cultural attitude that Germany refused to accept and it led to frenetic re-armament, a situation of racial paranoia, and a delirious organization of thought that sped to their conclusion in the Second World War, or, more properly, to the second phase of what was in fact a single World War. Defeat is a fact that has to be accepted and can of course be flanked by the payment of indemnities, to be regulated by international law. But guilt is a question of interpretation and it requires the psychological adhesion of the subject to which that interpretation is directed.

13 DEATH, DEPRESSION AND GUILT

1 This transformation has been reconstructed from two points of view. In terms of the modern history of ideas it has been analyzed primarily by Ariès, 1975. From the centrality of death in the Greek tragedies and the iconography of the Middle Ages, we have reached its present cancellation by way of various revisions of Christian culture and the leap from Christianity to secular materialism. Our society has covered the end of life with a taboo no less complete than the one with which the nineteenth century obscured sexuality, the origin of life. An anthropological point of view can be found in Baudrillard, 1976. Baudrillard returns to a French tradition of thought that finds its roots in Bataille, and further back in M. Mauss and E. Durkheim. His analysis insists on the way in which death in primitive societies is a social fact that includes a continuous relationship, dialog and symbolic exchange between the living and the dead. The dead occupy an extremely "lively" place in the economy of the psyche. The dead receive gifts, and they are a source of rebirth, as when they symbolically swallow youths on the eve of initiation and then restore them to the world as initiated adults. Initiation, which is essential in the lives of primitives, is understood as an exchange with the dead, as a process of death and rebirth. This circularity of the cultural process also regulates the rela-

tionship with things. Consider, for example, the sacred obligation to make certain gifts ("sacrifices," of which the etymological meaning is "that which renders sacred"); or the obligations incurred by their recipient, no matter whether man or god (which is what makes the relationship circular); or the reciprocal bond established by hospitality, even between enemies, and even within the traditions of our own antiquity. (See also my own essay, 1984.)

2 Pindar, *Pythian III*, 55ff.

3 One already finds this intuition in Dostoyevsky: Ivan Karamazov insists that if God does not exist, then everything is permissible. According to Jung, once Nietzsche had convinced himself that "God is dead" he unconsciously substituted himself for God, and became God; the final result was his madness. See Jung, 1988, lectures 2 and 3.

4 See Freud, 1930, p. 450.

5 *Agamemnon*, 1008ff.

6 In the course of the last few decades, the ever greater pressures exerted by external social events have become quite clear in countries like Italy. The possession of a television set, for example, was an exception for the Italian family of a generation ago. Programs were few, and there was only one channel. The exposure of the members of the family to the stimuli of the outside world was quite discontinuous and depended on what they decided to read, or on going to the cinema or visiting friends. Such activities were connected to relatively autonomous decisions, since their rhythms could be slowed when they grew too intense. Today, the possession of a television set is the norm, and it can receive more than twenty channels. Combined with a video recorder, it becomes an uninterrupted source of spectacle and stimulation. Entertainments are recorded even while we sleep or are at work and are then spewed back out at us in what we call our "leisure" time. Even people who do not buy books or periodicals are invaded by newsprint that arrives free of charge. The occupation of interstices that once were naturally empty is a typical feature of the whole invasion; it is one of the most salient aspects of the world of ceaseless spectacle. It has been calculated that every minute of television now contains twice as many words as it did a generation ago. Silence, the natural limit of the word, is rejected as unnatural. Convulsed and accelerated speech, which has always been a symptom of manic pathologies, tends to transform itself into the norm. Television chatter is the invasive next-door neighbor who shatters the enormity of history into tiny little pieces for daily consumption. The continuity of the spectacle and its stimuli has become so thoroughly a part of life as to make it extremely difficult for the individual "to pull the plug"; the role of the television set within the dynamics of the cohesion of the family system is today more important than that of the individual. When no longer able to bear the quantity and rapidity of in-coming stimuli, the individual is much more likely to pull the private plug of psychic communication, withdrawing towards depression.

7 "*Mnogo li zemli čeloveku nužno?*" (1885).

PRIMARY SOURCES AND BIBLIOGRAPHICAL NOTE

The author has found his primary sources in the following works:

Aeschylus, *Tragoediae*, ed. D. Page, Oxford, 1972.
Anthologia lyrica graeca, ed. E. Diehl, Leipzig, 1935–52.
Aristotle, *Athenaion politeia*, ed. M. Chambers, Leipzig, 1986.
—— *Ethica Nicomachea*, ed. I. Mywater, Oxford, 1954.
—— *Poetica*, ed. I. Bywater, Oxford, 1953.
—— *Politica.*, ed. W. D. Ross, Oxford, 1957.
—— *Rhetorica*, ed. R. Kassel, Berlin, 1976.
—— *Metaphysica*, ed. W. Jaeger, Oxford, 1957
Euripides, *Tragoediae*, ed. G. Murray, Oxford, 1901–13.
Die Fragmente der Vorsokratiker, ed. H. Diels and A. Kranz, Berlin, 1951–2.
Herodotus, *Histoires*, text complied by Ph.-E. Legrand, Paris, 1948–58.
Hesiod, *Theogonia – opera et dies*, ed. Fr. Solmsen, Oxford, 1970.
Hippocrates, *De Aeribus, aquis, locis*, ed. B. Diller, Berlin, 1970. (Corpus Medicorum
    Graecorum 1. 1.2.)
Homer, *Opera*, ed. M. Monro and Th. W. Allen, Oxford, 1917–20.
Horace, *Carmina*, ed. F. Klingner, Leipzig, 1959.
Ovid, *Metamorphoses.*, ed. R. Ehwahld, Leipzig, 1915
Pindar, *Epinicia*, ed. B. Snell and H. Maelher, Leipzig, 1971.
Plato, *Opera*, ed. J. Burnett, Oxford, 1905–10.
Sophocles, *Tragoediae*, text compiled by A. Dain, Paris, 1955–60.
Thucydides, *History of the Peloponnesian War*, 2 vols, ed. H.S. Jones and J.E. Powell,
    Oxford, 1942.
Tragicorum graecorum fragmenta, ed. A. Nauck, 2nd edn, Leipzig, 1889.

The translator has made use of:

The Dialogues of Plato, translated into English by B. Jowett, New York: Random
    House, 1937.
Ancilla to the Pre-Socratic Philosophers, a complete translation of the fragments in
    Diels, *Fragmente der Vorsokratiker*, by Kathleen Freeman. Cambridge, Mass.:
    Harvard University Press, 1957.

All other English translations from the Greek are those of the various volumes of
    the Loeb Classical Library.

The text consulted for Dante Alighieri's *Divina commedia* is the critical edition of
    G. Petrocchi, Turin: Einaudi, 1975. Goethe is quoted on the basis of the bilingual

218

edition directed by R. Fertonani: *Tutte le poesie*, volume I., books I and II, Milan: Mondadori, 1989.

Freud is quoted or referred to on the basis of *Gesammelte Werke: Chronologisch geordnet*, 18 volumes, London: Imago, 1940–52 and Frankfurt: Fischer, 1968. English quotations of Freud have been drawn from: *The Standard Edition of the Complete Psychological Works of Sigmund Freud*, 24 volumes, ed. James Strachey, London: The Hogarth Press, 1953–74.

Jung is quoted or referred to on the basis of *The Collected of Works of C. G. Jung*, 20 volumes, London: Routledge & Kegan Paul, 1953–78.

Nietzsche is quoted or referred to on the basis of *Werke: kritische Gesamtausgabe*, 30 volumes, ed. Giorgio Colli and Mazzino Montinari, Berlin: Walter De Gruyter, 1967–82.

The English versions of Oriental texts have been drawn from:

The Analects of Confucius, translated and annotated by Arthur Waley, London: George Allen & Unwin, 1938.
The Bhagavadgita, translated by S. Radhakrishnan, London: George Allen & Unwin, 1948.
The Dhammapada, translated by John Ross Carter and Mahinda Palihawadana, New York: Oxford University Press, 1987.
Tao Tê Ching, translated by Ch'u Ta-Kao, London: George Allen & Unwin, 1959.

For the Bible, the author has referred to the *Vulgata*, edited by R. Weber for the Deutsche Bibelgesellschaft, and to *Die apokryphischen gnostischen Adamschfriften*, edited by E. Preuschen, Giessen, 1900. The translator's quotations from the Bible are drawn from the Authorized King James Version published by the Oxford University Press.

REFERENCES

Ariès, Philippe, *Western Attitudes toward Death from the Middle Ages to the Present,* translated by Patricia M. Ranum, Baltimore: John Hopkins University Press, 1974. (Original: *Essais sur l'histoire de la mort en Occident du Moyen Age à nos jours.* Paris: Editions du Seuil,1975.)

—— *Le Temps de l'histoire,* Paris: Editions du Seuil, 1986.

Baudrillard, Jean, *L'échange symbolique et la mort,* Paris: Gallimard, 1976.

Benedict, Ruth, *The Chrysanthemum and the Sword: Patterns of Japanese Culture,* Boston: Houghton Mifflin, 1946.

Bengston, Hermann. *Griechische Geschichte.* Munich: Beck, 1986.

Boardman, John, Davis, J.K. Lewis, D.M. and Ostwald, M. (eds), *The Oxford History of the Classical World.* Oxford: Oxford University Press, 1986.

Bowra, C. Maurice, *Greek Lyric Poetry from Alcman to Simonides.* 2nd revised edition, Oxford: Clarendon Press, 1961.

Burckhardt, Jacob, *History of Greek Culture,* translated from German by Palmer Hitty, New York: Ungar, 1963. (Original: *Griechische Kulturgeschichte,* Leipzig, 1929.)

Burkert, Walter, *Ancient Mystery Cults,* Cambridge, Mass.: Harvard University Press, 1987.

Bury, John Bagnell, *The Idea of Progress: An Inquiry into its Origin and Growth,* New York: MacMillan, 1932.

Calasso, Roberto, *The Marriage of Cadmus and Harmony,* New York: Knopf, 1993. (Original: *Le nozze di Cadmo e Armonia,* Milan: Adelphi, 1988.)

Chantraine, Pierre, *Dictionnaire étymologique de la langue grecque,* Paris: Klinksieck, 1968.

Childe, V. Gordon, *What Happened in History,* London: Max Parrish, 1942.

Cipolla, Carlo M, *Guns and Sails in the Early Phase of European Expansion, 1400–1700,* London: Collins, 1965.

—— *Clocks and Culture, 1300–1700,* London: Collins, 1967.

—— "Le tre rivoluzioni," 1983, in *Le tre rivoluzioni e altri saggi,* Bologna: Il Mulino, 1989.

Colli, Giorgio, *La nascita della filosofia,* Milan: Adelphi, 1975.

Del Grande, Carlo, *Hybris. Colpa e castigo nell'espressione poetica e letteraria degli scrittori della Grecia antica da Omero a Cleante,* Naples: Ricciardi, 1947.

De Sanctis, Gaetano, *Storia dei Greci,* Florence: La Nuova Italia, 1975.

Detienne, Marcel, *Dionysus at Large,* translated by Arthur Goldhammer, Cambridge, Mass.: Harvard University Press, 1989. (Original: *Dionysos à ciel ouvert,* Paris: Hachette, 1986.)

220

REFERENCES

Dieckmann, Hans, "Schwierigkeiten der Sinnfindung in unserer Zeit," *Zeitschrift für Analytische Psychologie*, volume XIII, no. 2, pp. 93–116. Basle: Karger, 1982.

Di Lorenzo, Silvia, "L'eros e la scoperta dell'Io," in *Eros e amore*, Como: RED, 1988.

Dodds, Eric Robertson, *The Greeks and the Irrational*, Berkeley: University of California Press, 1951.

—— *The Ancient Concept of Progress and Other Essays*, Oxford: Oxford University Press, 1985.

Eliade, Mircea, *The Myth of the Eternal Return*, translated by Willard R. Trask, New York: Pantheon Books, 1964. (Original: *Le Mythe de l'éternel retour*, Paris: Gallimard, 1949.)

—— *The Sacred and the Profane: The Nature of Religion*, translated by Willard R. Trask, New York: Harcourt, Brace & World, 1959. (Original: *Le Sacré et le profane*, Paris: Gallimard, 1957.)

—— *A History of Religious Ideas*, translated by Willard R. Trask, Chicago: University of Chicago Press, 1978. (Original: *Histoire des croyances et des idées réligeuses*, Paris: Payot, 1978.)

Farrington, Benjamin, *Science and Politics in the Ancient World*, London: G. Allen & Unwin, 1946.

—— *Head and Hand in Ancient Greece: Four Studies in the Social Relations of Thought*, London: Watts, 1947.

Finley, Moses I., *The Ancient Greeks: An Introduction to their Life and Thought*, New York: Viking Press, 1964.

Flacelière, Robert, *Daily Life in Greece at the Time of Pericles*, translated by Peter Green, New York: MacMillan, 1965. (Original: *La Vie quotidienne en Grèce au siècle de Periclès*, Paris: Hachette, 1959.)

Florenskij, Pavel A., *Ikonostas*, Iskusstro, 1922.

Freud, Sigmund, *Creative Writers and Daydreaming*, standard edition, volume IX. (Original: *Der Dichter und das Phantasieren*, 1907.)

—— *Totem and Tabu: Resemblances between the Psychic Lives of Savages and Neurotics*, standard edition, volume XIII. (Original: *Totem und Tabu*, 1912–13.)

—— *Inhibitions, Symptoms and Anxiety*, standard edition, volume XX. (Original: *Hemmung, Symptom und Angst*, 1926.)

—— *The Future of an Illusion*, standard edition, volume XXI. (Original: *Die Zukunft einer Illusion*, 1927.)

—— *Civilization and its Discontents*, standard edition, volume XXI. (Original: *Das Unbehagen in der Kultur*, 1930.)

—— *New Introductory Lectures on Psychoanalysis*, standard edition, volume XXII. (Original: *Neue Folge der Vorlesungen zur Einführung in der Psychoanalyse*, 1932.)

Galimberti, Umberto, *Il corpo*, Milan: Feltrinelli, 1983.

—— *La terra senza il male*, Milan: Feltrinelli, 1984.

—— *Gli equivoci dell'anima*, Milan: Feltrinelli, 1987.

Glotz, Gustave, *Histoire greque*, Paris: PUF, 1986.

Graves, Robert, *The Greek Myths*, New York: G. Braziller, 1955.

Graves, Robert and Patai, Raphael, *Hebrew Myths: The Book of Genesis*, Garden City, N.Y.: Doubleday, 1964.

Guthrie, William Keith Chambers, *The Greeks and their Gods*, Boston: Beacon Press, 1951.

Hamilton, Charles (ed.), *Cry of the Thunderbird: The American Indians' Own Story*, New York: MacMillan, 1950.

Havelock, Eric, *The Greek Concept of Justice from its Shadow in Homer to its Substance in Plato*, Cambridge, Mass.: Harvard University Press, 1978.

Hillman, James, "Psychology: monotheistic or polytheistic?", *Spring*, 1971, pp. 193–208.

—— "An essay on Pan," in Wilhelm Heinrich Roscher, *Pan and the Nightmare, being the only Translation from the German by A. V. O'Brien of Ephiales: A Pathological-Mythological Treatise on the Nightmare in Classical Antiquity, together with* An Essay on Pan, *serving as a Psychological Introduction to Roscher's* Ephiales *by James Hillman*, New York: Spring, 1972.

Horkheimer, Max and Adorno, Theodor W., *Dialectic of Enlightenment*, translated by John Cumming. New York: Continuum, 1972. (Original: *Dialektik der Aufklärung: Philosophische Fragmente*, Amsterdam: Querido, 1947.)

Illich, Ivan, *Deschooling Society*, New York: Harper & Row, 1971.

—— *Energy and Equity*, New York: Harper & Row, 1974.

—— *Medical Nemesis: the Expropriation of Health*, New York: Pantheon Books, 1976.

Jaeger, Werner Wilhelm, *Paideia: The Ideals of Greek Culture*, translated by Gilbert Highet. New York: Oxford University Press, 1943–44. (Original: *Paideia: die Formung des griechischen Menschen*, Berlin: W. de Gruyter, 1943.)

Jaspers, Karl, *The Origin and Goal of History*, translated by Michael Bullock, New Haven: Yale University Press, 1953. (Original: *Vom Ursprung und Ziel der Geschichte*, Frankfurt on Main: Fischer, 1957.)

Jaspers, Karl and Bultmann, Rudolf, *Die Frage der Entmythologisierung*. Munich: Piper, 1953 and 1981.

Jung, Carl Gustav, *The Psychology of the Unconscious*, Collected Works, volume VII. (Original: *Über die Psychologie des Unbewussten*, 1917–43.)

—— *Psychological Types*, Collected Works, volume VI. (Original: *Psychologische Typen*, 1921.)

—— *Basic Postulates of Analytical Psychology*, Collected Works, volume VIII. (Original: *Das Grundproblem der gegenwärtigen Psychologie*, 1931–4.)

—— *Wotan*, Collected Works, volume X. (Original: *Wotan*, 1936.)

—— *Psychology and Religion*, Collected Works, volume XI. (Original: *Psychologie und Religion*, 1937–40.)

——"Diagnosing the dictators," 1938. Now in W. McGuire and R. F. C. Hull (eds), *C. G. Jung Speaking*, Princeton, N.J.: Princeton University Press, 1977.

—— *Aion: Researches into the Phenomenology of the Self*, Collected Works, volume IX, part II. (Original: *Aion*, 1951.)

—— *Answer to Job*, Collected Works, volume XI. (Original: *Antwort auf Hiob*, 1952.)

—— *Commentary on "The Secret of the Golden Flower,"* Collected Works, volume XIII. (Original: *Das Geheimnis der goldenen Blute: ein chinesisches Lesebuch*, 1929–57.)

—— *Nietzsche's Zarathustra. Notes on the Seminar Given in 1934–39*, Princeton, N.J.: Princeton University Press, 1988.

Kerényi, Károly, "Die Geburt der Helena," 1939. In *Werke in Einzelausgaben*, volume I, *Humanistische Seelenforschung*, Munich and Vienna: Langen Müller, 1966.

—— *The Gods of the Greeks*, translated by Norman Cameron. London: Grove Press, 1960. (Original: *Die Mythologie der Griechen*, Zurich: Rhein, 1951.)

Kirk, Geoffrey S., *Myth: Its Meaning and Functions in Ancient and Other Cultures*, Berkeley and Los Angeles: Cambridge University Press and University of California Press, 1971.

—— *The Nature of Greek Myths*, Harmondsworth: Penguin, 1975.

Kluckhohn, Clyde and Kroeber, Alfred, *Culture: A Critical Review of Concepts and Definitions*, New York: Vintage Books, 1952.

Lanza, Diego and Vegetti, Mario., "L'ideologia della città," 1975. Now in Mario Vegetti (ed.), *Marxismo e società antica*, Milan: Feltrinelli, 1977.

New Larousse Encyclopedia of Mythology, Feltham: Hamlyn, 1959.

REFERENCES

Latte, Kurt., "Schuld und Sünde in der griechischen Religion," *Archiv für Religionswissenschaft*, volume XX, 1920–2, pp. 254–99.

León-Portilla, Miguel, *El reverso de la conquista: relaciones aztecas, mayas y incas*, Mexico: Editorial J. Moritz, 1964.

Lévi-Strauss, Claude, *The View from Afar*, translated by Joachim Newgroschel and Phoebe Hoss. New York: Basic Books, 1984. (Original: *Le Regard éloigné*, Paris: Plon, 1983.)

Lévy-Bruhl, Lucien, *The "Soul" of the Primitive*, translated by Lillian A. Clare, Chicago: H. Regnery, 1966. (Original: *La Mentalité primitive*, Paris: Libraire F. Alcan, 1922.)

—— *Le Surnaturel et la nature dans la mentalité primitive*, Paris: PUF, 1963.

Lewis, D. M., Boardmann, John, Davis, J. K. and Ostwald, M. (eds), *The Cambridge Ancient History*, Cambridge: Cambridge University Press, 1992.

Linding, Wolfgang H. and Dauer, Alfons M., "Prophetismus und Geistertanzbewegung bei nord-amerikanischen Eingeborenen," in W.E. Muehlmann (ed.), *Chiliasmus und Nativismus*, Berlin: Reimer, 1964.

Mauss, Marcel, "Effet physique chez l'individu de l'idée de la mort suggerée par la collectivité," 1926. Now in *Sociologie et anthropologie*, Paris: PUF, 1950.

McLuhan, Marshall, *Understanding Media: the Extensions of Man*, New York: McGraw-Hill, 1964.

Meadows, Donella H., Meadows, Dennis L. and Randers, Jorgen. *Beyond the Limits*, Post Mills, Vermont: Chelsea Green Co., 1992.

Meadows, Donella H., Meadows, Dennis L., Randers, Jorgen and Behrens, William W., III. *The Limits to Growth: A Report for the Club of Rome's Project on the Predicament of Mankind*, New York: Universe Books, 1972.

Mondolfo, Rodolfo, *Polis, lavoro e tecnica*, Milan: Feltrinelli, 1982.

Mooney, James, "The ghost-dance religion and the Sioux outbreak of 1890," *Annual Report of the Bureau of American Ethnology*, volume XIV, no. 2. Washington, 1896.

Morris, Ivan, *The Nobility of the Failure: Tragic Heroes in the History of Japan*, New York: Holt, Rinehart & Winston, 1975.

Mühlmann, W. E. (ed.), *Chiliasmus und Nativismus*, Berlin: Reimer, 1964.

Mumelter, Martin, *Ums Leben Spielen: Vom Umgang mit Musik*, Anif. G. Salzburg: Müller-Speiser (forthcoming).

Mumford, Lewis, *The City in History: its Origins, its Translations, and its Prospects*, New York: Harcourt, Brace & World, 1961.

Murray, Gilbert, *The Rise of the Greek Epic*, 1907, Oxford: Oxford University Press, 1960.

Needham, Joseph, *Science and Civilization in China*, Cambridge: Cambridge University Press, 1954.

Nietzsche, Friedrich, *The Birth of Tragedy*, translated by Francis Golffing, New York: Anchor Books, 1956. (Original: *Die Geburt der Tragödie aus dem Geiste der Musik*, 1872.)

—— *The Use and Abuse of History*, translated by Adrian Collins, New York: MacMillan, 1957. (Original: *Vom Nutzen und Nachteil der Histoire für das Leben*, 1874.)

—— *A Book for All and None*, translated by Walter Kaufman, New York: Penguin, 1978. (Original: *Also Sprach Zarathustra*, 1883–5.)

—— *Beyond Good and Evil: Prelude to a Philosophy of the Future*, translated by R. J. Hollingdale, Harmondsworth: Penguin, 1990. (Original: *Jenseits von Gut und Böse*, 1886.)

—— *On the Genealogy of Morals*, translated by Walter Kaufman, New York: Vintage Books, 1964. (Original: *Zur Genealogie der Moral*, 1887.)

Ortega y Gasset, José, *The Revolt of the Masses*, translated by Anthony Kerrigana and edited by Kenneth Moore, Notre Dame, Ind.: University of Notre Dame

223

Press, 1985. (Original: *La rebelión de las masas: con un prólogo para francéses y un epílogo para ingléses*, Buenos Aires, Argentina: Cia. Editora Espasa, 1930.)

—— *An Interpretation of Universal History*, translated by Mildred Adams, New York: Norton, 1973. (Original: *Una interpretación de la historia universal*, Madrid: Revista de Occidente, 1966.)

Perrin, Noel, *Giving up the Gun. Japan's Reversion to the Sword 1543–1874*, Boulder, Col.: Shambala, 1979.

Pohlenz, Max, *Der hellenische Mensch*, Göttingen: Vandenhoeck & Ruprecht, 1947.

Popper, Karl, *The Logic of Scientific Discovery*, New York: Routledge, 1992. (Original: *Logik der Forschung: zur Erkenntnistheorie der Modernen Naturwissenschaft*, Vienna: J. Springer, 1934.)

—— *Conjectures and Refutations: The Growth of Scientific Knowledge*, New York: Basic Books, 1962.

Posnansky, Hermann, "Nemesis und Adrasteia," *Breslauer Philologische Abhand-lungen*, volume V, no. 2, 1890, pp. 1–184.

Quinzio, Sergio, *La croce e il nulla*, Milan: Adelphi, 1984.

Rohde, Erwin, *Psyche: the Cult of Souls and Belief in Immorality among the Ancient Greeks*, Chicago: Ares, 1987. (Original: *Psyche: Seelencult und Unsterblichkeitsglaube der Griechen*, Tübingen: J. C. B. Mohr, 1903.)

Roscher, Wilhelm H., *Ausführliches Lexikon der griechischen und römischen Mythologie*, 1884–1937, Hildesheim: Reprint Olms, 1978.

Rosenberg, Nathan and Birdzell, Luther E., Jr, *How the West Grew Rich: The Economic Transformation of the Industrial World*, New York: Basic Books, 1986.

Rousseau, Jean-Jacques, *Discours sur l'origine et les fondements de l'inéqualite parmi les hommes*, Geneva: Barillot, 1750.

Sahagun, Bernardino de, *General History of the Things of New Spain*, translated by Arthur J. O. Anderson and Charles E. Dibble, Santa Fe, N.M.: School of American Research Monographs, No. 14, 1975. (Original: *Historia general de las cosas de la nueva España*, volume XII, 1577, Mexico: I. Cumplido, 1840.)

Samuels, Andrew, *The Plural Psyche*, London and New York: Routledge, 1989.

Sinclair, Robert K., *Democracy and Participation in Athens*, Cambridge: Cambridge University Press, 1988.

Sini, Carlo, *Il silenzio e la parola*, Genoa: Marietti, 1989

Smith, Clifford Th., *An Historical Geography of Western Europe before 1800*, New York: Praeger, 1967.

Snell, Bruno, *Die Entdeckung des Geistes. Studien zur Entstehung des europäischen Denkens bei den Griechen*, Hamburg, Claassen, 1946.)

Tournier, Eduard, *Némesis et la jalousie des dieux*, Paris: Durand, 1863.

Toynbee, Arnold, *A Study of History*, Oxford: Oxford University Press, 1934–61.

—— *Civilization on Trial*, New York: Oxford University Press, 1948.

—— *An Historian's Approach to Religion*, New York: Oxford University Press, 1956.

—— *Hellenism: the History of Civilization*, New York: Oxford University Press, 1959.

Van der Leeuw, Gerardus, *Religion in Essence and Manifestation*, translated by J. E. Turner, Princeton, N.J.: Princeton University Press, 1986. (Original: *Phänom-enologie der Religion*, Tübingen: J. C. B. Mohr, 1956.)

Vernant, Jean-Pierre, *The Origins of Greek Thought*, Ithaca: Cornell University Press, 1982. (Original: "La formation de la pensée positive en Grèce arcaique," *Annales (E.S.C.)*, 1967, pp. 183–206, Paris.)

Vidal-Naquet, Pierre and Austin, Michel M., *Economic and Social History of Ancient Greece, an Introduction*, Berkeley and Los Angeles: University of California Press, 1977.

Volkmann, Hans, "Studien zum Nemesiskult," *Archiv für Religionswissenschaft*, volume XXVI, 1920–1, pp. 294–321.

REFERENCES

Weber, Max, "Die protestantische Ethik und der Geist des Kapitalismus," 1904. In *Gesammelte Aufsätze zur Religionssoziologie*, Tübingen: Mohr, 1920.

Zimmer, Heinrich, *Philosophies of India*, Princeton, N.J.: Princeton University Press, 1951.

Zoja, Luigi, "Working against Dorian Gray: analysis and the old," in Andrew Samuels (ed.), *Psychopathology: Contemporary Perspectives*, New York and London: The Guilford Press, 1991. (Original: "La pietra e la banana," in *Incontri con la morte*, Milan: Cortina, 1984.)

—— "Analytical Psychology and the metapsychology of feelings: possible connections between Jung and Melanie Klein," *Journal of Analytical Psychology*, no. 32, 1987, pp. 47–55, London. (Original: "Psicologia analitica e metapsicologia dei sentimenti," in Luigi Zoja (ed.), *La Psicologia analitica di fronte alle altre psicologie del profondo*, Verona: Bertani, 1986.)

INDEX